Validating Strategies

Linking Projects and Results to Uses and Benefits

PHIL DRIVER
Founder and CEO of OpenStrategies Ltd

 Routledge
Taylor & Francis Group

LONDON AND NEW YORK

First published 2014 by Gower Publishing

Published 2016 by Routledge
2 Park Square, Milton Park, Abingdon, Oxfordshire OX14 4RN
711 Third Avenue, New York, NY 10017, USA

First issued in paperback 2016

Routledge is an imprint of the Taylor & Francis Group, an informa business

British Library Cataloguing in Publication Data
A catalogue record for this book is available from the British Library

Library of Congress Cataloging-in-Publication Data
Driver, Phil.
 Validating strategies : linking projects and results to uses and benefits / by Phil Driver.
   pages cm
 Includes bibliographical references and index.
 ISBN 978-1-4724-2781-6 (hardback)
1. Strategic planning. 2. Project management. I. Title.
 HD30.28.D754 2014
 658.4'092--dc23
                                                                        2013040867

ISBN 13: 978-1-138-24795-6 (pbk)
ISBN 13: 978-1-4724-2781-6 (hbk)

Validating Strategies

Contents

List of Figures

List of Tables

Preface

The OpenStrategies story is an ongoing journey of accidental discovery, surprise, contemplation, focused exploration, intense conversations with hundreds of practitioners, engagement with thousands of strategy stakeholders and finally the development of the Integrated Strategic Information Management System known as OpenStrategies.

We started with what we now recognise was a naïve perception that in most organisations, the 'people at the top' knew what they were doing because they had developed and were implementing optimal strategies; that is, strategies which were implemented to effectively generate the desired outcomes and which did this better than alternative strategies. We discovered that not only did the top people in many organisations not have optimal strategies; many of them appeared unaware of this fact.

The few top people who realised that their strategies were ineffective usually tried hard, using traditional strategy development processes, to create optimal strategies. Occasionally they were effective; usually they weren't.

During the postgraduate courses I run in New Zealand and German universities for MBA students, we often search online for strategies of large companies or government departments and analyse them to see if they are actually strategies. To date, every such 'strategy' we have reviewed has not actually been a strategy. Many contained worthwhile *strategic ideas* but they were seldom translated into actual *strategies* or *strategic actions*.

I've also discovered that in all but the very smallest organisations, few people understood, had read or were even aware of their organisations' strategies. Many organisations were so complicated and the environments they worked in were so complex that no one individual could hope to fully understand all the issues and develop strategies on their own. Much better tools were required to draw together the strategic insights of significant numbers of stakeholders to create optimal strategies.

For example, in the 1990s the forward-thinking New Zealand Mussel Industry Council wanted an industry-wide strategy for investments in scientific research and technology implementation relevant to the industry. This sector had over 80 key stakeholders, including: mussel farmers; mussel processors; regulators; local authorities; central government; employees; environmental groups; community groups; recreational groups; the general public. Traditional strategy development and implementation techniques were unable to cope with this diversity and complexity of often competing perspectives so as to ensure that the resulting strategies met the majority of the needs of the majority of stakeholders. A new approach was needed.

At this time, I was introduced to radical thinker, sceptic and free-and-open-source software exponent Dave Lane (http://lane.net.nz). Dave posed the following profoundly important question:

> If it is possible to use open source paradigms and processes to write software, then is it possible to use open source paradigms and processes to develop strategies?

Open-source software is written by software developers all over the world and is then freely shared on the basis that if anyone further improves the software they also share it freely. Hundreds of thousands of minds are constantly being applied to the development and sharing of software and this has resulted in outstanding software which is adopted and supported throughout the world.

Could this be done with the development of strategies, albeit on a smaller scale within an organisation, or, as in the case of an industry sector such as the mussel industry, with clusters of organisations and individuals? Could many minds be focused on the development and implementation of optimal, shared strategies? If so, could such strategy development processes and paradigms be fully scalable from very small to very large organisations and multi-stakeholder groups?

Dave pointed out that open-source software development was predicated on a tightly defined set of 'rules', so that if code-writers adhered to these rules, each coder's software could be integrated seamlessly with other coders' software into large, cohesive packages. Each coder might have a narrowly defined area of interest but, provided they worked within the rules for open-source software, their pieces of software code could nevertheless be integrated with many other pieces of software to address complex world challenges.

We realised that the starting point for the open-source software community has many parallels with 'strategy communities', including:

1.   complex and challenging environments;

2.   similar problems around the world;

3.   diversity of stakeholders' interests (often competing with each other);

4.   some stakeholders who are motivated to focus on specific issues but other stakeholders who are focused on integrating many software modules (or strategies) into comprehensive packages to address large-scale challenges;

5.   intelligent stakeholders.

If the open-source software community thrives on the basis of commonly agreed rules, could there be a similar set of 'rules' that would enable the multi-stakeholder development and implementation of strategies? After all, 'software' and 'strategies' are both chunks of information assembled in structured ways.

We concluded that this concept was definitely worth exploring in depth.

We carefully reviewed the 'rules' of open-source software development and concluded that many of them were directly relevant or could be made relevant to strategy development processes. We then developed an equivalent set of 'rules of engagement' for multi-stakeholder strategies (all strategies are multi-stakeholder unless they are one-person strategies).

Along the way we identified:

•   great confusion about strategy concepts and words;

•   little common stakeholder understanding of each organisation's strategies;

•   complex demands (many stakeholders, many topics, many timescales, competing agendas, givers and receivers, different resources, etc.);

- minimal real strategy skills at top management level;

- little use being made of the collective wisdom of all stakeholders;

- an overwhelming control of strategy development by those controlling an organisation's resources with minimal input from those who had to actually implement the strategy or from those (other than the organisation itself) who would benefit from the strategy (customers, citizens, the environment);

- weak linkages from aspirational statements to strategies and from strategies to implementable action plans;

- poor stakeholder engagement;

- little cause-and-effect evidence that any particular chosen strategy was either a valid strategy or an optimal strategy;

- few strategies which could convincingly demonstrate that they were 'worth it';

- that poorly designed, poorly articulated and poorly understood strategies placed huge demands on leaders and managers to constantly guide what people were doing because most people didn't know what they were supposed to be doing;

- that it is hugely challenging to up-skill leaders and that it would often be more effective to improve systems so as to make it easier to be led rather than to improve the leaders;

- that people can hold seven +/– two interconnected ideas in their heads at any one time (Millers Law: http://en.wikipedia.org/wiki/The_Magical_Number_Seven,_Plus_or_Minus_Two);

- that people respond well to well-designed physical diagrams which contain up to about 20 pieces of information but that they struggle to understand larger diagrams;

- that the key role of almost every single organisation can be defined as: 'to create assets and enable customers/citizens to use them to create benefits' and that therefore 'strategy' should focus on improving and enabling this sequence.

Given the above observations and constraints, we decided to develop the simplest possible collaborative strategy development and implementation system which used *'the smallest amount of strategic information that had the highest value to the most people'* to define and guide the improvement of what organisations actually do. This suited my science and engineering background and also aligned with some sage advice once given to me by a colleague: 'anyone can design a complicated solution to a problem but a good engineer will design a simple solution.'

Our simple solution evolved based on the sequence: 'Organisations run *P*rojects which create *R*esults which customers/citizens *U*se to create *B*enefits (PRUB).' This sequence directly mirrors the key role of every organisation as defined above: 'to create assets and enable customers/citizens to use them to create benefits'. Everything that organisations wish to achieve can be described in this sequence so every strategy should be designed to optimise this sequence.

This Projects, Results, Uses and Benefits sequence turns out to be immensely powerful. The use of PRUB guides the rapid and effective development, validation, implementation and performance-management of strategies using our simple constructs of SubStrategies and OpenStrategies as described in this book. PRUB is scalable from single small strategic ideas in tiny organisations to large and complicated strategies in multinational companies and multi-stakeholder groups.

In many ways we feel that we 'discovered PRUB' rather than 'created it' because the Projects, Results, Uses and Benefits sequence simply reflects the uncompromising reality that the role of organisations and multi-stakeholder groups is to 'run *P*rojects which create *R*esults which customers/citizens *U*se to create *B*enefits', that is, 'to create assets and enable customers/citizens to use them to create benefits'.

Author's Note

The discovery of PRUB spawned a small and tightly defined taxonomy of OpenStrategies words ('Projects, Results, Uses, Benefits, Links, Evidence, Values, Validate, SubStrategies, OpenStrategies'). We identify the uniqueness of meaning of most of these words by using upper-case first letters and for the concepts of 'OpenStrategies' and 'SubStrategies', with an upper case 'S' for 'Strategies'.

Chapter 1

Introduction

1.1 What Is This Book About?

Most strategies have limited impact.

The OpenStrategies approach will guide you in an objective diagnosis of your existing 'strategies' and help you develop effective, validated strategies – ones that get implemented and have impact.

That's essentially what this book is about.

When you diagnose existing strategies to determine if they are meaningful and can be implemented, you may well discover that a large majority are not. Many are no more than aspirational outcomes which masquerade as strategies by adding vague verbs such as 'optimise' and 'ensure' in front of the descriptions of the desired aspirational outcomes. No wonder so few have any impact.

This book uses a system called OpenStrategies to diagnose traditional strategy statements and convincingly demonstrate their effectiveness or ineffectiveness. It then shows how to create and validate effective strategies, especially in large-scale multi-stakeholder environments.

We've created the simple yet robust OpenStrategies system that can be *easily understood and used by almost all stakeholders in almost all strategy environments.* OpenStrategies will enable you to:

1.   diagnose *existing* strategies;

2.   refine and validate *existing* strategies so they can be implemented;

3.   create *new*, validated strategies which can be implemented.

This simplicity is a defining feature of the OpenStrategies system and distinguishes it from more complicated systems such as Kaplan and Norton's *Strategy Maps* (Harvard Business School, 2004) and Bradley's *Benefits Realisation Management* (Gower Publishing, 2010). These systems are more generic, flexible and less prescriptive than the tightly defined OpenStrategies system and, as a result, they have wide applicability in the hands of experts who fully understand their intricacies. In contrast, the OpenStrategies system, with its unrelenting emphasis on simplicity, has been designed to immediately be effective in the hands of large numbers of strategy stakeholders who have had minimal training in either the general principles of strategies or in the OpenStrategies' system.

This book defines the concepts of Projects, Results, Uses and Benefits (PRUB) and 'OpenStrategies' and demonstrates how these simple yet powerful tools enable the *diagnosis, development* and *implementation* of *effective, validated* strategies.

The book addresses the pressing need for a simple, common strategy language and then shows you how to use precise strategy language to guide the development and implementation of effective, *validated* strategies.

Along the way we will address the concepts of strategy taxonomy (the classification of strategy concepts), strategy syntax (the linking together of strategic ideas) and strategy semantics (the meanings of strategies) and demonstrate how important it is to be precise and succinct when creating and implementing strategies which you need many stakeholders to understand.

Almost anyone can write a wordy and worthy strategy document, but unless it is *validated*, understood and implemented by the relevant stakeholders it will have minimal impact. That requires simplicity; a long-winded strategy is unlikely to be understood or even read by stakeholders.

Just as Pascal (1912) noted that it takes more effort to write a succinct letter than a long one (but that a succinct letter is more effective), so it takes more effort to create a succinct strategy than a long-winded strategy (but a succinct strategy will also be more effective):

> *Je n'ai fait celle-ci plus longue que parceque je n'ai pas eu le loisir de la faire plus courte.(I have only made this letter rather long because I have not had time to make it shorter). (Pascal, B. Lettres provinciales, December 1656.* In: Cassell's Book of Quotations, *London, 1912, p. 718).*

Have you:

- heard senior managers say, 'I do high-level strategy, I don't do details' and have you wondered if they are avoiding something?

- read high-level strategy documents and concluded that they contain almost no evidence or rationale that they will actually work, that they are little more than motherhood and apple pie?

- concluded that *anyone* could write such documents and that it is working out the details and *validating* a strategy that requires the hard work and an ability to handle complexity?

- tried to work with a high-level strategy to get into the detail of *exactly* what needs to be done to implement a strategy and then backed off because it became overwhelmingly complicated?

- been completely overwhelmed by huge amounts of strategic data and information coming in from many sources in dozens of different formats and magnitudes?

You are not alone.

How can we possibly communicate effectively if we all use a myriad of strategy jargon:

> *Projects, outputs, results, outcomes, themes, topics, high-level, low-level, generic, specific, measures, targets, missions, visions, schemes, cross-cutting themes, strategies, plans, platforms, collaboration, cooperation, competition, goals, objectives, frameworks, aspirations, values, structures, KPIs, performance indicators, tasks, accountabilities, responsibilities, tactics, strands, action plans, criteria, parameters, directions, issues, factors, priorities, principles, benefits, impacts, purpose, roles, capacity, capabilities, responsibility, expertise, resources, constraints, opportunities, boundaries, requirements, drivers for change, forecasts, data, information, knowledge, wisdom ... and ... maybe one day ... implementation ...*

around which there is little consensus on actual meanings?

Ask any group of people what the word 'outcomes' means and you'll get many different answers. Even in the public sector, which often claims to be 'outcomes focused', it is difficult to find anyone who knows what an 'outcome' actually is. Frequently it seems to be something that people hope will happen somewhere downstream in the strategy implementation process but for which no one wants to take responsibility.

If the primary reason for creating strategies is to guide the creation of outcomes, then if people aren't in agreement about what an outcome is, how can strategies be effective?

Try finding a common understanding of words such as 'frameworks, structures, outputs, tactics, values, vision, strategies …'

Most strategy documents contain large amounts of information which *contribute to* the strategy but which *are not the strategy itself*. Typical of such information is demographic data, drivers for change, economic constraints, environmental factors, legislation, political persuasions and so on.

A strategy is not the background strategic information or the external information or the scenario planning which feeds into a plan.

The strategy must state what will actually be done and support these actions with sound, evidence-based rationale.

As Freek Vermeulen of London Business School puts it:

> Let me not tire you with some real strategy textbook definitions but if I would just put it as 'you know what you are doing, and why', most firms would already fall short on this one. (Vermeulen, F. 2012. 'So, you think you have a strategy? Five poor excuses for a strategy'. The European Business Review, 14 January)

Therefore, to be effective, a strategy development system and process *must* guide the development of rationale-based strategies.

What information *does* constitute a strategy? Surely it must be:

> *the information which defines how the core functions of an organisation will be refined to produce better outcomes.*

Figure 1.1 identifies what organisations actually *do* and hence what their strategies should focus on. Fundamentally:

> *organisations create assets (products, services and infrastructure) and enable customers and citizens to use these assets to create benefits (outcomes) for themselves and others.*

This 'doing' is influenced by external factors (shown above the central box in Figure 1.1) and is supported by internal factors (shown below the central box in the figure). Strategies should define and provide a rationale for the way an organisation creates infrastructure, products and services and enables customers and citizens to use them to create benefits.

This describes what organisations actually *do* irrespective of whether they are in the private sector, public sector, voluntary sector or any other sector.

On this basis, the fundamental role of companies is *not* to 'make a profit'. Certainly a profit is a worthwhile outcome for a company, but there is no known machine or tool or process that 'makes a profit'.

The same basic rule applies to 'creating value'. There is no known machine or tool or process that 'creates value'.

Certainly there are machines and tools and processes that create valuable assets (products, services and infrastructure) for which customers pay and which they then use to create worthwhile outcomes. In the process, their payments contribute to the company making a profit.

So if a company wants to 'make a profit' or to 'create value', it can *only* do this by improving its core processes of creating assets and enabling people to use them to create worthwhile outcomes.

The same logic applies to the public sector that creates assets that citizens use to create beneficial outcomes and for which they pay their taxes.

While strategies need to take into account external factors – such as politics, legislation and global finance markets – and internal factors such as finance, human resources management, leadership and procurement – the strategies themselves should focus on improving what is happening. Have a look at the central box in Figure 1.1:

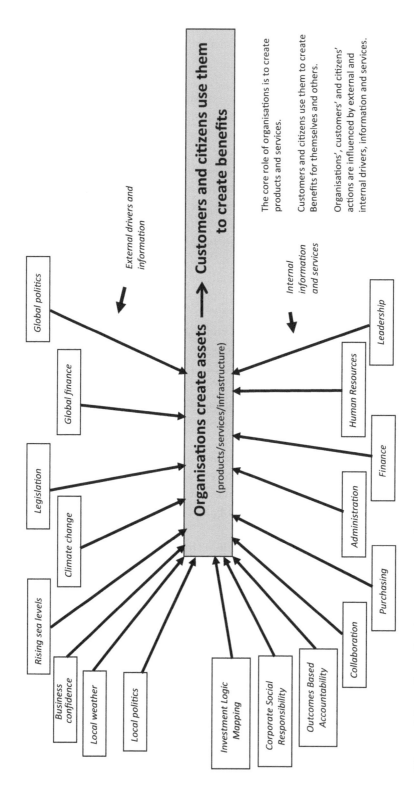

Figure 1.1   Organisations create products and services and enable customers and citizens to use them

organisations create assets (products, services and infrastructure) and enable customers and citizens to use these assets to create benefits (outcomes) for themselves and others.

So a strategy needs to define succinctly what organisations do, how their customers and citizens respond to what organisations do and why and how the organisation will do things better in future.

OpenStrategies thinking encapsulates this core function of organisations through a sequence of logic represented by the acronym PRUB: *organisations run Projects which produce Results which individuals and communities Use to derive Benefits* (see Figure 1.2), *that is, Projects create assets (Results) which customers/ citizens use (Use) to create benefits (Benefits) for themselves and others.*

This neatly represents the core of what organisations actually do. Therefore strategies should aim to improve an organisation's PRUB sequences and these should be at the core of every strategy.

Figure 1.2 shows how the PRUB sequence forms the *core* for any strategy to which other information *contributes*. Therefore, in order to strategically improve the core functioning of any organisation, a strategy should be based on PRUB. PRUB should be the core information structure for any strategy.

Given that the desired output of a strategy development process is 'a strategy' (that is, a plan supported by a rationale), the OpenStrategies approach involves starting any strategic planning process by defining the taxonomy, syntax and semantics of the final strategy. OpenStrategies uses this PRUB sequence to guide the strategy development process.

In particular the **P**rojects-**R**esults-**U**ses-**B**enefits sequence guides the strategy development process to first find robust information on Uses and their associated Benefits and to support this information with compelling cause-and-effect Evidence.

Subsequently PRUB guides the strategy development process to design Results which will enable the desired Uses and hence to identify the right Projects to produce these Results.

In doing so, the OpenStrategies approach guides the creation of *validated* strategies – in other words, strategies that are theoretically likely, can actually happen, and are worth the investment.

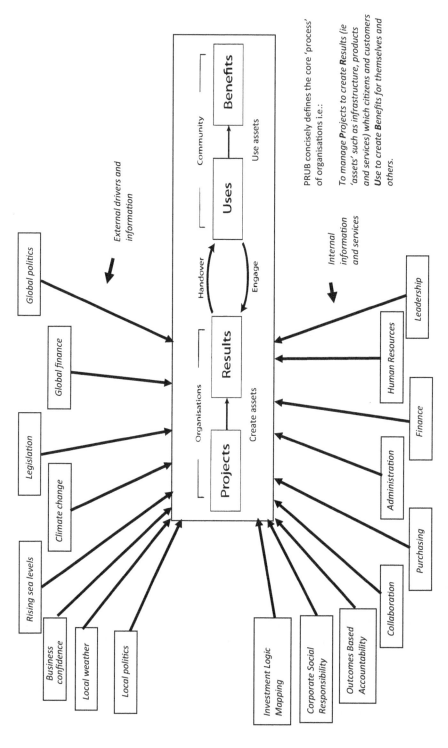

PRUB concisely defines the core 'process' of organisations i.e.:

*To manage **Projects** to create **Results** (ie 'assets' such as infrastructure, products and services) which citizens and customers **Use** to create **Benefits** for themselves and others.*

Figure 1.2   The core functions of an organisation can be defined by the sequence Projects-Results-Uses-Benefits

This OpenStrategies approach is in contrast to many traditional strategy development processes. These almost invariably start by creating a Vision and Mission and then undertaking huge amounts of strategy development activities (market research, environment scanning, brainstorming, development of multiple scenarios) with only the vaguest sense of the end-point of all this strategy development activity – the validated strategy itself.

As a consequence, many strategy documents are populated with huge amounts of *strategic information* but they contain very little information in the form of an *actual strategy*.

It is helpful to have an overall vision and mission for an organisation, but it is crucial to go much further than this – to create a strategy which encapsulates this vision and mission in a *validated* and *implementable* format.

Figure 1.3 shows a very small and simplified 'SubStrategy' based on PRUB. In this example there are several sequential asset-creation steps before the final product can be made available to customers.

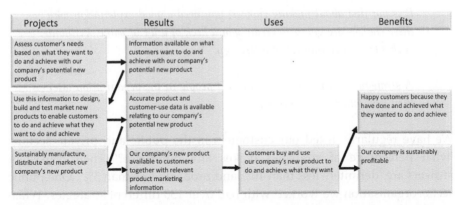

Figure 1.3   A very small and simplified 'SubStrategy' based on PRUB

The 'syntax', or logical flow, of SubStrategy figures such as this is explained and demonstrated throughout this book. In particular we will address factors such as the different 'levels' of strategies (aspirational, guidance and operational), how to create strategies which can actually be implemented, how many traditional so-called 'strategies' create 'Orphan Results' which cannot be used by customers and citizens, and how to 'validate' strategies so that they can be implemented with confidence.

1.2   The Ineffectiveness of Most Strategies

Many people have observed that few strategies have impact and that even fewer organisations actually have realistic strategies. Our experience working with numerous large, multi-stakeholder groups confirms this view.

The following quotes from Freek Vermeulen (2012), Associate Professor of Strategy at the London Business School, neatly summarise these observations:

> *Most companies do not have a strategy. Ok, I admit it, I do not have any solid statistics (if such a thing were possible) as evidence to back up this statement, but I do see a heck of a lot of companies, strategy directors, and CEOs present their 'strategies' and I tell you, I think 9 out of 10 (at least) don't actually have one.*

> *Most companies and CEOs do not have a good rationale of why they are doing the things they are doing and how this should lead to superior performance ... Without a proper rationalisation of why your choices are going to help you create value, I cannot call it a strategy.*

> *It is not just about making choices, you need a good explanation why these choices are going to create you a heck of a lot of value. Without such a logic, I cannot call it a strategy.*

> *A strategy is only really a strategy if people in the organisation alter their behaviour as a result of it.*

We have regularly asked our customers in the public and private sectors: 'what percentage of strategies makes any difference?' Their consistent answers are 'definitely less than 10% and probably less than 5%'. One public sector organisation we worked with had over 130 different strategies. When we questioned their staff we found very few people who were aware of *any* of these strategies, let alone read them, understood them or used them to guide their work.

Of the hundreds of strategies we've reviewed, fewer than 10% use robust taxonomy, syntax and semantics. As a result they are unclear on exactly what they are trying to achieve, why they are trying to achieve it, how they are going to achieve it and what confidence they have that their strategy has been validated, is optimal and can actually be made to happen cost-effectively.

In short, most strategies and strategic plans simply cannot be 'validated', as explained later in this book.

In a further quote, Vermeulen (2012) says:

I'd say there are 3 types of CEOs here:

1) CEOs who think they have a strategy; they are the most abundant;

2) CEOs who pretend to think that they have a strategy, but deep down they are really very hesitant because they fear they don't actually have one (and they're probably right); these are generally quite a bit more clever than the first category, but alas fewer in numbers;

3) CEOs who do have a strategy; there are preciously few of them, but invariably they head very successful companies.

If you can demonstrate that your organisation has an effective strategy that is being successfully implemented (type 3 above), this book is not for you. Otherwise, read on.

1.3 Why Do Strategies Fail?

People in the organisation have to know about the strategy and they also need to understand it and how they should manage their roles within the organisation consistent with the strategy.

Large organisations employ many people at many levels in an organisation, all of whom need to have a common understanding of the strategy.

Poor strategy language leads to few people understanding the strategy and that means that few people know what they are actually supposed to be doing. OpenStrategies and its underpinning PRUB strategic thinking provide clear strategy language.

The heart of this book addresses the taxonomy, syntax and semantics of strategies.

TAXONOMY (THE SCIENCE OF CLASSIFICATION)

PRUB and OpenStrategies *classify* core strategic concepts such as Projects, Results, Uses, Benefits, Links, Evidence, Values, Indicators, Targets and Measurements (see Chapter 2).

SYNTAX (THE RULES FOR CONSTRUCTING SENTENCES)

The *rules* for constructing and Validating 'SubStrategies' (see Chapter 2) from these concepts are defined by the PRUB-Validate process (see Chapter 6).

SEMANTICS (THE STUDY OF MEANING)

The *meaning* of a SubStrategy when it has been populated with strategic ideas defines the semantics of a SubStrategy or an OpenStrategy (see Chapters 2–8).

This book specifies the requirements for such a simple, minimalist *taxonomy + syntax + semantics of strategy language* and shows how to use the OpenStrategies system to create, validate and implement effective strategies.

1.4   The Complex World of Strategies

Almost everyone's strategic environment is complex. This complexity comes from:

- multiple levels of strategies (national, regional, local, aspirational, guidance, operational);

- multiple demographics characterised in many different ways (age bands, healthy/sick, male/female, obese/non-obese, smokers/non-smokers, employed/unemployed, skilled/unskilled, customer segments ...);

- multiple geographic regions characterised in many different ways (urban/rural, different geographical districts for police/NHS/education/local authorities, flat/hilly, dry/wet ...);

- multiple overlapping themes and sub-themes (drugs and alcohol, health, teenage pregnancy, education, transport, environment, waste, energy, climate change, economic development ...);

- multiple organisations and other stakeholders (customers, suppliers, government agencies, local authorities, police, NHS, schools and universities, third sector, industry and commerce, citizens, interest groups, politicians ...);

- multiple reporting and accountability requirements (to shareholders, customers, citizens, audit agencies, tax agencies, regulators, politicians, interest groups, media ...);

- with most of the above evolving constantly within constantly evolving strategic environments;

- and with most strategies using different language and different formats in each strategy document.

Is it any wonder that it is difficult to create, validate and implement strategies?

Snowden and Boone ('A leaders' framework for decision-making'. *Harvard Business Review*, November 2007) have characterised strategic decision-making environments as:

- simple (known knowns), or

- complicated (unknown knowns), or

- complex (unknown unknowns), or

- chaotic (unknowables).

We will adopt these four categories because they cover all the strategy environments addressed by this book.

Examples of these environments could be:

- Simple: for example laying bricks. How to lay bricks is well known and anyone can learn to do it.

- Complicated: for example fixing a Ferrari. How to do it is known to experts but it would be difficult for everyone to learn how to do it. However, anyone could learn to do single simple steps in the process.

- Complex: for example understanding a rainforest. It is not possible for anyone to fully understand a rainforest, although some people can understand some aspects of it. However, anyone could learn to take single simple steps towards understanding a rainforest.

- Chaotic: for example immediately after an earthquake. No one understands what to do in the event of an unexpected earthquake and it's not possible to find the right information before taking action. However, anyone could take single simple steps to help address the situation.

So irrespective of whether a strategic environment is simple, complicated, complex or chaotic, actual step-by-step actions must always be simple (known knowns) since it is physically impossible to implement unknown knowns, unknown unknowns and unknowables. The outcomes of these actions might be difficult to predict (unknown or unknowable) due to complexity, but *the actions themselves will and must always be simple (they must be known knowns)*.

A combination of many simple actions (that is, a suite of SubStrategies) may become complicated overall while each SubStrategy remains necessarily simple.

Therefore a key challenge for an effective strategy development and implementation system will be to distil and validate simple strategic actions from complex strategic environments.

This book describes how OpenStrategies does this.

1.5   The Three Levels of Strategy

In principle, strategies are created at three broad levels:

- aspirational strategies;

- guidance strategies;

- operational strategies.

ASPIRATIONAL STRATEGIES

These are the highest level strategies and, as the name suggests, describe what stakeholders aspire to. They contain statements which often *sound like* projects or actions (for example 'Protect the environment', 'Reduce levels of crime', 'Improve the health of women and children'), but these statements are not actually actions or projects because they cannot be directly implemented. In reality, they describe desired outcomes such as 'healthy environment' or 'safer citizens due to less crime' or 'healthy women and children' preceded by non-actionable verbs such as 'protect', 'reduce', 'improve'.

In essence they are little more than aspirational statements of outcomes masquerading as strategies by attaching verbs to the outcomes statements. Aspirational strategies are nevertheless valuable, often in a succinct and readable way. However, aspirational strategies tend to be very similar all around the world and are never specific enough to be implemented.

GUIDANCE STRATEGIES

Typically between high-level aspirational strategies and grassroots operational strategies (often called action plans) are a range of mid-level 'guidance strategies' which are more specific than the high-level aspirational strategies but which remain insufficiently specific to be implementable.

Guidance strategies include statements which *sound like* Projects (but which still are not able to be implemented), for example 'Reduce harm to endangered bird species', 'Provide prisoners with training in social and job skills' or 'Provide drop-in health centres for women and children'. Compared with the statements in aspirational strategies, guidance strategies focus on areas where the environment can be 'protected', or an action to minimise criminal offending or general actions to address 'women's and children's health'.

There can be many levels of guidance strategies between the aspirational-level strategies and operational-level strategies, but in each case, the guidance-level strategies cannot be directly implemented. *Only* operational-level strategies can be directly implemented.

OPERATIONAL STRATEGIES

These grassroots-level strategies or action plans define exactly what needs
to be done and why. Typical of phrases in such strategies are: 'design and
enforce legislation to prohibit the clearance of native trees', 'obtain and
follow the dietary advice of an internationally renowned athletics coach and
nutritionist', 'build and market the new super-widget and sell it to young
people through eBay'.

Operational strategies are the only strategies which can be
directly implemented.

To be implementable, an operational strategy or action plan must be:

- demographically specific (who are the users who will benefit?); *and*

- thematically specific (on what topics?); *and*

- geographically specific (where are actions taking place?); *and*

- organisationally specific (who are the service providers, including
  partnerships?); *and*

- specific in other areas as well, for example process specific (how
  things will be done?).

Most published strategies and action plans do not meet these specificity
criteria – they are aspirational or guidance-level strategies – so they have
little chance of being directly implemented. This does not necessarily mean
that they are a waste of time – it is just that they are *insufficient* to
be implemented.

An effective strategic information management system must distinguish,
yet also seamlessly interlink, all three levels of strategy.

1.6 The Crucial Role of End-users in Strategy Development and Implementation

In the implementation of most strategies, there are many times more end-users
than there are providers.

Therefore, for purely numerical reasons, end-users should have a key role in designing and implementing strategies.

In most strategies end-users are paying for the implementation of the strategy. In the case of companies, end-users provide the cash flow for ongoing strategy implementation through their purchase of goods and services. In the public sector, citizen end-users pay for the development and implementation of strategies through taxes and rates.

Therefore, for 'who is paying for this?' reasons, end-users should have a key role in designing and implementing strategies.

Only end-users can create Benefits (outcomes).

Therefore because only end-users can realise or create Benefits/outcomes, end-users should have a key role in designing and implementing strategies.

We will return repeatedly to this concept of Uses and users because it is vital to the development of effective strategies.

1.7   Stakeholder Engagement (see Chapter 5)

Most strategies involve multiple stakeholders in the development and implementation phases so 'stakeholder engagement' is a significant issue.

We will use the term 'engagement' to mean 'stakeholders *developing* strategies together' and 'collaboration' to mean 'stakeholders *implementing* strategies together'. In this context, 'engagement' includes 'inform', 'consult' and 'involve' whereas 'collaboration' includes 'involve', 'collaborate' and 'empower'.

More detailed descriptions of the different types of stakeholder engagement can be found at www.iap2.org/associations/4748/files/IAP2%20 Spectrum_vertical.pdf.

1.8   The Structure of This Book

Strategy development processes must exhibit certain characteristics if they are to be effective. We have distilled about 60 characteristics which a strategy development and implementation system needs to address (see Appendix 2 and www.openstrategies.com for details). While there is a widespread belief that almost anyone can dream up a 'strategy', until it is 'validated' it is meaningless. Therefore an effective strategy development process *must* include 'strategy validation'.

Chapter 2 defines Projects, Results, Uses and Benefits (PRUB-thinking) in some detail and then indicates how PRUB guides the diagnosis of existing strategies and the development of strategies which impact on organisations' core functions, that is, 'to create assets and enable people to use them to create benefits'.

By focusing on this core function of organisations, Chapter 3 explores why so many strategies have no impact, with a particular focus on the imprecise and often confusing language traditionally used in strategies.

Chapter 4 diagnoses many of the other challenges of strategy development and implementation.

Chapter 5 demonstrates how PRUB strategic thinking is an effective tool for diagnosing (and then enabling) large-scale stakeholder engagement.

Chapter 6 introduces the core OpenStrategies tool and shows how it guides the development and *validation* of 'SubStrategies'.

Chapter 7 addresses the interlinking or nesting of SubStrategies into large-scale OpenStrategies.

Chapter 8 provides a summary and checklist for anyone wanting to become proficient in using all or some of the OpenStrategies system.

Appendix 1 contains a glossary of the rigorously defined OpenStrategies terminology.

Appendix 2 summarises the specifications for an ideal Integrated Strategic Information Management System.

It is important to note that the development of this book and the OpenStrategies system have been guided by a great deal of empirical experience in addition to theory. By working with thousands of stakeholders who have wanted to create and implement large strategies in complex environments, we have identified what does and doesn't work in practice.

We have created the simple yet robust OpenStrategies system so that, *most importantly*, it can be *easily understood and used by almost all stakeholders in almost all strategy environments*.

OpenStrategies was not designed to be a sophisticated tool solely for academics and strategy experts. OpenStrategies is a tool for everyone wanting to engage in the process of developing and implementing strategies. As such, OpenStrategies and PRUB-Validate are a system and process which anyone can learn to use.

In this respect, people's engagement in strategy development and implementation has parallels with the concept of a flock of birds. Flocks of birds don't need to be told how to fly or how to eat or how to procreate but when flocking it pays for them to share, understand and follow a simple rule along the lines of 'stay at least one wingspan distance from your neighbours' – they can work the rest out for themselves.

Similarly, people involved in developing, validating and implementing strategies don't need to be told to do everything they need to do – they just need to be given minimal guidance (for example provided by the simple rules of PRUB) and they can generally work out the rest for themselves.

Nevertheless, having developed the OpenStrategies system so it is deliberately simple enough for almost everyone to understand it, we have discovered that the OpenStrategies system often works as effectively for strategy experts as it does for the majority of stakeholders who are not specialists in strategy development and implementation.

Also, PRUB and OpenStrategies have proven to be easily scalable from single Projects up to complicated, multi-stakeholder, multi-themed OpenStrategies.

While many of the examples and discussions in this book relate directly to collaborative strategy development and implementation in the public sector, almost without exception the same factors are relevant to the development and validation of private sector and voluntary sector strategies.

Chapter 2

Projects, Results, Uses and Benefits (PRUB) and OpenStrategies

This chapter expands on the concept of PRUB thinking as a succinct representation of an organisation's core functions and then develops this concept to show how this also guides the diagnosis of existing strategies and the development and validation of new strategies.

This chapter is therefore, necessarily, somewhat theoretical. We encourage you to bear with us as we explain the core PRUB and OpenStrategies concepts so that you can then understand how we use PRUB thinking as a tool for diagnosing why most strategies have minimal impact (Chapters 3–5).

2.1 What are PRUB and OpenStrategies?

The core role of organisations is to:

> Create assets and enable people to use them to create benefits.

We encapsulate this role in the OpenStrategies concept of PRUB thinking as:

> Organisations run **P**rojects to create **R**esults (assets) which people **U**se to create **B**enefits.

To be effective, strategies should directly impact on improving this core role of organisations, that is, on improving the core PRUB sequence. Therefore it is important to understand PRUB thinking in order to:

1. diagnose existing strategies (and to understand why perhaps 90% or more have no significant impact);

2.   refine them or create new strategies;

3.   validate them;

4.   where relevant, to interlink them with related strategies;

5.   where relevant, to engage effectively with all stakeholders;

6.   implement them;

7.   performance-manage them.

This chapter therefore explains more about Projects, Results, Uses and Benefits (PRUB) and briefly outlines how PRUB underpins the overall OpenStrategies system, consisting of:

1.   a concise taxonomy of strategy language;

2.   a simple syntax for strategy statements;

3.   evolving strategy semantics derived from the taxonomy and syntax encapsulated in Linked sequences ('SubStrategies') for each strategic idea;

4.   the precise positioning of key cause-and-effect Evidence on the Links within each SubStrategy;

5.   the precise definition of net Value;

6.   performance measurement and management;

7.   mechanisms for stakeholder engagement;

8.   a scalable system for aggregating collections of SubStrategies into complete OpenStrategies.

Once readers are familiar with our thinking, Chapter 3 will then use the Projects–Results–Uses–Benefits sequence as a powerful tool for diagnosing existing strategies and identifying some of the main linguistic reasons why most strategies have no impact.

2.2   Understanding Projects, Results, Uses and Benefits: The Simplest Strategy Building Block Which Accurately Represents What Organisations Actually Do

The core role of organisations is to create assets and enable people to use them to create benefits. As shown in Figure 2.1, OpenStrategies encapsulates this core role in the sequence:

> *organisations run **P**rojects to create **R**esults (assets) which people **U**se to create **B**enefits.*

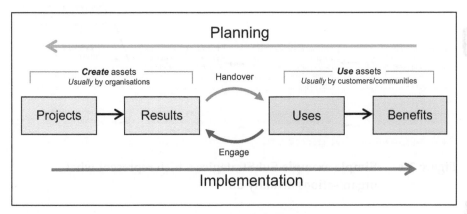

Figure 2.1   The core PRUB strategy building block

SUBSTRATEGIES AND OPENSTRATEGIES

The PRUB taxonomy, syntax and semantics define the concept of 'SubStrategies', which are the core building blocks of OpenStrategies.

Interlinked sequences of small numbers of Projects, Results, Uses and Benefits are known as SubStrategies. SubStrategies precisely encapsulate 'what needs to be done and why'. Typically a SubStrategy will contain up to about 20 Projects, Results, Uses and Benefits and can usually be encapsulated on a single page of A4 paper. A SubStrategy usually addresses a single theme.

Such SubStrategies represent the smallest 'unit of strategy' and are the building blocks for all larger SubStrategies and OpenStrategies. By this we mean that anything smaller than a SubStrategy cannot accurately define what needs to be done and why – so a SubStrategy is the smallest interlinked collection of strategic concepts that can be called a strategy.

Larger SubStrategies with more than approximately 20 PRUBs are defined as OpenStrategies.

Figures 1.3 (on page 9) and 2.2 give very simple examples of small SubStrategies.

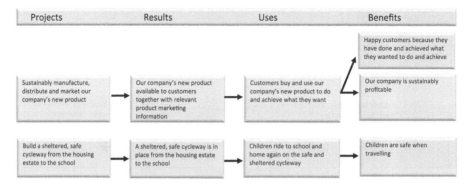

Figure 2.2   Simple example SubStrategies which represent what organisations actually do

You will see from these examples that Projects can only create Results – they cannot create Uses or Benefits. The only way to get from an organisation's Projects to the desired final Benefits is for the Results produced by the organisation to be Used (by customers or citizens) and it is precisely the Use of the Results which creates the Benefits.

Some might argue that users 'realise' Benefits but we believe that this implies that the Benefits somehow already exist or are inherently present in the Results and just need to be 'realised' by relatively passive users. The *first* or *primary* definition of 'realisation' in many dictionaries is along the lines of 'to become conscious or aware of' and this aligns with the sense (mistaken in our view) that the Benefits already exist prior to the Use. In contrast, the OpenStrategies team believe that Benefits need to be actually 'created' by Users and not just 'realised'.

PROJECTS

Organisations run **Projects** such as building a new local market, developing a communications campaign, developing health services, planting flaxes and trees around a wetland or building an irrigation scheme and filling it with water. Projects create and maintain assets such as products, services and infrastructure.

RESULTS

Organisations produce **Results** from these Projects such as a new local market, a communication campaign, a new health service, a restored wetland, or water being available to farmers. Results consist of assets such as products, services and infrastructure.

USES

Customers, citizens and communities (and 'the environment') **Use** these Results, for example by purchasing and using produce from a local market, reading the information from a communications campaign, engaging with service at a hospital, studying flora and fauna in the wetland, or farmers using water for irrigation.

BENEFITS

Customers, citizens and communities (and 'the environment') create **Benefits** from their Use of the assets that organisations produce, such as: healthier citizens due to eating healthier local produce, more engaged citizens, healthier citizens as a result of receiving more effective medical care, people having a sense of oneness with nature through their experiences in the wetlands, or farms being sustainably profitable. Benefits encapsulate the *reasons* for a strategy.

Using the Projects, Results, Uses and Benefits sequence produces SubStrategies containing:

the *smallest* amount of strategic information

that has the *highest value*

to the *most people*.

Every strategic idea or core organisational role can be described using this sequence either as a single P-R-U-B or as combinations of multiple Projects, Results, Uses and Benefits.

PRUB defines the absolute minimum set of sequenced information which is necessary to represent what organisations actually do and hence to enable them to create and implement strategies.

All other strategic information contributes to the sequence – but the PRUB sequence itself is 'the strategy'.

SubStrategies based on Projects, Results, Uses and Benefits are fundamental to the OpenStrategy system. They are the core strategy building blocks because they concisely represent the core function of organisations.

The purpose of an effective strategy is to improve this core function. Hence an effective strategy will:

- define exactly the organisation's core function in terms of what Projects the organisation needs to do, what Results they must produce, how these Results will be Used and how these Uses will create Benefits;

- partially 'Validate' this sequence by including compelling cause-and-effect Evidence that Projects really will produce the desired Results/assets, that the Results really will be Used, and that the Uses really will create Benefits;

- further 'Validate' this sequence by including compelling information that the Value of the Benefits exceeds the combined costs of the Projects and the Uses.

Using SubStrategies it is possible to create strategies for everything from single projects right up to large-scale multi-level, multi-stakeholder, multi-theme OpenStrategies.

The two simple SubStrategies in Figure 2.2 show how easy it is to follow the logical sequence from Projects through to Benefits.

They also demonstrate that it is not possible or logical to expect a Project to create a Benefit. A Project can only create a Result. That Result has to be Used to create a Benefit. This is crucially important:

> *There are no shortcuts from Projects to Benefits (outcomes) or from Results (outputs) to Benefits.*

Most strategic ideas will need to be represented by SubStrategies which are more complicated than the above two examples and will contain multiple inter-linked Projects, Results, Uses and Benefits.

A strategy based on PRUB Strategic Thinking (that is, an OpenStrategy) will be concise, clear and implementable. We are confident that:

- any simpler strategy will be too vague to implement;

- any more complicated strategy will be … more complicated.

2.3   Stakeholders

Organisations such as companies, service providers, government departments, local authorities and others undertake Projects to produce Results (organisational action followed by organisational output or consequence).

Almost without exception the role of organisations is to *create assets* (note that on occasions citizens also perform this role). The assets might be infrastructure assets such as roads, they might be products or they might be services.

Customers and citizens and communities Use the Results to produce Benefits (customers/citizens/community action followed by customers/citizens/community outcomes). Customers/citizens/communities play the roles of *Users* of assets (or consumers of assets).

Throughout this book we will use the phrase 'customers and citizens' to mean all Users, including 'communities' and 'the environment'.

Projects must necessarily be linked through Results and Uses in order to lead to Benefits. Therefore provider organisations must create the *right* Results in order for customers and citizens to (usually voluntarily) Use these Results to create Benefits.

As discussed in detail later in this chapter in section 2.14, these Results need to be 'handed over' or 'made available to' communities, *not delivered **to** or **at** or **for** them!*

Exercise 1 below (section 2.4) provides a set of statements and invites you to use our taxonomy to classify them as Projects, Results, Uses or Benefits. Once you are familiar with what constitutes a Project, a Result, a Use or a Benefit, you will have started down the road to using PRUB thinking to diagnose your existing strategies to determine whether or not they are *actually* strategies and whether or not they can be implemented.

In doing this exercise, remember that:

- Projects describe actions to create or maintain assets (products, services or infrastructure) and are usually run by organisations.

- Results are the consequences of Projects and consist of assets (products, services and infrastructure).

- Uses are actions by customers or citizens who are using these assets.

- Benefits are the consequences of customers' and citizens' Uses.

- Organisations run Projects to produce Results whereas it is customers and citizens who undertake Uses to produce Benefits.

2.4   Exercise I: Identifying Projects, Results, Uses and Benefits

Decide whether the items in Table 2.1 are Projects, Results, Uses or Benefits and write the corresponding letter (P, R, U or B) in the 'Item Type' column.

Table 2.1   Example Projects, Results, Uses and Benefits

	Example Item	Type
I	Healthier young people due to more walking and cycling	
2	Develop a campaign to promote exercise to young people as being 'cool'	
3	Traffic is flowing more smoothly through seven new roundabouts	
4	Young people in five secondary schools are exercising more due to a campaign that promotes exercise as being 'cool'	
5	Replace traffic lights with roundabouts to reduce congestion	
6	More cyclists are visiting the town centre and using bike parks	
7	Happier citizens due to shorter travel times via roundabouts	
8	Build a swimming pool to be used by all ages	
9	On-site parking is available, making it easier for people to use the swimming pool	
I I	Build a car park to provide on-site parking for a swimming pool	
12	Build a new library in a local residential area	
13	Develop swimming training and 'pool fun' programmes to encourage young people to use the swimming pool	
14	'Further learning' night classes are available to adult students	
15	Healthier and happier young people in the community	
16	Develop a 'library awareness' campaign to promote the use of local libraries	
17	Happier adult citizens through increased earning potential	
18	Undertake analysis of congestion reduction options	
19	A 'library awareness' campaign is in place to promote the use of local libraries	
20	A mobile library service is available for elderly and disabled residents	
21	A greater number of citizens make use of local libraries	
22	Standard of living for local residents is improved through better education and earning potential	
23	Adult students attend 'further learning' night classes and develop their employment potential	
24	A greater number of young people take part in productive after-school swimming and swim-training activities	
25	Use information available from analysis of congestion reduction options to develop action plan	
26	Better-paid jobs are available to 'further learning' night class graduates	

Table 2.2   Answers that Correctly Identify each Project, Result, Use and Benefit

	Example Item	Type
I	Healthier young people due to more walking and cycling	B
2	Develop a campaign to promote exercise to young people as being 'cool'	P
3	Traffic is flowing more smoothly through seven new roundabouts	U
4	Young people in five secondary schools are exercising more due to a campaign that promotes exercise as being 'cool'	U
5	Replace traffic lights with roundabouts to reduce congestion	P
6	More cyclists are visiting the town centre and using bike parks	U
7	Happier citizens due to shorter travel times via roundabouts	B
8	Build a swimming pool to be used by all ages	P
9	On-site parking is available, making it easier for people to use the swimming pool	R
11	Build a car park to provide on-site parking for a swimming pool	P
12	Build a new library in a local residential area	P
13	Develop swimming training and 'pool fun' programmes to encourage young people to use the swimming pool	P
14	'Further learning' night classes are available to adult students	R
15	Healthier and happier young people in the community	B
16	Develop a 'library awareness' campaign to promote the use of local libraries	P
17	Happier adult citizens through increased earning potential	B
18	Undertake analysis of congestion reduction options	P
19	A 'library awareness' campaign is in place to promote the use of local libraries	R
20	A mobile library service is available for elderly and disabled residents	R
21	A greater number of citizens make use of local libraries	U
22	Standard of living for local residents is improved through better education and earning potential	B
23	Adult students attend 'further learning' night classes and develop their employment potential	U
24	A greater number of young people take part in productive after-school swimming and swim-training activities	U
25	Use information available from analysis of congestion reduction options to develop action plan	P
26	Better-paid jobs are available to 'further learning' night class graduates	B

2.5   The Handover

The core role of organisations is to create assets and enable people to use them to create benefits.

Note the use of the word 'enable'. Organisations generally cannot *compel* people to use the assets the organisations have created:

Therefore you cannot assume that assets will automatically be used.

This is a profoundly important statement, especially in the public sector where many public servants believe that their job is to *'deliver'* services *to* and *at* and *for* people.

Assets will only be used if people *choose* to use them. This means that the assets must be the 'right' assets, where *'right' is determined by the users, not by the providers*.

When the core role of an organisation is represented by PRUB, this means that Results must be the right Results if they are to be Used by people to create Benefits.

Therefore, while SubStrategies show Links going from Results to Uses, it is important to note that this Link is almost always a voluntary Link.

This is why the core Projects, Results, Uses and Benefits (Figure 2.1) shows that between Results and Uses there is a curved Link going from Results to Uses, which is indicative of the fact that ideally the Results will be 'handed over' to Users who will Use them, rather than *delivered to* and *at* and *for* people.

In addition there is a second Linking arrow going from Uses back to Results. This second Linking arrow indicates that it is essential to learn from Users about their desired Uses prior to, and in order to, design the *right* Results so that end-users will in fact Use the Results.

In the OpenStrategies system we define this duality of Linking arrows (from Results to Uses) as:

- 'the handover' (when assets have been made available to end-users, that is, the top arrow), and as;

- 'engagement' (when learning from end-users about what their desired Uses are and hence be able to determine the right Results, that is, the bottom arrow).

Figure 2.1 therefore makes it crystal clear that there *must* be a two-way process between the providers or creators of assets (products, services and infrastructure) and users (the stakeholders who will Use the products, services and infrastructure).

Providers must *first* engage with end-users (indicated by the lower arrow going from Uses back to Results in Figure 2.1). They must do this in order to fully understand end-users' needs and then *and only then* can providers develop strategies which will create the right assets/Results for the end-users to Use.

Then the assets are handed over or made available to end-users. If they are the right assets, they will indeed be Used as hoped, to create Benefits. If they are the wrong assets/Results, it is unlikely that they will be Used.

It is possible to look at the distinction between Projects/Results (on the left of the handover) and Uses/Benefits (on the right of the handover) in different ways. You could view this distinction as what organisations do and achieve on the left and what customers and citizens do and achieve on the right. Alternatively, you can view Projects as the creation of assets (= Results) on the left, and the Uses of assets on the right to create Benefits.

Table 2.3   Two ways of thinking about the left- and right-hand sides of the PRUB information structure

Projects and Results	HANDOVER	Uses and Benefits
Public, private and third sector organisations – what they do and achieve		Customers and citizens* – what they do and achieve
Creating assets		Using assets

Note: * In some special circumstances, citizens can also run Projects – see Chapter 5.

Organisations can *control* their Projects and Results but they can only *influence* Uses and Benefits (see Chapter 5).

So an important point is that the stakeholder groups involved on either side of the handover will almost always be uniquely different stakeholders and therefore it is critical to engage groups from both sides of the handover in any strategy development and implementation process. This engagement will ensure that your strategy is genuinely driven by Benefits to all relevant stakeholders and that the Results of Projects will actually be Used.

2.6   Some Key Comparisons with Traditional Strategy Language

In traditional strategy language, what we define as 'Results' are often known as 'outputs'. In the PRUB taxonomy, Results are *desired* outputs and are always worded positively.

Similarly in traditional strategy language, Benefits (and sometimes Uses) are often known as 'outcomes'. In the PRUB taxonomy, Benefits are *desired* outcomes and are always worded positively.

Traditional strategy language also often loosely uses the terms 'goals' and 'objectives' to denote what we more rigorously define as Uses and Benefits.

Chapter 3 includes further discussion on the typically loose use of strategy language in traditional strategies.

2.7   Links

Projects, Results, Uses and Benefits defines a 'Linked' sequence of Projects which lead to Results which lead to Uses which lead to Benefits. In this sequence, 'Linked' means 'contributes to', or 'increases the likelihood that' or 'will have a definite and direct impact on'.

For example, a Project 'Build a cycleway' naturally Links to the Result 'A cycleway'. Similarly a Project 'Undertake and document research on' naturally Links positively to a Result 'A report on'.

Another example could be a Result 'Qualified staff are available to counsel young people', which increases the likelihood of a Use that 'young people attend a youth centre and receive counselling'.

Projects and Uses focus on actions so the *verbs* are the most important terms when describing Projects and Uses. In contrast, Results and Benefits focus on consequences of actions, so *nouns* are the most important terms when describing Results and Benefits.

Sometimes a Project, Result or Use increases the likelihood of something negative happening, for example a Use of 'chopping down native trees' would have a negative Link to a Benefit defined as 'a healthy native forest' while simultaneously having a positive Link to a potential Benefit of 'improved profit for a timber company'.

So if a Use has a negative impact (leads to a negative outcome), our syntax captures this in a 'negative Link' from the Use to a positive Benefit/outcome – that is, negativity is captured in Links. In this respect, Projects, Results, Uses and Benefits are *always* worded positively or neutrally and any negativity is captured in the Links.

There are strong psychological reasons for wording all strategies (and SubStrategies) positively. People are more motivated by being associated with positively worded strategies than with negatively worded ones.

Links can only connect adjacent items, that is, a Project can Link to a Result, a Result can Link to a Use and a Use can Link to a Benefit. A Project *cannot* Link to a Use or Benefit. This is vitally important. *There are no shortcuts from Projects to Benefits. Successful* Projects *must* Link to Results which *must* Link to Uses which *must* Link to Benefits.

2.8 Evidence

We have found that very few of the traditional strategies we have encountered in both the public and private sectors can be confidently described as being the 'right' or 'best' or 'optimal' strategy or to even be a 'Validated' strategy which has even a reasonable chance of success. Typically they are merely a selected set of strategic actions with minimal rationale or validation which would demonstrate that they are the right/best/optimal/Validated strategy.

In order to have the confidence to implement a strategy and to know that it is the 'right' or 'best' strategy, it is vital to have solid *cause-and-effect Evidence* to 'Validate' the strategies' proposed actions. Note again the use of upper-case letters for the words Evidence and Validate to make it clear that we have attached precise OpenStrategies meanings to these words (see the glossary in Appendix 1, page 197).

It is important to find *the most relevant and valuable* Evidence which is necessary to most convincingly Validate a strategy and not to waste time collecting irrelevant information.

After tens of thousands of hours working with large and small multi-stakeholder groups developing strategies, the OpenStrategies team has identified certain categories of cause-and-effect Evidence which appear to be the most valuable for Validating strategies. These pieces of Evidence are the ones which provide confidence in the cause-and-effect Links from Projects to Results, from Results to Uses and from Uses to Benefits.

> *In particular, the most valuable Evidence is the cause-and-effect Evidence that confirms that Results will actually be Used.*

Such Evidence can be obtained from market surveys, environmental scanning, scenario planning and many other strategic planning techniques. The key point here is that the *category* of Evidence that is the most valuable is the cause-and-effect Evidence which confirms the Links in the PRUB sequence and in particular the Evidence which confirms that Results will actually be Used.

It is vitally important to note that cause-and-effect Evidence is not the same as performance measurement data.

Cause-and-effect Evidence provides *cause-and-effect information* on the impact that a Project has on a Result, or a Result has on a Use, or a Use has on a Benefit. So Evidence is information which relates to the cause-and-effect nature of the Links between Projects and Results, between Results and Uses and between Uses and Benefits.

In contrast, performance measurement typically measures just the parameters *within* each Project, Result, Use and Benefit and does not contain cause-and-effect information. Performance measurements are merely 'data' which describe the *state* of a Project or a Result or a Use or a Benefit without providing cause-and-effect Evidence of *how* or *why* this state came about. This information is not Evidence of cause-and-effect – it is simply a measure of the 'effect'.

Therefore when seeking compelling Evidence to help Validate a strategy, it is essential to know 'what caused what to happen' (that is, cause-and-effect Evidence) rather than to merely measure the 'consequence of what happened' (performance measurement data).

2.9   Values

Prior to implementing a strategy it is also important to have confidence that 'it will be worth it', that is, that the value of the Benefits exceeds the costs of the Projects *plus* the costs of the Uses. This is a core component of PRUB-Validate (see Chapter 6).

Sometimes it is quite challenging to determine the value of Benefits and it can be even more challenging to translate people's 'values' into Benefits. For example, many first-nations' (native) people place a high value on natural, pure water but it is not always immediately obvious what this value represents in practical terms and hence how to design a strategy which will lead to this value being realised.

In such circumstances it is important to ask people to carefully describe their values and to then ask them what they would need to *see* or *experience* in order to be satisfied that their values were being realised. Generally the answers to this question will be Results, Uses or Benefits which can then be incorporated into a validated SubStrategy designed to realise the desired values.

2.10   Performance Management

The performance management of many traditional strategies is ineffective because the wrong parameters are measured.

We find that frequently the parameters that are measured are the ones that are easy to measure or the ones which matter most to some subgroups of stakeholders, especially finance-oriented stakeholders. We frequently find that financial *data* is collected in fine detail but few *cause-and-effect* measurements or observations are made on the operational processes that impact on financial performance. Financial data are often of minimal value for guiding stakeholders to improve the performance of their operations.

For example, there may be cost over-runs on the Projects within a strategy but merely measuring the costs (data) has minimal value for performance management. It is much more useful to monitor the *cause-and-effect Evidence* within the Projects in order to determine *why* there are cost over-runs and hence to identify actions that can be taken to rectify the problem.

The OpenStrategies system has identified that performance needs to be measured (data) and managed *within* each Project, *within* each Result, *within* each Use and *within* each Benefit. So, for example, in a SubStrategy to build a public swimming pool:

- The performance *data* of the Project may relate to the achievement of construction milestones within budget.

- The performance *data* of a Result may relate to the quality of the pool.

- The performance *data* of the Use may relate to the number of people using the pool.

- The performance *data* of the Benefit may relate to the health improvement of the people who use the pool.

You need to identify one or more 'Indicators' (*what* will be measured), Targets (the desired *level* for the measurement) and actual Measurements (the Measurements that are made when the Project, Result, Use or Benefit is being monitored) within each Project, Result, Use and Benefit.

You further must identify the management actions necessary to improve any performance parameter. Necessarily any such action must take place one step to the left in the PRUB sequence from where the measurement was made. To fix a non-performing Benefit you need to improve the Use (one step to the left in the Projects, Results, Uses and Benefits sequence). To fix a non-performing Use you need to improve the Result and to fix a poor Result you need to improve the Project.

For example, if a Target of 1,100 children per day had been agreed for the Use of a swimming pool but only 725 children per day are using the pool, the only way to increase the level of Use is to improve the Results. This might be achieved by having a better pool, better promotion of the pool, better support services such as public transport and lifeguards or the availability of better activities at the pool such as aquasize classes or sports training.

In assessing which Result needs to be improved in order to achieve the greatest impact on the non-performing Use you will need to understand the cause-and-effect Evidence which Links each Result to the desired Use.

This is why OpenStrategies emphasises the crucial distinction between performance measurement data (measures of consequences) and cause-and-effect Evidence (information on 'what causes what').

Performance measurement data sits *within* each Project, Result, Use and Benefit whereas cause-and-effect Evidence sits on the Links *between* each Project and Result, each Result and Use and each Use and Benefit.

2.11   Benefits, Uses, Results and Projects

You can enhance strategy development processes by first identifying and describing desired outcomes or Benefits and then determining what needs to be done to create these Benefits. Given that the role of organisations is to create assets and enable people to use them, it makes sense to start any strategy process by determining what people want to do (Uses) *before* deciding what assets to create.

This works well by simply reversing the standard PRUB sequence:

1.   define the desired Benefits, then

2.   work out what customers and citizens need to do (Uses) to create these Benefits, then

3.   work out what Results customers and citizens need in order to undertake these Uses, then

4.   work out what Projects are required to create these Results.

The beauty of this approach is that you can:

- •   start with Benefits to articulate your strategy and then

- •   start with Projects to implement it.

So the Projects, Results, Uses and Benefits sequence is simultaneously a strategy and action plan.

2.12   SubStrategies

Generally several Projects are necessary to produce a set of Results (outputs) which collectively are Used by customers and citizens to create one or more Benefits (outcomes) for themselves and/or others. For example we were once invited to review a local authority's strategy for a new £35 million leisure centre that was about to open. Their strategy accurately included the construction of the physical centre itself. Unfortunately their strategy did not include some of the other Projects and Results that were essential to make the leisure centre successful, such as an effective bus system for bringing large numbers of children to the centre during school hours. Their strategy was 'necessary' (it included the leisure centre) but not 'sufficient' (it didn't include the necessary bus system).

A related set of Linked Projects, Results, Uses and Benefits which is both 'necessary' and 'sufficient' is called a 'SubStrategy' – it is the next level of building block above a simple PRUB sequence.

If a strategy is described in terms of Projects, Results, Uses and Benefits:

- A small collection of PRUBs = a SubStrategy.

- A collection of SubStrategies = an OpenStrategy.

Everything organisations do and how customers and citizens Use and Benefit from the Results of what organisations do can be accommodated within a SubStrategy – *without exception*.

Every strategic idea, whether in the public or private sector, can be usefully translated into a SubStrategy.

2.13   Which Information has the Most Value to the Most People?

As a generalisation, many of a strategy's stakeholders are interested in a narrow range of information, some of which is of interest to almost all stakeholders and some of which is of interest to only a few stakeholders. In the above example of a local authority's leisure centre, all stakeholders were interested in the aspirational-level concept of a leisure centre. However, the builders primarily were interested in the Project to build the leisure centre but they were less interested in the health and well-being of the children who were expected to use it. In contrast, the community-oriented people in the local authority were interested in the social Benefits of people's Uses of the leisure centre and the NHS was interested in the associated health Benefits.

Far too often strategies become cluttered up with all sorts of information which is of interest to only small sub-sets of stakeholders. As a consequence few strategies are well understood by most stakeholders (and in fact many strategies are so complicated that stakeholders don't even read them!). As a result stakeholders do not buy in to the strategies, which then fail to be successfully implemented.

Our approach has been to identify:

> the smallest amount of strategic information that has the highest value to the most stakeholders.

This 'smallest amount of information' is encapsulated in SubStrategies and OpenStrategies based on the Projects, Results, Uses and Benefits sequence.

At the highest level, practically all stakeholders are interested in the principles and themes encapsulated in a high-level aspirational SubStrategy such as the above leisure centre example.

Most stakeholders are interested primarily in SubStrategies that are directly relevant to them. In the above example, the builder was interested in the Project and Result relating to the construction of the leisure centre, whereas the community people and NHS were more interested in the Benefits arising from the Uses of the centre.

Typically only a few stakeholders are interested in the *cause-and-effect* Evidence (on the Links) that partially Validates the strategy (and an even smaller set of stakeholders is interested in the net Value of the SubStrategy). For example the NHS people were very keen to understand *how* the Use of the centre by children would impact on the children's health.

Finally a typically very small group of stakeholders is interested in Performance Management, although if performance turns out to be unsatisfactory many stakeholders will suddenly become very interested in Performance Management. In the above example, the procurement officer at the local authority was deeply interested in the quality of the leisure centre (a measure of performance) and the leader of the local authority was very interested in the *number* of people using the centre and how *happy* they were because the number and happiness measures (data) impacted directly on his chances of re-election.

The varying significance to different stakeholders of the different types of strategic information is why the OpenStrategies system of strategy taxonomy, syntax and semantics focuses *first* on defining Projects, Results, Uses and Benefits (taxonomy). This is because most stakeholders get the most benefit from first understanding 'what's happening' or 'what are we trying to achieve?' (Projects, Results, Uses and Benefits). Fewer stakeholders are interested in the secondary emphasis of the OpenStrategies system, that is, how information is connected into SubStrategies (syntax). Finally, even fewer stakeholders are interested in the added meaning (semantics) that comes from adding Evidence, Values and Performance Management information to the SubStrategies and OpenStrategies. We have worked hard to minimise such jargon in the OpenStrategies system, but there is nevertheless a certain minimum set of information required for effective strategies:

> *SubStrategies based on Projects, Results, Uses and Benefits are*
>
> *the smallest amount of strategic information*
>
> *that has the highest value*
>
> *to the most stakeholders.*

2.14 Do Organisations Deliver Outcomes/Benefits?

The question of whether organisations deliver outcomes and Benefits and its answer are vitally important.

The word 'deliver' is commonly but unhelpfully employed by many organisations to combine the functions of Project, Result, Use and Benefit. Traditional strategic documents frequently use the expression 'to deliver outcomes'.

By using the concept 'deliver outcomes', organisations imply that some product or service or infrastructure is developed or provided (that is, a Project), that it is available for Use (that is, a Result or 'output'), that customers or the community are *having to use it* (a Use) and are enjoying a Benefit (or 'outcome') that the organisations have decided is good for them.

A typical example might be a local authority's 'delivery' of a waste collection service. In reality, the local authority cannot 'deliver' such a service. It can certainly make such a service 'available' in the form of waste collection trucks driving around enabled to collect waste, but the service will only happen *if Users put out their waste for collection.* So it takes the *combined efforts of both organisations and end-users to 'deliver services' and create outcomes/Benefits.*

Organisations Cannot 'Deliver' Outcomes/Benefits on Their Own

Organisations can make products and services and infrastructure *available* so that they are *ready* to be Used, but the Benefits (outcomes) only arise when the handover takes place and customers or citizens *actually* Use those services/ products/infrastructure. Organisations can seldom *make* Uses happen by *making* people Use Results, so *organisations cannot deliver outcomes.*

Once organisations realise this, it can be liberating.

If organisations run Projects to create the *right* Results and make them readily available, there is a good chance that customers and citizens will indeed create worthwhile Benefits by Using these Results. In this way organisations can definitely *deliver* Results (that is, assets such as products, services and infrastructure) but they can only *influence* Benefits.

Organisations Cannot Ensure/Deliver/Create/Produce Benefits/Outcomes

Organisations are only indirectly accountable for improved Benefits (outcomes) as they can only *influence* Uses and Benefits, not *deliver* them! In many instances, organisations may nevertheless be held accountable for the emergence of the desired outcomes/Benefits but they can only achieve this accountability through creating the *right* Results so that these Results are Used to achieve the desired Benefits.

Organisations *can* deliver Results (outputs) which are directly under their control and which they are directly accountable for. They can 'deliver' a swimming pool but they cannot 'deliver' healthy children. Children swimming in the swimming pool can potentially 'deliver' healthy children.

A company cannot 'deliver' happy customers. A company can 'deliver' (or 'make available') products and services but it is the Use of those products and services by customers which creates Benefits for the customers and hence happy customers.

Organisations are also accountable for consulting with customers and citizens in order to discover the customers' and citizens' desired Uses in order to create the right Results that are most likely to lead to those Uses and subsequent Benefits.

In most cases such Uses are voluntary. Customers and citizens seldom *have* to Use the Results created by organisations. Therefore in order to achieve high levels of Use and their subsequent Benefits, the Results must be *wanted* by customers and citizens.

There are no shortcuts from Projects to Benefits. To be effective, Projects *must* lead to Results which *must* lead to Uses which *must* lead to Benefits. This point is overwhelmingly important, so we repeat it: *there are no shortcuts from Projects to Benefits.*

So for any strategy to get from Projects through to Benefits it is absolutely essential to understand and enable Uses. Precisely understanding and enabling Uses is the most important component of every strategy because it is *Users not organisations who ensure/deliver/create/produce Benefits/outcomes.*

Sadly the majority of public sector strategies and even some private sector strategies we have encountered make minimal or no reference to Uses. They make false claims that Projects will create Benefits but the essential role of Users as the actual creators of Benefits is seldom acknowledged. This would be like a commercial business creating a strategy without understanding customer behaviour – understanding customers is crucial to business success – and the same applies to enabling the success of public service organisations.

So prior to undertaking a Project to produce a Result, it is essential to engage with end-users (customers and citizens) to secure:

- sufficient cause-and-effect Evidence that enough customers or citizens will actually Use the proposed Results;

- sufficient cause-and-effect Evidence that this Use will create Benefits of sufficient value to the Users to justify the costs of the Project plus the costs of the Uses.

2.15   PRUB and 'Orphan Results'

We find that 15–25% of all existing organisational actions produce Results that no one uses. Some of our colleagues have suggested that in the public sector, up to 40% of activities produce Results that no one uses. We call such Results 'Orphan Results' because they have been lovingly created but then abandoned.

The requirement for compelling cause-and-effect Evidence by the PRUB strategic thinking process explicitly identifies wasteful Projects that are producing Results that are not being or will not be Used. Therefore 'PRUBing a Project' can save money by identifying and stopping such wasteful Projects.

Figure 2.3 illustrates the concept of Orphan Results.

There are two main types of Orphan Results.

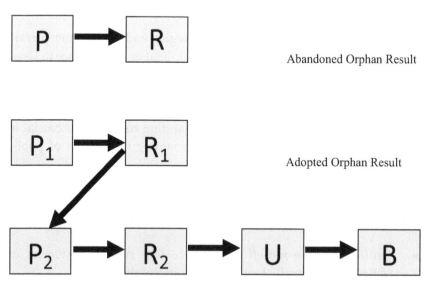

Figure 2.3   PRUB diagram showing the production of two types of
                Orphan Result

ABANDONED ORPHAN RESULTS

These are Orphan Results which cannot be Used by customers/citizens and also cannot be used by other organisations.

We call these 'Abandoned Orphan Results' (for example 'R' in Figure 2.3).

The corresponding Projects should either be modified so they create Useful or Adoptable Results or they should be stopped and money saved.

An example of an Abandoned Orphan Result is 'a report sent to central government which sits unread in a filing cabinet'.

ADOPTED ORPHAN RESULTS

These are Orphan Results which cannot be directly used by customers/citizens but which *can* be *Adopted and used* by other organisations to create useable Results.

We call these 'Adopted Orphan Results' (for example R_1 in Figure 2.3).

An example of an Adopted Orphan Result is 'a research Project P_1 which produces an engineering report as Result R_1 which can then be used (Adopted) by a second organisation to guide the construction P_2 of a swimming pool R_2 which individuals and communities can Use'.

We believe it should be non-negotiable that for every Project it must be incumbent upon the person who starts the Project and creates the Result (the Project leader) to:

- demonstrate compellingly that Users will Use the Result to create Benefits, or

- find someone to Adopt the Orphan Result.

Therefore *before* a Project starts, the project leader should be *responsible and held accountable* for finding either customers or citizens to *Use* the Result or to find an organisation to *Adopt* the Result. If neither of these can be identified or if compelling Evidence cannot be found that they genuinely will Use or Adopt the Result, the Project should not start.

Alarmingly frequently, especially in the public sector, organisations/ Project leaders produce Abandoned Orphan Results and then simply walk away from them, saying it is someone else's responsibility to work out what to do with the Results. What a sad waste of resources. So Projects should not be started until there is clear and compelling Evidence that either:

- the Result will cost-effectively be Used to create Benefits, or

- there is someone willing to Adopt (and ideally pay for) and use the Orphan Result.

Based on extensive discussions with many people in the UK and New Zealand public sectors, we estimate that savings of 15–25% and possibly as high as 50–70% could be achieved immediately in many public sector organisations simply by withdrawing funding from Projects which are producing Abandoned Orphan Results.

2.16   PRUB is a 'Plan and Rationale'

A strategy is all about 'what needs to be done and why' given the current and forecast circumstances. It is about actions/plans (Projects) backed up by reasons for taking those actions (summarised in PRUB as Benefits and as the cause-and-effect Evidence that Links Projects to Results to Uses to Benefits).

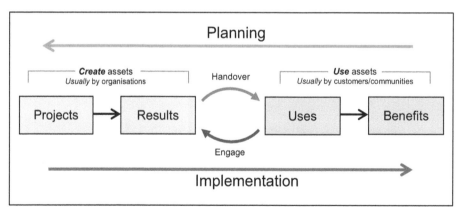

Figure 2.4   PRUB defines the core function of every organisation as it interfaces with its customers and communities

After thousands of hours of research and discussions with hundreds of public, private and third sector people, we're convinced that 'what needs to be done and why' can be best represented by Figure 2.4.

Every other piece of information as shown in Figures 1.1 and 1.2 (Chapter 1) is important in its own specific way for *informing* and *guiding* a strategy, but when all such information has been collected, collated, analysed, tested, brainstormed, mind-mapped, scenario-planned, debated, refined, understood and finally agreed … you still won't have a strategy!

For example 'drivers for change' are not strategy – they *impact on* strategy.

Similarly demographics, geographic factors, themes, economic and financial constraints, legislation and political perspectives all *impact on* strategy – they are not strategy – a strategy must be represented by a sequence of Projects, Results, Uses and Benefits.

So when you have completed your information analysis, you need to take action which reflects all this information.

PRUB reflects 'what needs to be done and why' by organisations (Projects to create Results) and customers/citizens (Uses to create Benefits).

Certainly there is other very important information that should be part of a strategy or action plan, for example:

- precisely who is responsible for a Project or SubStrategy;

- exactly who the customers and citizens (Users) are;

- what resources are required and what are available to support a Project (such as cash, people, infrastructure, and so on);

- start and finish dates for a Project or SubStrategy;

- more detailed information about each Project, Result, Use and Benefit;

- performance measurement information.

Important as this information is, it is of secondary importance to the core PRUB information – indeed it *fits within* each PRUB item.

2.17 Aggregating and Disaggregating SubStrategies

Many strategies are inherently complicated or complex because they must take into account many (often divergent) parameters. They typically involve numerous stakeholders, each with their own agenda.

Therefore few strategic activities can be usefully described with a single Linked sequence made up of a single Project, a single Result, a single Use and a single Benefit.

A number of Projects are usually required to produce several Results which may have one or more Uses to achieve one or more related Benefits. For example, a swimming pool on its own is not sufficient to enable children to swim and get fit. There is also a need for (amongst other things) car parking as well as a range of swimming training and 'poolfun' programmes to encourage young people to use the swimming pool.

This simplistic example has been portrayed in Figure 2.5 as a SubStrategy using PRUB to address an aspirational wish that 'large numbers of young people are taking part in swimming activities'.

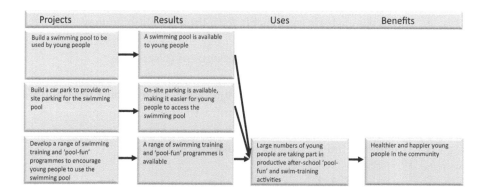

Figure 2.5   A simple SubStrategy

The three Projects shown in Figure 2.5 may still not be enough to enable the desired Use. Other Results that are likely to be required include: trained lifeguards, safety equipment, buses to the swimming pool, cycle routes to the swimming pool, secure cycle parks, promotional campaigns and so on.

A SubStrategy is a tidy and effective way of displaying all the Projects and Results that are *both necessary and sufficient* to enable a Use to happen.

Similarly, many traditional strategies impact on other strategies. For example, a cycling strategy may overlap with a road-use strategy, which may overlap with a freight-transport strategy and a community safety strategy.

We therefore need a mechanism for interlinking multiple strategies in order to identify overlapping Projects, Results, Uses and Benefits, which will then enable us to determine what impact each strategy will have on all other strategies. Once strategic ideas have been translated into the common format of SubStrategies it becomes relatively straightforward to do this interlinking, as discussed in more detail in Chapter 6.

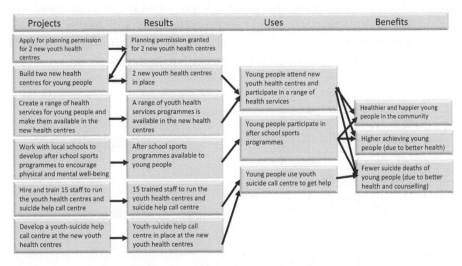

Figure 2.6   **An example of a modest-sized SubStrategy relating to aspects of young people's health**

Figure 2.6 shows a modest-sized SubStrategy created by aggregating several Single SubStrategies on the topics of:

- building a new health centre;

- a campaign to promote the new health centre;

- development of after-school programmes;

- building and staffing a youth suicide call centre.

This is typical of the manner in which single SubStrategies can be aggregated into a larger thematic SubStrategy while simultaneously:

- retaining the distinctness of each SubStrategy;

- interlinking the SubStrategies.

The first Project produces an Orphan Result which is Adopted by the second Project. Further Projects and Results are likely to be required to make this SubStrategy complete (for example to promote the youth health centre to young people). However, even this simplified SubStrategy shows how multiple Projects can easily be interlinked into cohesive SubStrategies.

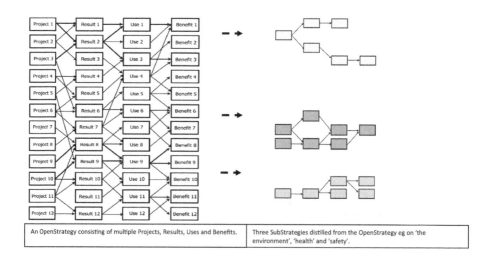

An OpenStrategy consisting of multiple Projects, Results, Uses and Benefits.	Three SubStrategies distilled from the OpenStrategy eg on 'the environment', 'health' and 'safety'.

Figure 2.7   **A number of PRUBs aggregated into an OpenStrategy as well as three SubStrategies distilled from the OpenStrategy**

Figure 2.7 similarly shows schematically how once strategic plans have been encapsulated into SubStrategies they can first be aggregated into collections of ideas or SubStrategies to create an overall OpenStrategy and secondly that they can be disaggregated into the same or different SubStrategies. The left-hand part of Figure 2.7 shows an example of a small OpenStrategy made up of 48 Projects, Results, Uses and Benefits together with the links between these PRUB items.

Such an OpenStrategy could contain half a dozen or more SubStrategies on specific themes or demographic or geographic groupings.

The right-hand part of Figure 2.7 shows three thematic SubStrategies which have been distilled from this OpenStrategy.

By using PRUB, individual Projects, Results, Uses and Benefits can be aggregated, disaggregated and re-aggregated easily to form new SubStrategies, for example on cross-cutting themes or focusing on particular demographic groups.

In the example in Figure 2.7 it would be easy to create a combined 'environmental, health and safety SubStrategy' by simply combining the three distilled SubStrategies.

Similarly it would be straightforward to add 'recreational' PRUBs to the Environmental SubStrategy to create an 'Environmental and Recreational SubStrategy'.

So a fundamental principle of OpenStrategy is that SubStrategies are scalable and can be aggregated into OpenStrategies – and then disaggregated again.

For example:

- A Transport OpenStrategy can be an aggregation of SubStrategies on cycling, walking, horse riding, road transport, rail transport and aviation.

- An Environmental OpenStrategy can be a distillation and an aggregation of SubStrategies on biodiversity, trees, protected areas, recreational open spaces, cycling, walking, horse riding and waste management.

As described in the bullet points above, the cycling, walking and horse riding SubStrategies can each be part of *both* a Transport OpenStrategy *and* an Environmental OpenStrategy.

An aspirational-level OpenStrategy based on raising children's health through physical exercise could contain operational-level SubStrategies on a swimming pool, gymnastics, football, horse riding, cycling, rowing, martial arts and other themes.

At the same time the swimming pool SubStrategy could be part of an older persons' OpenStrategy while also being part of the local authority's Capital Works OpenStrategy.

So once all activities have been 'PRUBd' into SubStrategies they can be aggregated and disaggregated and re-aggregated into many different OpenStrategies based on themes, demographic groupings, geographic areas and indeed many other combination of SubStrategies.

Therefore instead of an organisation needing 50 or 100 strategies they can have a single 'library of SubStrategies' which can be aggregated and disaggregated into whatever combinations of OpenStrategies are desired.

A strength of the OpenStrategies approach is that the same SubStrategies can appear in multiple OpenStrategies without having to redraft them (see Chapter 7 for more information on the aggregation and disaggregation of SubStrategies).

So PRUB-based SubStrategy building blocks enable enormous flexibility in the shared, transparent development, aggregation and re-aggregation of strategy components (Projects, Results, Uses and Benefits) to create new SubStrategies (new combinations of strategic ideas) using the same Projects, Results, Uses and Benefits.

Such re-aggregation enables a strategic refocusing as and when required on specific themes, demographics, geographical areas or all of the above.

A key point to note here is that strategy implementation happens at the level of SubStrategies. The implementation of any strategy necessarily consists of multiple actions and each such action is the first step, that is, a Project in a SubStrategy.

The effective implementation of a large strategy or OpenStrategy by implementing many SubStrategies will certainly require coordination amongst all the SubStrategies in order to achieve the (Open)Strategy's overall intent, but every organisational action will nevertheless just be a Project within a SubStrategy.

Where there are multiple PRUBs, as in a large SubStrategy or OpenStrategy, the sum total of the Benefits is closely related to the reasons for implementing a strategy – that is, the 'vision' of the stakeholder organisations and their communities.

The total set of Benefits approximates the Vision of an OpenStrategy's stakeholders.

Similarly, the total set of Results approximately defines the mission of the OpenStrategy's organisational stakeholders.

2.18   Summary

When strategies are created as interlinked suites of operational-level SubStrategies using the OpenStrategies taxonomy, syntax and semantics, they:

- exactly represent the core function of organisations, which is to 'create assets and enable people to use them to create benefits';

- precisely define the strategic actions which need to be adopted and improved in order to optimise the performance of the organisation;

- can be directly implemented, because Projects are explicitly defined;

- demonstrate explicitly how Projects (inputs) contribute ultimately via Results and Uses to Benefits (outcomes);

- confirm that there are no shortcuts between Projects and Benefits – Users *have* to be engaged to create Benefits;

- identify where it is most important to have convincing cause-and-effect Evidence to Validate Projects and SubStrategies;

- can be aggregated, disaggregated and re-aggregated into different combinations and sizes to create strategies on chosen themes or demographic or geographic groups using the same PRUB strategic building blocks;

- enable the interlinking of national, regional and local strategies while preserving the integrity of each SubStrategy;

- enable effective communications because all stakeholders use the same PRUB strategy language;

- show simply and transparently what sub-groups are doing, thereby assisting collaboration;

- evolve fluidly over time;

- save money by explicitly identifying those Projects/actions which create Abandoned Orphan Results and hence such Projects should be stopped and money saved;

- can be 'Validated'.

PRUB thinking is also a powerful tool for diagnosing existing strategies.

WHAT BURP/PRUB HELPS YOU ACHIEVE

The sequence 'Benefits, Uses, Results and Projects' helps you to diagnose existing strategies and to create validated strategies and SubStrategies. Subsequently the sequence 'Projects, Results, Uses and Benefits' guides you to implement SubStrategies.

A FINAL RECOMMENDATION

OpenStrategies identifies that stakeholders should implement interlinked SubStrategies instead of implementing individual Projects because SubStrategies encapsulate the core processes that organisations actually *do*: 'create assets and enable people to use them to create benefits'.

It is rare for a single Project to lead via a Result and a Use to a Benefit, so generally it will require the implementation of multiple interlinked Projects, Results, Uses and Benefits (that is, a SubStrategy) to achieve the desired Benefits.

So we strongly recommend that you: *'Implement SubStrategies, not Projects'*.

PART I

Why Most Strategies Fail to Have Any Impact

Chapter 3
Strategy Language (Taxonomy)

3.1 Introduction

The next three chapters use Projects, Results, Uses and Benefits thinking and the concept of three levels of strategies as lenses to explore some of the linguistic reasons why so many strategies fail to have any impact.

This chapter evaluates traditional uses of strategy words (strategy language taxonomy), in particular the verbs used to describe strategic actions.

Chapter 4 continues to use PRUB thinking to diagnose the many ways that strategic environments impact on the structure (syntax) and meaning (semantics) of strategic thinking.

Chapter 5 then uses PRUB thinking to define many issues relating to stakeholder engagement and explains how these issues impact on the effectiveness of strategies.

3.2 The Validity of All Three Levels of Strategy

All three levels of strategy are valuable, each in its own context and each with its own taxonomy of 'strategy words', especially as they relate to the verbs ('Project-verbs') used within the Project descriptions. This applies irrespective of whether the OpenStrategies system of strategy taxonomy, syntax and semantics is used or if some other strategy system is used:

- 'Aspirational strategies' use high-level aspirational, Benefits-oriented 'Project-verbs' and result in relatively small documents such as are required at the very top of any organisation or multi-stakeholder group.

- 'Guidance strategies' use a mix of aspirational and practical 'Project-verbs' and result in medium-sized documents such as are required by managers within an organisation or multi-stakeholder group.

- 'Operational strategies' must use 'Project-verbs' which can actually be implemented and typically result in very large action-planning documents such as are required by the grassroots people who actually implement strategies.

If all strategies were aspirational strategies, there would be insufficient detail for any implementation to take place. So there is definitely a need for strategies which are more detailed than aspirational strategies.

However, if all strategies were operational-level strategies, there would be far too much information in massive strategy documents that few stakeholders would read or understand. So there is definitely a need for aspirational strategies which are succinct summaries of the main strategic issues as well as operational-level strategies which define exactly what needs to be done at the operational level.

In between these two extremes of succinct aspirational strategies and detailed operational strategies (action plans) are the guidance-level strategies which guide management-level stakeholders by providing sufficient strategic guidance without micro-managing each situation.

The need for these three levels of strategies leads to a requirement to clearly distinguish between the different levels so that:

- each strategy is clearly an aspirational strategy or a guidance strategy or an operational strategy and is not a mixture of the three types of strategies;

- stakeholders are crystal clear about whether they are developing an aspirational, guidance or operational strategy;

- stakeholders who are developing, for example, an operational-level strategy can engage meaningfully with other stakeholders who are developing an aspirational-level strategy or a guidance-level strategy because there are clear taxonomic, syntactical and semantic rules for delineating and interlinking the different strategy levels.

A key parameter which delineates the level of a strategy is the verbs used when describing Projects. This chapter focuses on the different categories of 'Project-verbs' (that is, verbs used in descriptors of Projects) as they relate to aspirational and operational strategies because the failure to use the correct Project-verbs is a key reason why so many strategies fail to be understood or to have any impact.

By understanding how different Project-verbs are appropriate to different levels of strategy, it becomes easy to evaluate existing strategy documents to:

- determine what level they are;

- distil the different levels from a (typically confusingly) multi-level strategy;

- create an interlinked set of aspirational, guidance and operational-level strategies.

3.3 The Different Categories of Project-verbs for the Different Levels of Strategies

Many strategies use words and phrases that *sound like* strategies but which can't be implemented.

In some instances such strategies are legitimate, high-level aspirational strategies which were designed to give an outline of what a stakeholder group is trying to achieve without getting into operational details.

More often such strategies are *intended* to be implemented but they still cannot be implemented because the action words they use cannot actually be actioned.

A verb such as 'ensure' cannot actually be implemented. 'Ensure' sounds like a good, strong action word for a strategy but there simply is no action which can be identified within the term 'ensure'. Verbs such as 'ensure' are pseudo-action verbs.

For example, it might be possible to exclude predators from a breeding colony of rare birds by building a protective fence and such an action might help to 'ensure' that the birds are safe, but there is simply no action known as 'ensure'.

As discussed in more detail below, the same arguments apply to words such as 'protect' and 'conserve' and 'provide'. None of these action words can be implemented.

Instead, such action words point to Benefits.

For example, a high-level aspirational strategy Project such as 'Protect rare and threatened birds' points to a desired Benefit of 'rare and threatened birds are safe/protected'. However, this phrase provides no indication or action statements that describe *how* this protection/safety will be achieved.

So the verb 'protect' cannot be implemented and has no place in an operational-level strategy, although it can be a perfectly useful word in a high-level aspirational strategy.

Similarly, stakeholders may want a Benefit along the lines of 'citizens are confident that there are lower levels of criminal activity' and this may be expressed in a traditional high-level aspirational strategy document as a pseudo-action statement such as 'ensure low levels of criminal activity'. However, as with the previous example, there is no action known as 'ensure'.

So, traditional high-level strategies typically take outcomes-related (Benefits-related) concepts such as 'protec*ted* rare birds' and then try to make them into actionable strategic statements by 'verbalising' them, that is, by creating *Project-like* statements such as '*protect* rare birds'. However, such verbalising of the high-level aspirations does not make them actionable, even if it does capture a general sense of strategic intent.

In contrast, operational-level strategies use actionable Project-verbs in their Project descriptions to define exactly what needs to be done.

Is this all 'just' a matter of semantics? It *is* a matter of semantics, but it is not *just* a matter of semantics.

At first glance it may appear as if insisting on the precise use of strategy taxonomy (including precisely categorised Project-verbs), syntax and semantics is merely being pedantic. In reality it turns out that the loose use of strategy taxonomy, syntax and semantics leads to the widespread development of poor strategies which are poorly understood by stakeholders and which either do not get implemented or which do not have any positive impacts when they do get implemented.

Using taxonomically, syntactically and semantically precisely defined strategic information definitely provides illuminating clarity for strategies and in particular guides the development of implementable, validated strategies that actually make a difference.

The following sections discuss the categories of verbs which are appropriate to aspirational-level strategies and to operational-level strategies while noting that guidance-level strategies typically contain a mixture of the types of verbs used in aspirational-level and operational-level strategies.

VERBS FOR HIGH-LEVEL ASPIRATIONAL STRATEGIES

The Project-verbs in Table 3.1 are suitable for high-level aspirational strategies but are ineffective for operational-level projects. In essence, these verbs define abstract 'pseudo-actions' which cannot actually be undertaken by anyone. They imply actions but they cannot be implemented.

To translate these aspirational Project-verbs into implementable Project-Verbs they each need to be followed by ... 'by doing xyz' where 'xyz' is a specific implementable action.

For example, an aspirational statement such as 'grow our business in South East Asia' can be made into a more operational-level strategy by expanding it into something such as 'grow our business in South East Asia *by negotiating agency agreements with another 55 distributors within 12 months'*.

In this instance the implementable action is 'negotiating', leading to new agency agreements with distributors which in turn will (hopefully) lead to more sales and ultimately to growth in the business in South East Asia.

Although the table of aspirational Project-verbs (Table 3.1) is separate from the subsequent list of operational Project-verbs (Table 3.2), in reality there is some overlap. For example, the word 'maintain' can be used loosely in an aspirational strategy (for example 'maintain services') or a bit more precisely in a guidance strategy (for example 'maintain the spare parts service for the company's products').

However, even though the level of precision is increasing from the aspirational to the guidance strategy, in the above example the action of 'maintain' is still quite vague. Therefore at the operational level the use of a Project-verb such as 'maintain' would ideally be accompanied by a statement of *how* the maintenance would happen. For example, the above guidance-level statement could be made more readily implementable by expanding it into a suite of Projects along the lines of:

'maintain the spare parts service for the company's products by:

1. training all spare parts staff at least once per year in customer relations skills;

2. repainting all spare parts depots in the company's new colour scheme;

3. installing a stock management computer system;

4. holding an agreed minimum number of each spare part consistent with last year's levels of demand'.

In this example the actual actions which come under the aspirational-level verb 'maintenance' relate to 'training', 'repainting', 'software-installing' and 'stock-holding'.

Table 3.1   Project-verbs for aspirational-level strategies

Verb	Comment
'Exploratory' Project -verbs	**'Exploratory' Project-verbs hint at issues that need to be considered and they indicate a need for further investigations before the issues can be properly addressed in any strategy.**
Explore Investigate Review Consider	These Project-verbs are very loose, open-ended non-committal words which can be useful in early-stage, high-level aspirational strategies where there is as yet minimal clarity about exactly what needs to be done. The Results of these Project-verbs are almost invariably Orphan Results such as 'reports' which then need to be Adopted by other Projects to guide such actions as 'make a decision', which produce another Orphan Result of 'a decision'. The decision then needs to be Adopted into yet another Project which actually implements the decision. Project-verbs such as *explore/investigate/review/consider* can be useful in early-stage, aspirational-level strategies but they are less useful in operational-level strategies where they *tend to be used as delaying tactics to avoid actually taking any real concrete or substantive actions.*
Address	*Address* is a Project-verb which initially appears to be a worthwhile concept but which actually does not have much substance to it because it gives no guidance on *how* to *address* the topic to be addressed. All that the concept of *address* does is to bring an issue into a strategy, but it says absolutely nothing strategic about what to do with the issue. *Address* should ideally be avoided in any level of strategy.

Table 3.1 Project-verbs for aspirational-level strategies (*continued*)

Verb	Comment
Recognise Take into account	*Recognise* and *take into account* are also Project-verbs which initially appear to be robust and worthwhile concepts but which have minimal substance to them. They sometimes have some value in aspirational or guidance-level strategies – for example, in guiding stakeholders to *recognise* or *take into account* the values of ethnic minorities – but these words provide absolutely no guidance as to *how* to recognise or take into account any issue.
'Improvement' Project-verbs	**'Improvement' Project-verbs are useful in high-level aspirational strategies because they hint at a need for change in a strategy but they provide no indication of how that change will be implemented.**
Enhance Improve Increase Consolidate	*Enhance/improve/increase/consolidate* imply a change in a Result or a Benefit without providing any clarity on *how* the change will be achieved. They are useful words for conveying a stakeholder group's broad intent but they need to be translated into more specific and more actionable Project-verbs if they are to be included in guidance-level or operational-level strategies. An effective operational-level strategy will specify the level of the final end-point for any *enhancement/improvement/increase/consolidate* Project rather than just use these vague terms. For example, an implementable operational-level SubStrategy may include a measurable Use along the following lines: 'The number of customers purchasing and using the company's products will have increased from 1,200 per day in 2012 to 2,300 per day in 2018.'
Prioritise Focus on	*Prioritise* and *focus on* are popular Project-verbs which sound particularly convincing and worthwhile because they imply some sort of astute judgement about the importance of the issues being *prioritised/focused on*. However, like so many aspirational-level strategy verbs, they give absolutely no indication of how the issues will be *prioritised* or *focused on*. Nevertheless, these terms do have value in aspirational-level strategies because they provide some indication of the level of importance of some issues relative to others, but they have minimal or no value when used in operational-level strategies.
Optimise	*Optimise* is also a particularly popular strategy word because it conveys a warmly comforting sense of improvement in all facets of an issue without needing to provide any information on how the improvements will be achieved in each such facet, which facets are most important to improve and the extent to which it is economic to improve each facet. Strategies frequently contain phrases such as 'optimise shareholder value', which seems especially redundant because what's the alternative – to *not* optimise shareholder value? Indeed, it can be convincingly argued that *all* strategies should be attempting to optimise *all* facets of a strategy, hence the use of the Project-verb *optimise* is redundant.
Encourage Promote	*Encourage* and *promote* are loose, catch-all concepts which, like so many other aspirational-level Project-verbs, do little more than identify an issue that needs to be addressed and hint at the fact that the issues need to be encouraged and promoted by at least some of the stakeholders. Surely if an issue is going to be included within a strategy, it will, by default, need to be *encouraged* and *promoted*, so in many instances these words are redundant (like *optimise*).
Support/help	Many strategies include concepts such as *support* and *help*. While these words convey a generally positive expression of an organisation's intent, they are too vague to be used operationally as they provide no indication of *how* the support or help will be made available. Even when used in aspirational strategies, these Project-verbs do little more than draw attention to an issue and convey the fact that the strategy will *contribute to* the issue rather than actually manage it within the strategy.

Table 3.1   Project-verbs for aspirational-level strategies (*continued*)

Verb	Comment
'Certainty' Project-verbs	**'Certainty' Project-verbs are words which appear to convey absolute confidence that the strategy will have its desired effects without making it clear how or why there is reason for such confidence.**
Ensure	This word is one of the most popular words in strategies because it conveys a sense of determination to actually implement the strategy. However, simply putting this word into a strategy doesn't make the strategy happen, especially because there is no such action as *ensure*. Organisations may be able to take actions which have a high probability of producing a desired Result but they cannot *ensure* that the community will Use them, nor can they *ensure* that the community will Benefit. Organisations can only produce Results that encourage or provide the incentive for something to happen and then make these Results available to end-Users. If they are the right Results, there is a high probability that end-Users will Use them and so create the desired Benefits, but organisations can't *ensure* that this will happen (except in rare, legislatively mandated and enforced situations such as prisons). Therefore, to maximise the probability that a desired outcome (Benefit) will be achieved, an organisation will wish to *influence* (not *ensure*) Users' behaviour by making their Results as attractive and accessible as possible, accompanied by well-distributed, convincing information on the merits of the Results, the recommended Uses and the anticipated Benefits. So if you see the word *ensure* in a strategy document we encourage you to carefully consider whether it is in fact possible to *ensure* whatever the strategy is attempting to *ensure* and if not (which we believe to be the case almost 100% of the time), to replace the word *ensure* with more meaningful and implementable Project-verbs.
Prevent Restrict Limit Reduce Enforce	*Prevent* and *restrict* and *limit* and *reduce* and *enforce* are Project-verbs with similar characteristics to *ensure*. Except in legislatively mandated and enforced situations, they quite simply cannot be *made* to happen. As with *ensure*, the correct approach to these concepts is for stakeholders (typically organisations) to take practical actions which create the right Results that increase the probability of *preventing/restricting/limiting/reducing/enforcing* some desired behaviour or situation. These practical actions will use much more specific Project-verbs than the abstract concepts of this set of aspirational verbs, for example they might include Project-verbs such as '*build* fences ...' or '*develop* policies ...' or '*monitor* behaviours and *issue* infringement notices ...', all of which are implementable steps which will ideally lead to the desired *prevention/restriction/limitation/reduction/enforcement* of some desired behaviour or situation. So if you see the words *prevent/restrict/limit/reduce/enforce* in a strategy document, we encourage you to carefully consider whether it is in fact possible to *prevent/restrict/limit/reduce/enforce* whatever the strategy is attempting to *prevent/restrict/limit/reduce/enforce* and, if not (which is likely), to replace these words with more meaningful and implementable Project-verbs.
'Cooperation' Project-verbs	**'Cooperation' Project-verbs relate to a general process that can be applied to Projects, that is, for stakeholders to work together.**

Table 3.1   Project-verbs for aspirational-level strategies (*continued*)

Verb	Comment
Collaborate Cooperate Engage	*Collaborate, cooperate* and *engage* are Project-verbs which have become very popular in recent years, especially in the public sector, where it is considered to be important to engage (or appear to engage) with stakeholders when developing and/or implementing a strategy. There is a widespread belief that collaboration, cooperation and engaging are almost universally good things to do even though they are usually expensive and difficult to carry out in a manner which will achieve meaningful Results or Benefits from these processes. Indeed, these processes are often deemed to be so beneficial that they are embarked upon purely as *collaboration/cooperation/engagement* exercises with no clear concepts of what is to be achieved in terms of Benefits through such joint working. Because these three concepts are so universally believed to be 'good things to do' they appear in many strategy documents with little information on *why* these processes are believed to add value to a strategy or *how* these processes will be applied during the development or implementation of the strategy. As with other aspirational-level strategy words, they give no indication of *how* collaboration or cooperation or engagement is to occur or what value it will generate. The OpenStrategies team is an enthusiastic proponent of *collaboration, cooperation* and *engagement* but nevertheless we generally advise against undertaking *collaboration* or *cooperation* or *engagement* processes until the stakeholders we are working with can provide convincing arguments as to why they believe that these processes will be effective and add value in their particular circumstances. These processes have no independent life of their own and they have no inherent value in themselves – they must involve *collaboration/cooperation/engagement about* an issue in order to *improve* the way the issue is addressed to create better or more Benefits. Be very wary of strategies which propose *collaboration/cooperation/engagement* in isolation from what these processes will be applied to or when there is minimal information on why these processes will add sufficient value to the issues to justify their substantial costs.
Other aspirational Project-verbs	**The following 'Project-verbs' are frequently used in traditional strategies and need to be used carefully and mindfully if they are to be effective.**
Educate	*Educate* is a very provider-driven concept which is at odds with modern thinking about *learning. Educate* implies that the primary actor is the educator, whereas *learning* implies, more realistically, that the main actors are the learners. Learning is a voluntary activity by the end-Users so it quite simply cannot be *made* to happen by the educators. Therefore, it is simply not possible to *educate* anyone. So like other provider-driven Project-verbs such as *deliver* and *provide, educate* is generally an inappropriate concept for any level of strategy, whether aspirational, guidance or operational.
Enable	*Enable* is a particularly well-meaning, end-User-focused Project-verb which recognises that most end-Uses are voluntary and therefore it is important to make it easy for end-Users to use the Results of Projects. So philosophically and psychologically, *enable* is well attuned to modern strategic thinking which recognises that the key actions in any strategy are the actions of the end-Users. However, like most aspirational-level Project-verbs, *enable* gives no indication of *how* end-Users will be *enabled* to Use a Result, so this verb should only be used in aspirational-level strategies.

Table 3.1   Project-verbs for aspirational-level strategies (*continued*)

Verb	Comment
Conserve Preserve Protect	These three Project-verbs are common in all levels of traditional strategies even though they provide no guidance on *how* to *conserve* or *preserve* or *protect*. In general, these three words merely suggest that some issue is especially worthwhile because at least some stakeholders believe the issue is worth retaining in some way (by *conserving*, *preserving* or *protecting* it). These three concepts should be restricted to aspirational-level and occasionally to guidance-level strategies but they are insufficiently specific to guide the implementation of operational-level strategies.
Deliver	The Project-verb *deliver* has been discussed in several places in this book, but it is nevertheless worth revisiting it here because it is such a widely used, widely believed and widely misunderstood verb in strategy documents, especially in the public sector. The word *deliver* is popular in public service strategies (that is, the public service generally believes its role is to '*deliver* public services to citizens') but the verb is misleading because most such services are not, and cannot be, *delivered*. Instead, a much more accurate concept, which has profound philosophical and psychological ramifications, is the concept of 'make available'. So public services are 'made available to' citizens, not '*delivered* to' or '*delivered* at' or '*delivered* for' citizens. In this model, citizens come and 'Use' the services; they don't have services '*delivered* to/at/for' them. Why is this so important? It is about power, control and effectiveness. The concept of *deliver* implies that the deliverer is controlling the interaction – that the deliverer has power in the interaction with citizens and that citizens are merely passive, willing and indeed grateful participants in the *delivery* process. In reality: citizens are generally the ones who are paying for the service either via taxes or by direct payment for the service, so the public servants are being paid by the citizens to enable citizens to enjoy better lives. The citizens generally have the option of using, or not using, the service (legislatively required services not withstanding). Therefore, for each service, it is the citizens who actually have the power to dictate whether or not the service is Used. Also, there are generally many more Users than there are providers of a service, so in terms of sheer numbers, the Users collectively have much more power than the providers. Therefore, the power inherent in the Use of most public service resides with the Users. This means that the concept of 'to *deliver*' as applied to public services is quite wrong and a more correct concept is 'to make available' or 'to hand over' a Result to enable its Use by end-Users.
Manage	*Manage* is a popular and seemingly comforting Project-verb in traditional strategies because it conveys a sense of intention and/or control over an issue. However, as noted earlier, most end-Users simply cannot be *managed* because they are free agents who can choose to Use, or not Use, any Result created by a provider organisation. Therefore, the concept of *managing* the end-to-end implementation of any strategy which has free-agent end-Users is no more than a fantasy. However, it will often be possible to *manage* a Project to confidently produce a desired Result even though it is not possible to *manage* the subsequent Use-step. As with other aspirational-level strategy words, *manage* provides no indication of *how* the managing will be done. *Manage* is therefore a Project-verb which should be used only in aspirational strategies and occasionally in guidance-level strategies, but it is too vague to make any useful contribution to operational-level strategies.

Table 3.1   Project-verbs for aspirational-level strategies (*concluded*)

Verb	Comment
Maintain	*Maintain* has similar characteristics to *manage* because it also conveys a sense of intention and control over an issue. However, *maintain* provides no strategic guidance on *how* the maintenance will be carried out so this word has value primarily in high-level aspirational strategies which are aiming to identify those things that need maintaining rather than identifying how they will be maintained (as would be required for an operational-level strategy).
Provide	Like the terms *improve* and *deliver* (see above), *provide* combines a number of concepts and suggests Projects, Results, Uses and Benefits all rolled up together. In PRUB these need to be separated so that there is clarity about what the Project is (how a product or infrastructure or service will be created), what the Result is (that is, what is available to hand over to the community), what the Use is (that is, who is using it and how) and finally what the Benefit is to the community.
Introduce Take steps to ...	*Introduce* and *take steps to* ... frequently appear in strategy documents when there is a lack of clarity on what needs to be done. They are redundant phrases because the implementation of *any* strategy will involve *introducing* or *taking steps*, so such words and phrases should not be included in any meaningful strategy.

PROJECT-VERBS FOR OPERATIONAL-LEVEL STRATEGIES

Operational-level strategies must be directly implementable. Therefore, the Project-verbs used in their Project descriptors must be actions that can actually be taken.

It is relatively straightforward to determine if a Project-verb is actually implementable: simply try envisaging someone 'doing' the Project-verb.

- Can you visualise someone 'ensuring'? No, so it is not an operational-level, implementable Project-verb.

- Can you visualise someone 'building' or 'designing' or 'facilitating'? Yes, so these are operational-level, implementable Project-verbs.

There are hundreds of operational-level, implementable Project-verbs, so the short list of operational-level Project-verbs in Table 3.2 includes only a few typical examples of Project-verbs that can definitely be directly implemented.

Table 3.2   Project-verbs for operational-level strategies

Project-verbs for operational-level strategies
Build a bridge.
Write a promotional brochure.
Design and build a new commercial product.
Facilitate a workshop.
Develop a marketing strategy.
Paint a piece of infrastructure.
Train staff.
Manufacture a car dashboard.
Draft new legislation.
Patrol the streets.
Write a computer program.
Construct a building.
Mediate between parties.
Negotiate and sign a contract.
Fill in a form for planning permission.
Install lighting in a stadium.

3.4   Other Strategy Words and How They Are Typically (Mis)Used

The words in Table 3.3 appear frequently in strategy documents. A key challenge is that many of them have different meanings to different people.

In Table 3.3 we highlight the *observed* differences in meanings for these words together with some of the ways that we have observed these words being used and misused in practice. We emphasise that these meanings and differences in meanings are the *observed* meanings and differences in meanings and are not in any way related to dictionary-based meanings of these words.

We have not attempted to select any preferred meaning or preferred usage for these words because in our experience this is a futile task which is heavily influenced by one's biases and historical, personal usage of the words. Also, dictionary definitions are inconsistent.

Readers who are interested in international attempts to develop consistent meanings for the dozens of words commonly found in strategies are encouraged to connect with StratML (Strategy Mark-up Language) at http://xml.gov/stratml/index.htm.

In our case, instead of attempting to work with this existing, imprecisely defined strategy terminology, we developed the simple PRUB taxonomy, syntax and semantics as a minimalist, master-set of precisely defined strategy terms together with rules for their use. We believe that our taxonomy/syntax/ semantics including Projects, Results, Uses, Benefits, Links, Evidence, Value, and PRUB-Validate and our carefully defined performance monitoring terminology constitute the most succinct and effective such package of strategy language that has been developed so far. We welcome feedback on this assertion together with recommendations for making the OpenStrategies system even more effective.

Table 3.3 **Traditional strategy words and their *observed* meanings and uses/misuses**

Word	Comment
Goals Objectives	There are many dictionary definitions of *goals* and *objectives*. However, *in practice* we find that most stakeholders are unclear about what goals and objectives actually are. Some people believe that a set of goals contributes to an objective and some believe that a set of objectives contributes to a goal. Some refer to internal goals/ objectives (which we could call Results) and to external goals/objectives (which we could call Uses or Benefits). This means that the terms *goals* and *objectives* are typically used loosely and unhelpfully to refer to any of the three factors which we have rigorously delineated as Results, Uses and Benefits.
Impact	The word *impact* is a loosely defined term which is sometimes used to define the accumulation of outcomes (Benefits) at a community or larger scale. For example, if a Benefit such as 'healthy individuals' applies to many people, the *impact* might be defined as the overall change in health of the community, taking into account such things as the percentage of people in the community who are creating and/or receiving the Benefit. In the OpenStrategies system we accommodate the concept of *impact* within each Benefit by including cumulative performance information (for example, how many people are Benefitting).
Mission	The definition of the *mission* of many organisations is typically as unclear and non-specific as its *vision*. OpenStrategies recommends that a useful organisational mission can be distilled and consolidated from the Results in a guidance-level OpenStrategy because these Results define exactly what assets the organisation is intending to create – that is, its mission ('organisations create assets which people use to create benefits'). When this type of mission is combined with the type of Benefits-based vision recommended by OpenStrategies, the output is more or less an aspirational SubStrategy for the organisation.
Outcomes	Despite the UK and New Zealand public sectors both being ostensibly *outcomes*-focused, we have discovered that fewer than 10% of the public servants we have listened to are able to define an *outcome*. Generally they have indicated that an *outcome* is something that happens long after they have completed their tasks and that *outcomes* are something to do with end-Users. *They seldom take any responsibility for 'outcomes'!* Amongst the definitions that have been offered for an *outcome* are descriptions which we would variously categorise as Results, Uses and Benefits. Therefore, in our experience the term *outcome* is too vague to be useful in strategies and is better replaced by the exact terminology of Results, Uses and Benefits.

Table 3.3   Traditional strategy words and their *observed* meanings and uses/misuses (*continued*)

Word	Comment
Outcomes-based Accountability	The methodology known as *Outcomes-based Accountability* has its own set of definitions for *outputs* and *outcomes* (including internal outcomes and external outcomes) and these are useful within the context of this methodology. We believe that the OpenStrategies taxonomy, syntax and semantics offer a more concise, integrated and more widely understood information set for strategy analysis, strategic planning, strategy implementation and performance management.
Outputs	As with people's limited understanding of the word *outcomes*, few people are able to provide us with a clear definition of the popular strategy word *output*. Where people are able to offer a definition it comes closest to the OpenStrategies term *Result*, that is, something that exists as a consequence of an action by an organisation.
Performance measurement and management Indicators Targets Measurements	Only a small percentage of stakeholders exhibit an understanding of performance management and the meaning of terms such as *indicators*, *targets* and *measurements*. There is also limited awareness of *what* needs to be measured in order to generate useful information to inform subsequent management decisions to improve performance. All too often factors are measured because they are easy to measure and not because the results of the measurements are useful for improving performance. As one client advised: 'you don't fatten the pig by measuring it', yet so often that is what people attempt to do – to measure, measure and measure some more in the fond hope that something will improve as a consequence of all this measuring. The OpenStrategies system identifies one or more *indicators* (what will be measured), *targets* (the desired level for the measurement) and actual *measurements* (the measurements that are made when the Project, Result, Use or Benefit is being monitored) within each Project, Result, Use and Benefit. The OpenStrategies system further identifies that management actions to improve any performance parameter must necessarily take place one step to the left in the PRUB sequence from where the measurement was made (see section 2.10 in Chapter 2).
Plan Strategy	The words *plan* and *strategy* have many and varied meanings in the minds of different people. For some they are lists of actions, whereas for others they are aspirational documents which describe desired outcomes. For some they are documents which define what is allowed to be built in different zones of a city and for yet others they are a sequence of actions on a single issue. It is specifically because of this wide variation in meanings which we *observe* to be given to these words by different people that we have developed our alternative precise and unique definitions for SubStrategies and OpenStrategies and their three different levels (aspirational, guidance and operational) together with a rigorously defined taxonomy, syntax and semantic for the OpenStrategies system. In reality there is an unbroken continuum from aspirational strategies down to operational strategies. In this respect, we have yet to find any traditional 'strategy' which does not neatly fit into the format of a PRUB-based aspirational SubStrategy.

Table 3.3 **Traditional strategy words and their *observed* meanings and uses/misuses (*concluded*)**

Word	Comment
Simple Complicated Complex Chaotic	Many strategies confuse the complexity of the real world with the complexity (or otherwise) of their strategies (see Chapter 4). Snowden and Boone (A leader's framework for decision making. *Harvard Business Review*, November 2007) usefully categorised strategic environments (that is, the world) as: simple (known knowns) complicated (unknown knowns) complex (unknown unknowns) chaotic (unknowables). Much of the world is complicated or complex but *strategic actions are always simple*. This is because every action must necessarily be a simple known-known (you cannot implement an unknown-known or an unknown-unknown or an unknowable), even if the consequences of the simple action are not completely known. So whereas the strategic *environment* and the strategy development *process* may be complicated and complex, the elements of the strategy itself must necessarily be simple. So SubStrategies must be simple. However, a collection of SubStrategies making up an OpenStrategy may be perceived by some stakeholders as complicated because some of the SubStrategies will be 'unknowns' to them even if they are 'knowns' to other stakeholders (hence these SubStrategies are unknown knowns and hence 'complicated').
Silos	*Silo* is a word that is frequently used to define a business unit or some other grouping of stakeholders that appears to work independently of and in isolation from other groups. Many people bemoan the fact that such *silos* exist and that they have a *silo mentality* of isolation and non-collaboration. We frequently hear that *silos* should be *broken down* to enable collaboration. We challenge this perspective. Many *silos* need to retain their identity and not be broken down because they *must* retain clarity about their areas of responsibility and accountability, especially financial accountability. OpenStrategies therefore encourages the *joining up of silos* rather than the *breaking down of silos* in order to achieve collaboration/cooperation while retaining the accountability of each *silo*. When strategies are written using the OpenStrategies taxonomy, syntax and semantics, it makes it much easier for silos to *join up* and work together (usually on SubStrategies) compared with when each silo-entity creates its strategies in traditional, inconsistent formats.
Vision	It is rare to find a *vision* that uniquely defines the ultimate end-point that an organisation wishes to achieve. Far too often a *vision* contains almost meaningless concepts such as 'we provide solutions' or 'we will exceed customers' expectations'. Such *visions* provide almost no guidance as to what makes the organisation different from every other organisation that is also offering 'solutions' in ways which 'exceed customers' expectations'. It is because of the vagueness of most *vision* statements that OpenStrategies recommends that a more useful form of *vision* for a strategy equates to the consolidated sum of the Benefits that are intended to be created.

3.5   Other 'Strategy Phrases' and How They Are Typically (Mis)Used

The following statements have been distilled (and slightly edited to obscure their sources) from existing traditionally created strategies which are available in the public domain. In all cases these statements have come from the strategies of substantial organisations such as multinational companies, government departments and territorial local authorities.

The reader is invited to diagnose each of these statements using the Projects, Results, Uses and Benefits sequence and the information in the above tables and to then decide whether or not the statements are useful strategic statements that can be validated and implemented.

For example:

> 'All activities will be carried out with the objective of protecting and growing shareholder value.' This is often abbreviated to 'Optimise shareholder value.'

How helpfully strategic are these statements? What's the alternative? *Not to* optimise shareholder value or *not* to protect and grow shareholder value?

So a diagnosis of these phrases leads to the conclusion that they describe blindingly obvious *aspirations* and as such they apply to almost all organisations which have shareholders. Also the verbs *protecting* and *growing* and *optimise* cannot be directly implemented – they are 'aspirational verbs' which need to be translated into operational or implementable verbs before the above statements could claim to be providing strategic guidance.

Here are some more 'strategic statements' distilled from the actual strategies of various large organisations. Are they genuinely useful strategic statements? Are they blindingly obvious? Are they 'givens'? Can they actually be implemented or are they just aspirations masquerading as 'strategies'?

1.   'Take environmental factors into account.'

2.   'Increase net profits from 6% to 10%.'

3.   'Consistent with these principal activities, we will pursue activities designed to ensure:

a) the safe and effective utilisation of its assets and human resources;

b) the prudent management of its business risks across markets and geographies.'

4.   'To achieve these objectives, (we) will maximise long-term shareholder value by:

a) seeking sustainable competitive advantage from excellence in generating electricity at optimal value through to meeting customer needs for energy and wider complementary and adjacent products and solutions;

b) actively developing and participating in competitive energy markets to provide products and services that deliver value to our customers and to enable (us) to optimise its risk position;

c) undertaking new investments that over their lives are:

- aimed at yielding a positive risk-related net present value,

- managed in a manner that will maximise the commercial value of the business;

d) undertaking prudent risk management in relation to its business activities;

e) minimising operating costs;

f) acting with a sense of social responsibility and reporting on its actions;

g) providing healthy and safe places of work for its people;

h) building and maintaining relationships with the communities in which it operates;

i) pursuing its commitment to the environment and the sustainable management and development of the natural, physical and human resources utilised in the business.'

5.   'The following business strategies have been set for the period:

 a) to build a sustainable physical network that offers the flexibility to align to changes in demand;

 b) to develop and deliver, in an economic and sustainable way, a good customer experience, by providing effective products and services;

 c) to ensure long-term value creation for the Group through the further development and growth of [subsidiary];

 d) to ensure the internal structure, processes and frameworks in operation at [company name] are positioned to offer the most efficient and profitable outcome for the Group;

 e) to ensure that our people have the skills and capabilities they require to succeed, and to create a culture in the organisation that enables and encourages our people to strive for great customer outcomes; and

 f) to create a range of digital services to meet changing customer needs.'

You may wish to also search for corporate and government strategies available online and similarly diagnose whether or not they contain genuinely useful strategic statements. During the global MBA courses I run in Germany and New Zealand I often challenge the students to do exactly this – to find and diagnose publicly available strategies of international corporations, government departments and other large organisations. Every single time we have done this in class (*totally randomly* seeking and diagnosing such strategies), we have collectively assessed the so-called strategies as being ineffective.

Try it – I think you will be alarmed at what you find. I am confident that it will confirm for you Freek Vermeulen's statement quoted in Chapter 1 of this book that 'most companies do not have a strategy' and our assertion that 'less than 10% of "strategies" make any difference', because as you will have confirmed for yourself, *they aren't actually 'strategies'*.

Chapters 4 and 5 provide more insights into why most traditional strategies are ineffective. Subsequent chapters demonstrate how the OpenStrategies approach can guide you to create meaningful, implementable strategies.

Chapter 4
Strategy Structure (Syntax) and Meaning (Semantics)

4.1 Introduction

This chapter uses our Projects, Results, Uses and Benefits thinking as a lens for analysing the real world by breaking down real-world strategic concepts, firstly into Projects, Results, Uses and Benefits, and then identifying subtle variations within these broad categories. In doing so our approach demonstrates that while the world is primarily complex, actual actions (strategies) must necessarily be simple (known knowns), even if the consequences of those simple actions may not be entirely predictable and hence are complex (unknown unknowns).

As noted in the Chapter 1, Snowden and Boone segmented the world of strategic management into four broad categories:

- simple (known knowns);

- complicated (unknown knowns);

- complex (unknown unknowns);

- chaotic (unknowables).

The concept was expanded in Chapter 1 to demonstrate that irrespective of whether we are working in a simple, complicated, complex or chaotic world, our strategic actions will necessarily *always* be simple (known knowns – we can implement *only* known knowns because it is impossible to implement anything which has any component of 'unknown' in it), even if the outcomes may be unpredictable.

So for example even in the complex world of environmental management (unknown unknowns), strategic actions must necessarily always be 'simple' (known knowns).

So when evaluating traditional strategies we need to review whether or not the strategic actions are inherently simple (if they are small strategies) or are complicated (if they are collections of simple actions in larger strategies) and also whether or not these strategies reflect and address the complex and chaotic nature of the real world.

Looking at this issue through the PRUB-thinking lens, at the operational level the Projects, Results, Uses and Benefits sequence encapsulates simple known knowns within its Projects while acknowledging that the subsequent Results, Uses and Benefits may not be known knowns but instead may emerge and evolve as the Projects are implemented.

So a Project (an action by an organisation) must be simple, planned and deliberate, that is, a 'known known'. The Result of such a Project will generally also be a 'known known' (the Project's managers will 'know' what it is they are intending to create and will have a high level of control over actually creating it). However, the Uses may be either the intended Uses (known knowns) or they may be unexpected Uses (unknown knowns – which are unknown to the initiator of the Project but known to the User). So the *actual* Use, as distinct from the *intended* Use may emerge in a complex fashion even though each Project and Result are simple 'known knowns'.

If a SubStrategy has been based on high-quality market research, the actual Uses will be the same as the intended Uses because the 'right' Results will have been created by the 'right' Projects. So a robust and well-validated strategy based on high-quality market research will be primarily 'simple'.

In contrast, a poorly validated SubStrategy based on speculative market research will be more likely to generate Results which are Used in unintended ways (or not Used at all). Such a strategy is unlikely to achieve the outcomes intended by the developers of the strategy.

It therefore makes good strategic sense to encapsulate strategic ideas within *desired and simple* SubStrategies and to then closely monitor actual Results, actual Uses and actual Benefits and to modify the Projects if the Results, Uses and Benefits diverge from the desired ones.

As this chapter uses our thinking to evaluate and explain the complex world of strategies, the sequence of Projects, Results, Uses and Benefits itself nevertheless remains a simple concept – it is the world that is complex! This chapter shows that PRUB thinking incorporates many subtle powers (for example the identification of different types of Uses and hence the need for different types of Results) while still remaining as a simple concept.

Perhaps of greatest importance are the subtly different categories of Uses (that is, how people use assets) because these subtleties shape the requirements for the necessary and sufficient sets of Results (assets) that are required to enable those Uses. Hence the syntax and semantics of strategy documents are important if the strategies they describe are to be successfully implemented.

So we encourage you to remember that PRUB simply represents 'what organisations do', that is:

> Organisations create (**P**rojects) assets (**R**esults) and enable people to use them (**U**ses) to generate benefits (**B**enefits).

Throughout this chapter we use PRUB thinking as a simple tool for evaluating strategies in terms of what organisations actually do.

4.2   Starting with Projects or Starting with Benefits? (PRUB or BURP?)

Based on an intention to strategically 'improve what organisations actually do', strategy development should start with defining the final outcomes (Benefits) that end-users desire and then work back to identify what people need to be doing to create these outcomes and therefore what assets (Results) an organisation should be developing. This strategic thinking sequence is concisely represented by Benefits, Uses, Results and Projects (BURP), which in turn represents the exact reverse of the sequence 'create assets and enable people to use them to generate Benefits'. That is, it represents the reverse of what organisations actually do by strategically thinking backwards from the desired end-points (Benefits).

The sequence Projects, Results, Uses and Benefits correlates with the time sequence of strategy *implementation* ('organisations create assets (Results) and enable people to use them (Uses) to create Benefits') and is the sequence that people readily relate to. People (at least in the Western world) think from left to right when imagining things happening in a time-based sequence, so people really do understand that Projects lead to Results which need to be Used to create Benefits.

So given people's total comfort with this logical real-world sequence and the fact that it succinctly and accurately represents what organisations actually *do*, we use PRUB as a tool to evaluate existing strategies and as the core of the OpenStrategies system.

However, within minutes of people becoming comfortable with PRUB as an accurate representation of what needs to be done, they starting asking whether or not their strategic *thinking*, as distinct from *implementation*, should perhaps follow the BURP sequence. Most people quickly realise that understanding the desired Benefits should generally be the starting point for designing or developing a strategy.

As a consequence they readily accept that strategic thinking (and strategy evaluation) should ideally follow the Benefits, Uses, Results and Projects sequence and that strategy implementation should then follow the Projects, Results, Uses and Benefits sequence. This makes sense because a strategy needs to be designed or evaluated (using BURP) before it can be implemented (using PRUB).

So people are comfortable with retaining the left-to-right PRUB sequence as the core graphical representation of what organisations need to do and to think from right to left (BURP) when doing strategy analysis or development.

Why is it so important to start with Benefits rather than Projects when evaluating and developing a strategy?

Correctly using BURP thinking for strategic planning focuses first on outcomes and the reasons for doing things (that is, focusing on effectiveness – doing the right things).

In contrast, incorrectly using PRUB thinking for strategic planning focuses first on inputs and then on refining those inputs (that is, focusing on efficiency – which risks the undesirable consequence of doing things right, even if they are the wrong things).

BURP thinking defines Benefits and Uses before attempting to determine what Results are required to enable those Uses. In doing so it recognises that Results must be designed to meet the needs of the users so that the *right* Results are created. In contrast, PRUB thinking all too often creates Results and then goes looking for Uses for those Results, or even worse, assumes that some as yet undefined Uses will turn up to make Use of the Results.

So starting by thinking about Benefits reduces the risk of accidentally designing Orphan Results because the process specifies the Benefits and Uses *before* it specifies the Results.

Therefore, when using BURP thinking, each Result arises only as a direct consequence of an identified need for that Result to enable a Use.

It is particularly important when evaluating or refining existing traditional strategies (which seldom define Uses in any detail) to assess every single Result to determine whether or not it is being Used, if it is the *best* possible Result or if it is an unused Orphan Result. Such an assessment should look closely at the current Uses to see whether or not they are the desired or optimal Uses and if they are happening at the desired level.

So whether auditing an existing strategy, creating a new strategy from scratch or modifying an existing strategy, we strongly recommend that you start by quickly identifying Benefits and then focus the greatest effort on precisely understanding Uses, that is, on what users want to be 'doing' in order for them to create Benefits.

By identifying what people want to be doing you will sometimes uncover the fact that users actually don't need any significant new Results to be created by 'provider' organisations. In this sense it is important *not* to ask users to define how they intend to use a specific Result but rather to focus simply on what they want to 'do'. Any required Results can then be identified *after* there is clarity on what users want to be *doing*.

There are subtle reasons why focusing on Uses is more helpful than focusing on Benefits. It turns out that Benefits (outcomes) are very similar in a great many different strategies as they all focus around the somewhat generic 'four well-beings' (economic, social, environmental and cultural well-beings). So while it is important to identify the desired Benefits, they seldom provide a great deal of clarity or guidance about what is required in the local context.

In contrast, Uses are much more locally and demographically specific because they necessarily focus on specific user groups and their specific behaviours within their specific local environments. As such, a detailed

understanding of local Uses provides much more valuable guidance for the
development of strategies and the selection of Results and Projects than does
an understanding of the typically more generic Benefits/outcomes.

4.3   Active vs. Passive Wording

We need to address the importance of using active language when creating
strategies irrespective of whether or not the strategy is developed using
traditional approaches or the OpenStrategies approach. The use of *active* rather
than *passive* wording for strategies might at first appear trivial but, as shown
below, active wording can profoundly alter the focus on who are the active or
passive players in the effective implementation of a strategy.

In particular, it is essential to phrase Uses (how people use assets) actively
in order to crystallise the actions that the users need to take in order to
consciously and deliberately Use a Result.

We stressed in Chapters 2 and 3 that providers of Results or assets cannot
deliver their services/products, they can only *make them available* to users and
it is the conscious and deliberate actions of the users which are the primary
actions required to 'create' (and not just 'realise') Benefits/outcomes.

Consider the following two wordings of a Use relating to people
participating in an anti-obesity programme:

> *Use version 1:*

> *Obese people receive training, delivered by the council, in healthy
> eating.*

> *Use version 2:*

> *Obese people eat more healthily because they learned about healthy
> eating when they participated in the council's anti-obesity training
> programme.*

Version 1 is typical of the wording found in many public sector strategy
documents. It describes an active council (which 'delivers' the training) and
passive obese people (who 'receive' training). It gives no indication that the
obese people need to take an active part in the process. In this version, the

council can inappropriately (!) consider that it has completed its task once it has 'delivered' the training. The council effectively washes its hands of any responsibility for achieving the desired outcome of 'reduced levels of obesity'.

In contrast version 2 identifies the obese people as the *key actors in the process*. They no longer passively 'receive' training but instead they actively 'eat more healthily' as a consequence of actively participating in the training. The focus is unequivocally on the active engagement of obese people and less so on the so-called delivery function of the council.

This is most important with respect to the handover of assets/Results to users because it requires the users to be *proactive*. If we use verbs such as 'provide', 'ensure', 'deliver' and 'supply' to describe our Projects, it is too easy to imagine that the Uses and Benefits are assured and will somehow just happen automatically. This is seldom true!

So it is essential to understand fully what conscious and deliberate actions the users need to take to use an asset to create Benefits because in most situations the users cannot merely be passive. They must consciously *act* – so we must know what actions they need to take and *whether or not they will actually take those actions*. This is why it is profoundly important to phrase Uses as active not passive statements.

The same applies to Projects which are Adopting Orphan Results. It is essential you understand what actions need to be taken by the owner of the Adopting Project and to know that they will actually do the Adopting.

The danger of over-using passive verbs to describe Uses as an easy option is that it allows a focus on the creation of an asset or service rather than on whatever may be involved in activating or encouraging its effective uptake, that is, whether the real customers/citizens/community will actually use the assets. There cannot be successful outcomes until customers or citizens actively take over and use the available assets.

Is this just a matter of semantics? It is a profoundly important matter of semantics because of the way it shifts the focus for action on to the (typically many) users and away from the (typically few) providers.

Our experience shows that many people in the public service strongly resist giving up their cherished concept of '*delivering* public services'. Many have a deeply engrained perception that the public sector knows what is best for people and hence this 'best' needs to be 'delivered to' and 'at' and 'for' people, with the public being merely passive recipients of a service or product.

The concept that end-users might in fact have a better understanding of their needs and how to meet them and that the *end-users must necessarily be the main players in the implementation of a strategy* is a challenging concept to many people in the public sector.

Let's now look more closely at how the precise taxonomy, syntax and semantics of Benefits, Uses, Results and Projects help us to analyse and transform existing strategies into effective strategies which can be implemented and will make a difference.

4.4   Benefits

JUSTIFICATION

Benefits (outcomes) provide justifications for a traditional strategy, SubStrategy or OpenStrategy. They represent the final goals or the consequences of all earlier actions.

VISION

Few 'visions' in traditional strategy documents provide any useful insight because they are so lightweight and/or obvious.

In contrast, the aggregation or consolidation of the Benefits in an OpenStrategy adds up to, or provides the basis for, a worthwhile and meaningful vision for a strategy. Thus the vision for a strategy often emerges and evolves as the strategy develops rather than being a concept that is focused on in depth before the strategy gets under way. Certainly it is worth creating an interim vision early in the strategy development process, but then it is almost always invaluable to allow the strategy to evolve and for a refined vision to emerge and evolve from the aggregated or consolidated Benefits.

THE FOUR WELL-BEINGS

Generally Benefits represent one or more of the 'four well-beings':

1.   economic well-being;

2.   social well-being;

3.   environmental well-being;

4.   cultural well-being.

Typical examples of Benefits include: economic prosperity, sustainable businesses, happy citizens, mentally/emotionally/physically healthy citizens, healthy ecosystems, enhanced values, more money to spend, stronger and more stable communities, higher levels of education – essentially all of the above being variations on the four well-beings.

FINAL BENEFITS

Benefits need to be carefully selected so as to define the end-point of a particular strategy. For example, the end-point Benefit of an Educational Strategy might include 'qualified young people' whereas the end-point Benefit of an Economic Strategy might include 'wealthy young people (because they have good jobs because they are well qualified)'.

So it is important when establishing any strategy to be clear about the final end-point Benefits *for that strategy* and to not confuse them with other desired Benefits which may be part of other strategies.

ONLY USERS CREATE BENEFITS

It is worth repeating that outcomes/Benefits cannot be 'delivered' or 'created by' or 'provided by' organisations. *Only* users can create Benefits. There are no shortcuts from Projects to Benefits or from Results to Benefits. For a Project to successfully lead to a Benefit the Project *must* lead to a Result and the Result *must* be Used and the Use *must* lead to Benefits.

MEASUREMENT OF OUTCOMES/BENEFITS

There are various degrees of difficulty in measuring or assessing the value of outcomes/Benefits.

The first rule is: 'ask the users'. If the users are in fact using an asset/Result, *they* will know why they are doing so and what value they perceive from their Use. So while an external observer may struggle to assess the value of Uses and Benefits, the users themselves are likely to find it much easier to do so.

For example, many 'first nations' or indigenous people place a very high value on being able to drink natural unpolluted water which has not needed to be treated in any way.

In contrast, many Westerners are quite content to drink treated water and so Westerners often struggle to place a value on pure, untreated water. To first nations' people the value of pure water is unquestionable, it is a given, it is simply part of their life-force.

So in assessing the value of a Benefit, the key people to converse with are the users and beneficiaries in order to identify *their* values and how *they* measure them.

Some Benefits are inherently easier to measure than others. Obesity levels are easy to measure objectively and physically, whereas 'community well-being' or 'citizen happiness' or 'customer satisfaction' are much more nebulous. However, as noted above, communities, citizens and customers themselves generally have a good feel for their own values and what matters to them in terms of Benefits.

Frequently it is possible to *infer* the importance of Benefits by monitoring other factors such as Uses. For example, if large numbers of children are using a swimming pool, this indicates that they must be gaining some Benefits from doing so. While the Benefits themselves may be nebulous (for example levels of happiness), a measure of the numbers of children coming to the pool provides an indirect indicator that Benefits are being achieved. Having said that, it is nevertheless helpful to accurately determine exactly what Benefits are being generated and/or desired so that the Uses, and hence the Results, can be optimised to generate the maximum Benefits.

OWNERSHIP/BENEFICIARIES OF BENEFITS

The beneficiaries of a Use may or may not be the users. For example, a Use of: 'dog owners walk their dogs on leashes' leads to a Benefit of '*other* citizens feel safe and not threatened by uncontrolled dogs'.

Similarly, there may be a Benefit to the user which the user is reluctant to acknowledge. For example, a Use of 'smokers smoke outside their offices' may feel most unattractive to the smokers and as a consequence they smoke less, so that gives them a Benefit of 'improved health'.

Also, a single Use may impact positively on one Benefit and negatively on another. For example, a Use of 'many citizens use the roundabout' may lead to the citizens having a Benefit of 'arriving at work on time', whereas it can simultaneously have a negative impact on noise levels for people living next to the roundabout.

Frequently there are demands on public resources to produce assets to enable Uses by selected members of society but to be funded by ratepayers or taxpayers. Classic examples include stadiums, public swimming pools and conference centres which lobbyists argue should be funded from public funds but which in reality will be used by only limited sections of society.

So when identifying and describing Benefits it is important to not just define the Benefits but also to identify *exactly who* the beneficiaries are. This then guides the making of wise decisions which correlate the Benefits and the values of the Benefits to the beneficiaries and in turn with the costs to those who are paying for the development of the assets and/or the costs of the Uses.

ACTUAL BENEFITS, NOT USES

Many Uses sound like Benefits. For example, 'wealthy tourists spend more money in the region' is a Use, not a Benefit, even though it sounds beneficial. A likely actual Benefit from this Use is 'more sustainably profitable communities and businesses in the region'. So always check the wording of Benefits by asking 'why is this a Benefit?' because often this identifies that the true Benefit has not actually been identified. Also check that the Benefit is worded as a consequence of an action and not as the action itself (the Use).

LEVEL OF SPECIFICITY

Benefits can range from very generic Benefits such as 'a healthy population' through various levels of specificity to detailed Benefits such as 'physically, emotionally and mentally healthy pregnant teenage mothers in South London'. In this respect, OpenStrategies has identified that there are four main 'specificities' which recur most often when people attempt to fine-tune their strategies and Benefits.

These key specificities are:

1.   Demographic specificity – exactly who are the users?

2.   Thematic specificity – exactly what will be done?

3.   Geographic specificity – exactly where will it be done?

4.   Organisational specificity – exactly who will do it?

The description of a SubStrategy needs to include all four of these specificities in order to accurately define the process leading to the desired Benefits. Not only that, each of the four specificities needs to be specified at a similar level of detail.

For example, if the demographic specificity is 'pregnant teenage mothers', the organisational specificity would ideally be more specific than just 'local authorities' and instead might be 'the social services division of south London councils working collaboratively with the women's health section of the NHS'.

This definition of levels of specificity applies equally to Projects, Results and Uses as it does to Benefits. The fine-tuning of the four specificities for each Project, Result, Use and Benefit is often a good way of tightening up any loosely worded components of a strategy.

4.5   Uses

Precisely understanding Uses is fundamental to any strategy or OpenStrategy.

This section discusses two key aspects of Uses:

1.   What exactly do users want to *do*, as distinct from what do users say they *want*?

2.   What are the characteristics of these Uses and how will these characteristics guide the development of the necessary and sufficient set of Results?

DOING VS. WANTING

In a classic local government setting, when people are asked what they *want* in terms of transport options in a city, they frequently say they 'want more cycle paths and better public transport'.

However, when asked what they want to *do*, many of the same people say they want to drive their cars in the city when *everyone else* is riding bikes and using public transport.

Similarly, many anti-obesity and anti-smoking strategies exist which offer all sorts of training and exercise programmes, yet few of these programmes appear to have any understanding of what obese people or smokers are *actually prepared to do* to address their obesity/smoking. As a consequence they offer assets (products, services or infrastructure) which simply do not get used in any effective way. Such strategies are ineffective because they do not factor in what people are prepared to actually *do*.

This issue of needing to *really* understand what people want to *do* applies in both the public and private sector strategies.

It is therefore essential to understand what people will actually *do*, not just what they *say they want* or what *someone else believes that they ought to do.*

Another characteristic of this *doing vs. wanting* dichotomy is that when people are asked what they *want*, they typically think about *what the questioner can give them*, that is, their focus shifts to the provider and away from themselves. As a consequence, their thinking focuses on the resources (often perceived to be unlimited) of the *provider* rather than on their own needs and capabilities.

In contrast, asking people what they want to *do* or are prepared to *do* focuses their attention on themselves: *their own* needs, *their own* resources and what *they* are prepared to *do* about it.

This is not just semantics. It is crucially important semantics. Understanding what people are actually prepared to *do* is immensely informative when it comes to creating strategies whether in the public or private sectors. This is because it is Uses, not Projects and not Results, which create Benefits, so it is essential to understand and enable actual, real-world Uses of assets (Results) if Benefits are to be realised.

CHARACTERISTICS OF TYPES OF USES

We have so far defined three broad categories of Uses in any strategy:

1.   time-based Uses (ongoing, evolving, end-point and one-off Uses);

2.   involvement-based Uses (optional, non-optional, unconscious/ automatic, opt-out, invisible and exclusive/non-exclusive Uses);

3.   resource-impacting Uses (abstractive/non-abstractive Uses, consumptive/non-consumptive Uses and destructive/neutral/ enhancing Uses).

Within each of these categories of Uses are a number of sub-categories.

These categories and sub-categories are real-world factors which fortunately can be readily understood using PRUB thinking.

Why are these categories of Uses important?

Different categories of Use require different categories of Result to enable the Use. For example, a 'non-optional Use' requires 'legislation', 'monitoring' and 'enforcement' Results or assets in order to compel or very strongly encourage the desired non-optional Use.

In contrast, an 'optional Use' requires Results which are attractive and well known in order that end-users *voluntarily choose* to engage in the strategically desired Uses. A one-off Use requires one-off Results, whereas an ongoing Use requires ongoing Results. While these examples may seem trivial, it is surprising how often strategy documents expect certain Uses to happen even though the providers have created the wrong categories of Results to enable those Uses.

TIME-BASED USES

Ongoing, evolving, end-point and one-off Uses are *time-based* categories of Uses because they each define a specific time period or a type of change that occurs over time.

Ongoing Uses

Ongoing Uses are Uses which are continuing without any changes in Use taking place, for example children using a swimming pool, pedestrians using footpaths and customers buying petrol.

Ongoing Uses include Uses which are intermittent (Intermittent Ongoing Uses) but repeating, for example the weekly Use of a stadium by sports teams. Ongoing Uses require Results to be similarly available on an ongoing basis.

End-point Uses

End-point Uses define the actions that users are expected to be doing at a set point in time. Wherever possible, end-point Uses should be used in preference to 'evolving Uses' (see below) so as to make it crystal clear what preferred actions are required, even if they can't be achieved instantly. Examples of end-point Uses might be 'in 2015 20% more people are eating five pieces of fresh fruit and vegetables per day', or 'in 2015 at least 1,000 people per day are buying the company's new product'. End-point Uses require Results which change over time to enable the Use to achieve its desired end-point.

Evolving Uses

Evolving Uses are Uses that involve change, ideally for the better. However, a caution here is to use such evolving Uses with great care because it is all too easy to use them lazily to imply some vague improvements instead of putting in the time and effort required to identify more measurable and definitive Uses.

Therefore, wherever possible, we recommend that evolving Uses such as 'people are eating more healthily' be quantified and changed into a desired end-point Use of 'in 2015 20% more people are eating five pieces of fresh fruit or vegetables each day'. Evolving Uses tend to include words such as 'increased' or 'more' and 'improve', which are somewhat nebulous, hence our recommendation to always try to convert evolving Uses into end-point Uses and to then use specific quantified amounts ('10% more', 'double', and so on). Evolving Uses require Results which are similarly evolving over time.

One-off Uses

One-off Uses include such activities as people attending a one-off event like a rock concert or sporting event. They require matching Results which are also one-off (for example catering for the event), although at the same time they may use venues which are ongoing (for example a stadium or conference centre).

INVOLVEMENT-BASED USES

Optional, non-optional, unconscious/automatic, opt-out and invisible Uses are *involvement-based* categories of Use because they define the nature of a user's involvement. It is helpful to understand the difference between these different types of Uses because some are easier to influence than others and typically each type of Use requires a different type of Result.

Optional Uses

Most Uses are optional!

Only in rare situations are Uses compulsory, so it should be generally assumed that the default position is that Uses are optional. Optional Uses are simply Uses where the users can choose to Use the available Results or choose not to. There is no compulsion. Therefore optional Uses require Results which are attractive to the user, are easily accessible and are well known. Such optional Uses involve choices by the users so it is essential that providers fully understand how the users will make these choices and what factors they will take into account. Frequently optional Uses require a real change of behaviour by people who are required to make a conscious choice. This means a lot of work has to go into listening to and then informing, encouraging and persuading people to choose to make an optional Use.

So an absolutely crucial message is that most Uses are optional and that, therefore, to be successful, every strategy must understand users and Uses and then design the right infrastructure, products and services that lead users to choose to implement their optional Uses.

Non-optional Uses

Non-optional Uses contain elements of compulsion, such as a legal requirement to not drink and drive or a legal requirement to register a dog or firearm. Non-optional Uses require Results such as 'legislation' and 'monitoring' and 'enforcement' and 'penalties' as well as 'awareness campaigns'. Even with non-optional Uses people can still choose to obey or disobey the rules but the general principle is that non-optional Uses 'should' be obeyed. With non-optional Uses a true change of behaviour is also usually required and an element of compulsion is involved. People are required to comply with legislation/regulations which they may resist, so monitoring and enforcement measures may then be necessary Results to increase the probability that people will comply (Uses).

Automatic or Unconscious Uses

Automatic or unconscious Uses can be simultaneously subtle and powerful. For example, if fast food providers change to healthier cooking oil, consumers will automatically or unconsciously eat the new and healthier fast food but will be unaware that they have made any change in behaviour.

Typically users are given little choice (and have little awareness of) automatic or unconscious Uses so that there is a risk that such Uses can be used to manipulate users. Automatic Uses are therefore significant because they have the potential to be the *easiest* way to influence citizen behaviour. This is because people are not even making a choice or changing their behaviour as a result of a different attitude, they are simply extending pre-existing behaviours in a (hopefully better) new way. From the Users' point of view, the Uses simply happen, and for this reason they can be a very effective way of bringing about desired Benefits. So automatic/unconscious Uses typically require Results which most people don't even notice.

Opt-out Uses

Opt-out Uses are where people consciously choose to not do the planned Use and to do something different instead. When developing a strategy it is worthwhile to understand what the opt-out Uses might be in a given situation because they may turn out to be more attractive options than the planned Uses. This information can provide guidance as to how to improve the attractiveness of the desired Uses by changing the Results/assets. An opt-out Use may be passive (that is, the user chooses not to make the effort to adopt the desired Use) or active (that is, the user consciously decides to not adopt the desired Use and adopts a different one instead). Opting out can be conscious, deliberate and totally valid and is an excellent source of ideas for new strategies, products and services.

Invisible Uses

Some Uses are profoundly important to some stakeholders yet these Uses don't appear obvious. For example, in a regional water management strategy in New Zealand, many people mentioned that one of their 'Uses' of water was to lie in bed knowing that mountain water was flowing freely and purely down through the great alpine rivers to the sea. For many Maori, this free flowing of alpine waters (without any mixing with lowland waters) is a crucially important 'Use' even though there is generally no outward sign of this Use occurring. Other people referred to their Uses of water being such things as taking photographs of rivers, lakes and waterfalls or simply walking alongside them. It is essential to identify such invisible Uses because they are often of enormous significance to the users even if they are not obvious to casual observers or regulators.

Exclusive/non-exclusive Uses

An exclusive Use is where a Use prevents other Uses. Abstractive Uses tend to be exclusive but even non-abstractive Uses (for example the sole use of a stretch of water for a rowing carnival) can be exclusive even if only temporarily so. The importance of recognising exclusive Uses is that they prevent other Uses and in so doing they reduce other people's options. Exclusive Uses should therefore generally be required to generate particularly valuable Benefits in order to justify the closing off of other options and Uses.

RESOURCE-IMPACTING USES

Some Uses change the Results or resources that they depend on, whereas others don't.

Abstractive/non-abstractive and Consumptive/non-consumptive Uses

Abstractive/consumptive Uses such as using river water for irrigation irreversibly change the resource they draw on (the river), which impacts on the river as well as on other users of the river.

In contrast, a non-abstractive/non-consumptive Use such as fishing in the river does not change the river (although it may change the density of fish stocks) and it doesn't impact (other than to a very minor extent) on other users of the river. Semi-consumptive Uses (for example damming a river to generate electricity and then returning the water to the river) tend to have intermediate impacts between those of fully abstractive and fully non-abstractive Uses.

A key issue here is that abstractive/consumptive Uses of a resource will generally be required to have much stronger levels of justification to permit their Use than will non-abstractive/non-consumptive Uses.

Destructive/neutral/enhancing Uses

A variation on this category of Use is the concept of destructive, neutral and resource-enhancing Uses. Abstractive Uses tend to be destructive of a resource whereas some non-abstractive Uses can enhance the resource (for example fishing in a river in circumstances in which the fishing societies re-stock the rivers).

USES WITH COMBINED CHARACTERISTICS

Most Uses exhibit characteristics that are a combination of time-based, involvement-based and resource-impacting Uses.

For example, the Use of a river by canoeists at weekends is an ongoing/intermittent, optional, non-exclusive, non-resource-impacting Use which requires Results which are similarly ongoing/intermittent, attractive and available at the right times to be Useful. Because this Use is intermittent it opens up the possibility that the same resource could also be used intermittently at other times by other users.

In contrast a Use of 'people build and live in houses which are compliant with government standards' is an end-point, non-optional, exclusive and resource-consuming Use which requires legislation, enforcement and penalties to ensure it happens.

Understanding the exact characteristics of each Use can influence the way organisations attempt to change people's behaviour by providing relevant Results.

When it is understood what the opt-out Uses are (which might be existing Uses), it might become clearer that the desired Use is simply too big a change for users, so they opt out and do something different. To achieve change in such circumstances a more attractive Use (and hence more attractive Result) needs to be enabled.

Here's an example: if a health board wanted local people who typically ate too much fast food to be eating more healthy foods, there could be several different ways they could try to bring this about. Looking to bring about a non-optional Use would be inappropriate in this situation because it is not socially acceptable to force people to eat differently, so the health board would need to consider optional or automatic Uses.

One approach

One of the optional Uses the council might try to influence could be that *'more people are including fresh fruit and vegetables in their home cooking'*. As this Use requires a change of behaviour and so is likely to be difficult to influence, the Results necessary to drive this would be focused on information and awareness-raising, rather than on infrastructure or services. This example is set out in Figure 4.1 using the PRUB information structure.

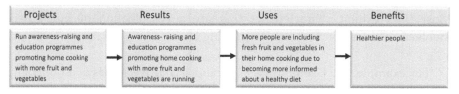

Projects	Results	Uses	Benefits
Run awareness-raising and education programmes promoting home cooking with more fruit and vegetables	Awareness- raising and education programmes promoting home cooking with more fruit and vegetables are running	More people are including fresh fruit and vegetables in their home cooking due to becoming more informed about a healthy diet	Healthier people

Figure 4.1   One approach to influencing people's eating behaviour

A Second Approach

An alternative approach to an optional Use of getting local people to eat more healthy food might be to set up a series of fast food restaurants that serve healthier foods and smaller portions and/or convince existing restaurants to offer healthier meal options.

Getting people to eat different meals at the same restaurants or at different restaurants might be perceived as requiring a relatively small change in behaviour with just a shift to using a new service. The Results required to drive it would therefore consist primarily of changing the healthiness of meal options in restaurants.

This example is set out in Figure 4.2 using the PRUB information structure.

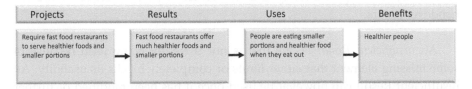

Projects	Results	Uses	Benefits
Require fast food restaurants to serve healthier foods and smaller portions	Fast food restaurants offer much healthier foods and smaller portions	People are eating smaller portions and healthier food when they eat out	Healthier people

Figure 4.2   A second approach to influencing people's eating behaviour

So precisely understanding the nature of a desired Use provides informative guidance as to the types of Results which are most likely to enable (and indeed encourage) the desired Use to actually happen.

In the above two examples, the second approach is probably more likely to be Used by the people who traditionally eat a lot of fast food that has been prepared for them, rather than following the first approach, which requires them to substantially change their behaviours and cook their own food.

4.6   Results

As with Uses it helps with strategy design to understand the different categories of Results so that Results are matched as effectively as possible with Uses.

There are two main types of Result: Used and Unused. When we look more closely into why a Result is Used or Unused, we can break the categories down into further sub-categories:

- sufficient/insufficient;

- necessary/unnecessary;

- wanted/unwanted;

- mistaken.

SUFFICIENT/INSUFFICIENT RESULTS

A *sufficient Result* is ready to be handed over and used by customers or the community; nothing is missing and no further steps are needed before the handover occurs.

An *insufficient Result* is one that is not currently being used because of some missing element that either limits or completely blocks its usability. An insufficient Result can however be used once it has been modified or further developed in some way.

For example, a cycleway which is too narrow or unsafe to be used at present will become useful once it has been widened or made safe. A swimming pool that is currently inaccessible will become useful once it has been connected to an extended bus route. In each of these examples, the initial Result (narrow cycleway, swimming pool) was insufficient. In the first instance the cycleway itself became sufficient once it was widened. In the second instance the swimming pool needed a second, parallel Result (an extended bus route) so that the swimming pool *plus* the bus route *together* became sufficient.

Similarly, a Result may only become sufficient (and hence useful) to a community once people are made aware of its existence – in which case a publicity campaign may be required. In this instance the original Result *plus* a publicity campaign are required to collectively create a sufficient and hence usable set of Results.

NECESSARY/UNNECESSARY RESULTS

A *necessary Result* is one which must be present in order to achieve the desired Use and Benefit. It may or may not also be sufficient.

An *unnecessary Result* is one where something sufficiently similar already exists and so the unnecessary Result has led to duplication. Alternatively, a Result may be unnecessary because it is simply not required by end-users.

WANTED/UNWANTED RESULTS

A *wanted Result* is one which the community sees as having value to them and thus is something they want to Use.

An *unwanted Result* is one which lacks Evidence of customer/citizen need or desire and where consequently there is no pick-up or Use by the customers/citizens. The unwanted Result may be given a relatively neutral reception by the customers/citizens because people feel indifferent, or on the other hand it may be received with anger and resentment. Unwanted Results frequently occur where there is inadequate consultation with customers and the community or where customers and the community believe there has been a degree of deception or injustice.

However, perhaps most frequently, unwanted Results arise when service providers operate under the mis-perception that it is their job to 'deliver' services/products *to* or *at* or *for* customers and that as service providers they know best what end-users want. In the experience of the OpenStrategies team, 15–25% of all public sector Results are unused or unwanted.

MISTAKEN RESULTS

Some Results are *mistaken*. This can occur as a result of asking community stakeholders the wrong questions or using the wrong information as a basis for deciding which Projects to run. This leads to the wrong Results being created which, while fully usable and perhaps even wanted by some sections of the community, are actually not what the strategists and community wanted (for example they may have unintended consequences).

ORPHAN RESULTS

The Orphan Result concept is useful because it highlights the way in which Results that are unusable, unnecessary and/or unwanted can be transformed into Results which are sufficient, necessary and wanted. Table 4.1 shows that an Adopted Orphan Result cannot be sufficient or wanted by the community because it is not enough on its own to deliver a Use; it is not sufficient or likely to be wanted by users as it is not Usable by them.

Table 4.1   Different types of Result

	Abandoned Orphan Result	Adopted Orphan Result	Usable Result
Necessary	–	✓	✓
Unnecessary	✓	✓	✓
Sufficient	–	–	✓
Insufficient	✓	✓	✓
Wanted	–	–	✓
Unwanted	✓	✓	✓
Mistaken	✓	✓	✓

To be Usable, a set of Results must be simultaneously sufficient, necessary and wanted.

Table 4.1 also shows that a sufficient Result might or might not be necessary and might or might not be wanted (or valued). A wanted Result might or might not be sufficient and might or might not be necessary.

Unusable Results are insufficient and/or unnecessary and/or unwanted. They are unable to be directly and immediately Used by the customers and citizens.

In practically every instance of an unusable Result, the pathway to modifying the unusable Result so it becomes usable will include developing an in-depth understanding of the desired Uses.

4.7   Projects

Projects consist of actions to create, refine, modify and maintain assets such as products, services and infrastructure.

However, many traditional strategies do not make clear distinctions between non-implementable aspirational-level 'Project-like' statements such as 'protect native birds' and operational-level, genuinely implementable Projects such as 'build fences around the colony of banded dotterels prior to nesting and maintain them until all the birds are fully fledged and able to fly'.

Because it is so important to phrase Projects correctly (and differently) for aspirational-level, guidance-level and operational-level strategies, Chapter 3 was devoted primarily to this topic.

4.8   General Wording of Projects, Results, Uses and Benefits

THE FUTURE-PRESENT

Many traditional strategies contain statements that are unclear about the desired outputs or outcomes and instead focus primarily on actions to make vaguely worded and imprecisely timed 'improvements'.

In contrast, in the OpenStrategies taxonomy, Projects, Results, Uses and Benefits are all precisely worded in the *future-present* to clearly define the desired outputs (Results) and outcomes (Benefits). By this we mean that they are described in the present tense by someone living in the future.

For example, if the intent of a strategy is that at a future point in time such as in 2015 people in the city *will be* eating an average of four pieces of fruit and vegetables per day, the Use would be written as 'in 2015 people in the city *are* eating an average of four pieces of fruit per day'. So the Projects, Results, Uses and Benefits describe the desired situation as it will be seen by someone living in the future.

This approach creates a clear picture of the desired future state.

DEFINITE STATEMENTS

We strongly believe that any strategy should be 100% definite about what it is reasonably intended to achieve, even if there is some doubt as to whether or not such achievement is definitely possible. Any doubt about a strategy should reside *outside* the strategy, but the strategy itself should be definite about its desired consequences.

Therefore, using PRUB thinking, Projects, Results, Uses and Benefits are all described as if they are actually happening or are in place at some point in the future. SubStrategies and OpenStrategies define the desired future state. Whether or not such future states do in fact happen is a quite separate issue from the strategic *intentions* encapsulated in PRUB-based SubStrategies.

It is the choosing whether or not to implement a strategy which will dictate whether or not the Projects, Results, Uses and Benefits actually happen.

Therefore, the wording of Projects, Results, Uses and Benefits must not use phrases such as 'consider whether to …', or 'try to …' or 'may …' or 'might …'. SubStrategies should instead be worded convincingly and definitely – any uncertainty then arises *external* from the strategy in terms of whether or not to implement the strategy and/or how many resources to commit to the strategy to make it work and to reduce the risk of failure.

POSITIVITY

All strategies should focus on the positive changes that stakeholders wish to create – there is not much point in having a negative strategy. This is because most people would prefer to engage with positive ideas rather than negative ideas, so psychologically it makes sense to focus on positively worded concepts.

All Projects, Results, Uses and Benefits must be worded either positively or neutrally. Any negativity in a SubStrategy or OpenStrategy is accommodated in the Links between items. This rule avoids any risk of double negativity, such as a negative Link to a negative item implying an overall positivity. For example, a Use of 'people use the parking area beside the beach' would have a positive Link to 'people are happy at the beach' but possibly a negative Link to 'people living near the car park are happy because their area is peaceful and free of cars'.

THE INFORMATION CONTENT OF PROJECT, RESULT, USE AND BENEFIT STATEMENTS

To be readable, understood and implemented by stakeholders, effective strategies should contain a hierarchy of information based on how important various categories of information are to the most stakeholders (or to the most significant stakeholders).

The OpenStrategies taxonomy, syntax and semantics have identified that *the most valuable information for the most stakeholders* consists of the four concepts of Projects, Results, Uses and Benefits followed in terms of widespread relevance by the second-tier concepts of Links, Evidence, Value and Performance Management.

In addition, some stakeholders want more details of each of these concepts. We therefore recommend that each Project, Result, Use and Benefit contains the following third-tier information:

- a summary of the Project, Result, Use and Benefit;

- a longer description of the item, ideally with references to sources of even more detailed information;

- start and finish dates (where relevant);

- budget requirements (where relevant);

- key stakeholders who are responsible for each item;

- other information as may be required on a case-by-case basis.

NEEDING MULTIPLE PROJECTS TO ACHIEVE A RESULT, MULTIPLE RESULTS TO ENABLE A USE AND MULTIPLE USES TO ACHIEVE A BENEFIT ... AND VICE VERSA

As noted under the discussion on necessary and sufficient Results on pages 95–8, a single Use of an asset often requires multiple other assets/Results. For example, the Use of 'children are swimming in a swimming pool (the asset)' needs (as a minimum) the following Results:

- a swimming pool;

- a means of the children getting safely to the swimming pool;

- lifeguards at the pool.

Similarly the Result/asset of 'a swimming pool' may require a Project to build the pool as well as a Project to put a cover over the pool and another one to build the access to the pool.

A variation on this theme is that often there will be several different assets which could potentially be Used in the same way. For example, the assets of 'a swimming pool', 'clean rivers suitable for swimming' and 'clean beaches and sea suitable for swimming' all enable a loosely defined Use of 'people are swimming'. To determine which of these Uses is the 'right' Use for the strategy it is essential to precisely understand the Use and to define it much more precisely than just 'people are swimming'.

It is therefore important that the *right* Result is created to enable the desired Use which is why it is always essential to identify and precisely define the *exact* Uses *before* identifying potential Results/assets which could enable those Uses.

In this respect, it's always worth bearing in mind the statement:

> *For every problem there is a solution that is simple, obvious ... and wrong.*
>
> > [attributed to Albert Einstein]

The same applies to Uses:

> *For every Use there is a Result that is simple, obvious ... and wrong.*

On a related theme, some Uses require a sequence of Projects and Results along the lines of P1-AR-P2-AR-P3-R-U-B where AR = Adoptable Result. Projects P2 and P3 are Projects which Adopt Results and use them to create further Results.

So, for example, the following sequence of Projects and Results may be required to achieve a single Use:

1. Project 1: Design a new consumer gadget.

2. Result 1 (Orphan Result): Design for a new consumer gadget exists.

3. Adopting Project 1: Build a prototype new consumer gadget using the new design.

4. Result 2 (Orphan Result): A prototype new consumer gadget exists.

5. Adopting Project 2: Build commercial consumer gadget.

6. Result 3 (Usable Result): New consumer gadgets available for sale.

7. Use: Consumers buy and use the new consumer gadget.

8. Benefit: Consumers are satisfied with whatever the new consumer gadget has enabled them to achieve.

Note that irrespective of the sequence that is followed, for Projects to contribute ultimately to a Benefit the Projects *must* produce Results which *must* either be Adopted or Used and *must* lead to Uses which create the desired Benefits. There are no shortcuts from Projects to Benefits or from Results to Benefits.

COMPOUND PROJECTS, RESULTS, USES AND BENEFITS

Strategic statements often describe more than one action or consequence and this issue can be well understood using PRUB thinking.

For example:

- Compound Project statement: 'Measure and manage traffic flows at key city intersections.'

- Compound Use statement: 'People are eating healthier food and taking more exercise.'

- Compound Benefit statement: 'City centre streets are cleaner and safer.'

Such statements are what we call 'compound Items' because they each contain two components.

The Project statement above contains two actions: 'measure' and 'manage'. Similarly, the Use statement contains 'eat' and 'take exercise' and the Benefit statement includes the two concepts of 'clean' and 'safe'.

While such wording of compound Items is useful for achieving conciseness in higher-level aspirational and guidance strategies, it is generally helpful to break compound Items into their component parts when creating new SubStrategies or analysing an existing strategy.

Each of the paired concepts in the above Items will require its own corresponding Items in other parts of the SubStrategy. For example, 'measure' will require 'measurement skills' whereas 'manage' will require 'management skills'. Similarly, 'eat' will require food and 'take exercise' will require places and resources to enable exercising.

Breaking down compound Items:

- enables you to separate the different 'strands' of Items or a strategy to find out how specific components of one Item are influencing components of other Items;

- enables you to identify which Projects will lead to Orphan Results and where further Projects and Results are needed;

- makes it easier to check for unforeseen consequences in Projects planned for the future;

- is an effective diagnostic tool by helping to analyse why an existing SubStrategy is not performing as anticipated so that you can then decide where you will increase efficiency or cut costs;

- is a good way of effectively mapping and highlighting different positive and negative impacts of strategic actions.

Compound Items may be used when developing high-level aspirational strategies or SubStrategies where the emphasis is on creating a broad strategic overview. Compound Items need to be broken down when the high-level aspirational strategy needs to be developed into an operational-level strategy to enable implementation.

Let's now look at one of the above examples in some detail:

Project statement: 'Measure and manage traffic flows at key city intersections.'

This infers an initial Project of 'measure traffic flows'. This Project will produce an Orphan Result of 'a database of measurements of traffic flows'.

This Orphan Result then needs to be adopted by a second Project along the lines of 'use the table of measurements of traffic flows to design a new traffic flow system', which in turn will produce another Orphan Result of 'a design for a new traffic flow system is available'.

A third Project will then be required to 'use the new traffic flow design to guide the construction of the new traffic flow system', leading to a Result of 'a new traffic flow system' which can then be Used by citizens.

Depending on the level of complexity, a fourth Project may then be required to operate and maintain the new traffic flow system.

So the initial single compound Project ('measure and manage') actually contained four Projects: to 'measure', to 'design', to 'construct' and to 'operate/maintain'.

So by disaggregating the initial compound Project into its constituent and sequential parts, it becomes obvious that four distinct Projects are required to enable the desired Use. Most importantly, two of the Projects will produce Orphan Results, so it is essential to be confident that these Orphan Results will in fact be Adopted and Used by Adopting Projects and Adopting organisations.

It is equally important to break down compound Uses into their component parts because doing this frequently identifies the fact that different Results are required for different components of the desired Use.

Consider an example Use of: 'people are eating healthier foods due to there being subsidies on healthy food, on the availability of fresh produce at farmers' markets and to being more informed about nutrition.'

By recognising the components of this compound Use, it becomes clear that three distinct Results are required:

- subsidies on healthy foods;

- fresh produce readily available at farmers' markets;

- information on food nutrition readily available to consumers.

4.9   Prioritising Strategies

Prioritising traditional strategies is inherently challenging, especially for large-scale multi-stakeholder, multi-themed strategies. This challenge can be at least partly addressed through the OpenStrategies process.

The OpenStrategies team recommends that stakeholders prioritise complete, Validated SubStrategies rather than prioritise single Projects. Individual Projects seldom lead to complete sets of Benefits, so there is not much point prioritising Projects in isolation from the SubStrategies which they contribute to.

When competing strategic ideas are encapsulated in fully Validated SubStrategies, it becomes possible to compare and prioritise them. Such prioritisation can be based on a number of clear parameters which each SubStrategy exhibits, including:

- the quality of the logic underpinning each SubStrategy;

- the quality of the Evidence supporting the Links in each SubStrategy;

- the 'Value' of each SubStrategy.

Complex multi-stakeholder strategies typically contain many strategic ideas and hence many SubStrategies. Sometimes there will be alternative ideas 'competing' on the same topic and frequently there will be ideas on different topics which are competing for the same funding and resources.

Validated SubStrategies provide a clear set of validated cause-and-effect information about each strategic idea so that ideas can be compared like-with-like during the prioritisation process. For example, there may be three different SubStrategies, each describing an option for a swimming pool, plus there may be 10 other SubStrategies describing alternative recreational options for cleaning up the local rivers for swimming or for developing cycling paths or horse trekking routes. Typically there will be limited funding and resources so not all these SubStrategies can be supported.

Multi-stakeholder groups therefore need to prioritise or select such competing ideas for implementation, so ultimately stakeholders need to make their own judgement calls about which Benefits and cost–Benefit ratios are most important to them. Validated SubStrategies encapsulate in a succinct format the exact information required for these judgement calls.

SubStrategies define the Users and the providers involved in the implementation of a SubStrategy and also capture information on who is providing the funding and other resources. This helps clarify the differing interests of these different stakeholder sub-groups, which in turn helps groups with similar interest to cluster around SubStrategies which are of direct interest to them.

The OpenStrategy team has reviewed this issue of prioritisation and concluded that in multi-stakeholder societies there is seldom an absolute set of priorities which will work for all stakeholders. Instead, different sub-groups have different sub-sets of priorities.

A traditional prioritisation process such as getting stakeholders to 'vote' on their preferred SubStrategies typically generates a prioritised list with the *least controversial SubStrategies at the top*, even if they aren't the most important SubStrategies for key stakeholder sub-groups.

So instead of just prioritising SubStrategies using a traditional voting system, the OpenStrategy 'rating system' (see below) also enables stakeholders to identify the *importance to them* of each Item or SubStrategy and through this process to identify like-minded stakeholders with whom they can engage (develop the strategy together) and collaborate (implement the strategy together).

This may mean that a sub-group of stakeholders implements a SubStrategy because it is important to the sub-group, even if the SubStrategy is not a priority for all stakeholders.

The OpenStrategies team encourages prioritisation based on a three-step process:

1.   A *'voting' process* in which all stakeholders vote for what they believe are overall the most important SubStrategies: the priorities arising from this process tend to be those SubStrategies which are the least controversial and/or those which will create widespread Benefits for many stakeholders.

2.   A *'ratings' process* in which stakeholders attach ratings to those SubStrategies which are important to them: this has the effect of clustering stakeholders around SubStrategies in which they have common interests. As a result a SubStrategy which may not be a priority for the overall group may turn out to have enough support from a sub-group for it to be worth implementing.

3.   A *'clumping' process* whereby SubStrategies are interlinked and clumped together until they contain enough concepts to attract enough stakeholders to support them: this has the effect of

encouraging the 'owners' of currently unsupported SubStrategies to modify their SubStrategies and join them with other SubStrategies so as to achieve a critical mass of supporters and resources.

Validated SubStrategies provide an excellent basis for the 'voting', 'rating' and 'clumping' prioritisation steps.

4.10   Fundamental Principles

Many traditional strategies contain statements and ideas which are not actionable. When analysed using PRUB thinking, it becomes clear that these ideas do not fit the categories of Project, Results, Uses or Benefits. Examples include statements such as:

- 'We will treat all people equally irrespective of their ethnicity.'

- 'We will never mix alpine water with lowland water.'

- 'Decisions will be made as close as possible to those who are affected by the decisions.'

- 'We will operate as openly and transparently as we can without compromising commercial confidentiality.'

- 'We will optimise shareholder value.'

In the OpenStrategies taxonomy we define these types of statements as *Fundamental Principles* because they apply to almost every action within a strategy. They define behavioural characteristics that relate to how everything will be done in an entire strategy rather than describing actual individual actions.

It is appropriate that Fundamental Principles be included in strategies as guiding principles, but in doing so it is important to acknowledge that Fundamental Principles do not actually describe implementable strategic actions but instead they define characteristics that all implementable actions must exhibit.

4.11   Searching, Auditing and Reporting on OpenStrategies

Large-scale multi-stakeholder strategies necessarily impact on many people and organisations, many of whom will want to view reports on the strategy, whether to simply find out what is happening, to audit the strategy or to promote/defend it.

Many traditional strategies are not readily amenable to such review or auditing because they use inconsistent strategy language (taxonomy, syntax and semantics) and are in hard-copy format.

Strategies developed and documented using the succinct and consistent OpenStrategies taxonomy, syntax and semantics are straightforward to search, report on, audit and promote/defend because they succinctly and consistently encapsulate *the smallest amount of information that has the most value to the most stakeholders*.

4.12   The Difference between 'Cause-and-effect Evidence' and 'Performance Measurement Data'

There is a vital difference between 'cause-and-effect Evidence' and 'performance measurement data'. This is significant for all strategies, whether or not they are based on PRUB thinking.

However, PRUB thinking provides a succinct tool for differentiating between such 'evidence' and 'data':

- Cause-and-effect Evidence provides information on *how/why* a Project impacts on a Result, or a Result on a Use, or a Use on a Benefit.

- Performance Measurement simply measures the status of parameters *within* each Project, Result, Use and Benefit and does not contain cause-and-effect information.

For example, a piece of information such as '150 people per day are buying our new product' is simply a piece of Performance Measurement data. It tells us nothing about the cause-and-effect reasons for *why* 150 people per day are buying our product. In contrast, if we changed our product from being green to being pink and the number of people buying it each day jumped from

150 to 175, we would have useful cause-and-effect Evidence that the colour change caused a change in people's purchasing decisions.

Similarly, a piece of Performance Management data such as '350 people per day are using the gym' tells us nothing about the reasons why these people are using the gym. Are they motivated to go to the gym to get fit or to meet their friends or to avoid something unpleasant in their lives (such as a cold house, whereas the gym is heated)? If we can determine exactly why people are coming to the gym, we can grow the gym business by improving the user experience by addressing their motivational reason for coming. For example, people may be motivated to go to the gym because it is a warm and friendly place to go, but a *by-product* of this motivation is the fact that they get fit. Such a gym might grow its business by promoting its warmth and friendliness rather than the quality of its get-fit equipment.

A great deal of information is merely 'data' which describes the state of a Project or of a Result or of a Use or of a Benefit. This information is not Evidence of cause and effect – it is simply a measure of the 'effect'.

Cause-and-effect Evidence on the Link from a Result to a Use provides Evidence that an asset/Result will actually be Used. Hence, Evidence on the Result–Use Link answers the implementation question 'will it actually happen?'

Similarly, cause-and-effect Evidence on the Link from a Use to a Benefit provides Evidence that the Use will generate a valuable Benefit. Hence, Evidence on the Use–Benefit link answers the value question 'is it worth it?'

Therefore, when seeking compelling Evidence to help Validate a strategy, it is essential to know 'what caused what' to happen (that is, Evidence) rather than to merely measure the consequence of 'what happened' (Performance Measurement data).

Understanding cause-and-effect Evidence is a key component for effective risk management. The Evidence that is generally of greatest value, yet is frequently the most difficult to obtain, is the cause-and-effect Evidence that Results will actually be Used. Therefore, when you are seeking to validate your strategies and minimise risk, it is essential that your market research determines exactly what users want to be doing, what Results they need to do these things and whether they will actually pay for and Use the Results that you intend to create through the implementation of your strategy.

Some performance indicators are 'lead indicators' and some are 'lag indicators'.

Lead indicators give an early indication of whether or not the implementation of a strategy or SubStrategy is proceeding well, whereas lag indicators give later indications of whether or not the implementation of the strategy is producing the desired Uses and Benefits.

Performance indicators of Projects and Results are lead indicators whereas performance indicators of Uses and Benefits are lag indicators.

4.13   Implementing Strategies

As explained throughout this book, many traditional strategies, as documented, cannot be implemented.

A key strength of the OpenStrategies system is that it provides explicit guidance on how a strategy needs to be written if it is to be at an aspirational level (non-implementable), guidance level (non-implementable) or operational level (implementable).

The PRUB sequence in an operational-level, PRUB-Validated SubStrategy (see Chapter 6) or OpenStrategy confidently defines exactly which Projects need to be undertaken, how the Results will be Used and what Benefits will arise. Therefore, such SubStrategies and OpenStrategies are, at least theoretically, straightforward to implement.

However, actual implementation is frequently governed by factors outside the strategy, especially in environments in which local and central government control many of the resources required by the strategy. In such circumstances SubStrategies and OpenStrategies which are fully Validated (logically sound, compellingly Evidenced and worthwhile in terms of net Values) may still not get implemented because they may not align with politicians'/decision-makers' ideologies.

The OpenStrategies approach therefore cannot guarantee that well-Validated SubStrategies will ever be implemented. What the OpenStrategies approach can guarantee is that if SubStrategies are rigorously developed using the OpenStrategies taxonomy, syntax and semantics, they will provide a clear basis for strategic decision-making and will guide strategy implementation.

Chapter 5
Working with Stakeholders

This chapter uses PRUB thinking to evaluate the challenging philosophies and psychologies of working with multiple stakeholders, the different types of stakeholders and their operational preferences and the OpenStrategies approach to stakeholder engagement (for strategy development) and collaboration (for strategy implementation).

5.1   Philosophy and Psychology

REASONS FOR MULTI-STAKEHOLDER STRATEGIES

Strategies are required for many different reasons, many of which overlap with other reasons and/or end up transitioning from one reason to another.

For example, a strategy focusing on a theme such as cycling is likely to overlap with a strategy focusing on young people. Similarly, a strategy on swimming pool use by older people is likely to overlap with a strategy on public health. A strategy on making it more attractive for consumers to buy wine (for example with wine companies giving discounts or other incentives) will invariably impact on a public sector strategy to minimise excessive drinking by young people.

In parallel with these overlaps in strategies will be differences between stakeholders in their levels of interest in different parts of a strategy. For example, in a children and young person's strategy, some stakeholders will be focused on health issues, some on sporting achievements and some on cultural activities.

Also, as strategies develop, stakeholders sometimes change their focus as they come to realise that other aspects of the strategy are especially important, perhaps more so than the issues that they first believed to be the most important. A slight variation on this theme is that sometimes strategies evolve into larger strategies once stakeholders recognise the inter-connections between different strategies.

Therefore, almost any overall strategy, especially in the public sector, will contain smaller strategies on different but related topics and the different components of the overall strategy will be of interest to different people. At the same time most stakeholders will also be interested in the big picture provided by the overall strategy while wanting a strategy system that continually evolves to accommodate changes in the environment and in stakeholders' preferences.

Traditional strategy processes typically do not possess sufficient evolutionary flexibility or abilities for strategy integration across themes, demographics, geographies and levels of strategies.

Strategies created as suites of SubStrategies provide the necessary versatility which enables all the above aggregations, disaggregations and evolution of strategies. This means that as the foci of stakeholders' preferences evolve and merge and de-merge, their SubStrategies and OpenStrategies can similarly evolve and stay up to date if they use the OpenStrategies system.

EQUALITY OR INEQUALITY OF STAKEHOLDERS

In any multi-stakeholder strategy development and implementation process, there is always tension due to the perceived inequality of stakeholders, some of whom (the 'providers') typically control most of the resources.

Usually these stakeholders believe that because they control the strategy's resources, they should also control most of the strategy development and implementation process. This presumption is frequently wrong.

The OpenStrategies system recognises that stakeholders are *not* universally unequal just because some of them have more resources than others.

There are strong arguments to support the perspective that the key stakeholders in any strategy development and implementation process should be the Users/Beneficiaries and there are further cogent arguments to suggest that 'strategic thinkers' should take a leading role rather than strategies being controlled primarily by providers.

The OpenStrategy system recognises stakeholders as:

1.   equal when they are generating ideas and creating an OpenStrategy;

2.   unequal in terms of their capacity to implement their SubStrategies;

3.   unequal in terms of their opportunities to use the assets/Results to create Benefits.

So stakeholders are simultaneously equal and unequal:

They are equal in terms of the value of their ideas.

They are unequal in terms of:

- *their resources and abilities to implement a strategy,*
- *the extent to which they Benefit from the strategy.*

Openly acknowledging and managing this apparent dichotomy of equality/ inequality needs to be done carefully because stakeholders who have traditionally taken control of strategy development processes (typically those stakeholders who control the most resources) usually strongly resist the notion that stakeholders without resources may nevertheless still have plenty of good strategic ideas, especially if they represent Uses and Benefits.

Provider-stakeholders far too frequently consciously or unconsciously invoke the so-called 'Golden Rule', that is, 'whoever has the gold makes the rules'. Yet by reading the first four chapters of this book, it should by now be crystal clear that in almost all strategies, the users are in fact the key players because unless they are motivated to use the assets that the providers (the ones with the 'gold') create, the strategy will fail. Therefore, there are overwhelmingly good reasons why end-user input should be a powerful feature of all strategy development and implementation processes.

Particularly strong resistance to end-user involvement is often exhibited by local and central government people when it is suggested that end-users/ beneficiaries may have very useful strategic suggestions to make and that these end-users' Uses and Benefits should be the primary drivers for the design, development and implementation of the strategy. However, as discussed many times in this book, understanding Uses (that is, what end-users want to be doing with assets) is crucially important for the development of *effective* strategies, so end-user stakeholders have absolutely crucial roles to play in formulating and implementing strategies.

In practical terms the OpenStrategies team recommends that when you are running multi-stakeholder workshops you invite participants to introduce themselves by stating just their names and their interests in participating in the workshop. Ask them to *not state their position in the organisational hierarchy* because the purpose of the strategy development workshop is to generate strategic ideas, not implement them at this stage. During this period everyone is equal in terms of their ability to generate strategic ideas.

Experience shows that while many people can operate under this rule, some provider stakeholders struggle to not mention that they are the 'manager' of some relevant function – they just cannot resist wanting to establish their perceived seniority in the hierarchy of power in a multi-stakeholder community. When they do this it immediately undermines the effectiveness of the strategy development process because, in essence, these hierarchy-bound stakeholders are saying right at the start that irrespective of what good ideas people come up with, these managerial stakeholders will make the final decisions. At the same time non-hierarchy-oriented people are invariably sensitive and smart enough to see the flaws in the behaviour of the hierarchy-dominated people and hence lose respect for them.

It is therefore vitally important to identify hierarchy-dominated individuals as soon as possible in any strategy development process so that they can be encouraged to 'let go' of their hierarchical tendencies, at least during the strategy development phase, in order to allow other stakeholders the freedom to come up with effective strategic ideas.

It is definitely worth persisting with the concept of stakeholders being equal in terms of their abilities to generate strategic ideas (and indeed end-users are probably more than equal when generating Uses), even when they are unequal in terms of their abilities to implement the strategic ideas.

At the same time it is important that various stakeholders take a level of leadership in terms of 'owning' or 'moderating' the development of the strategy and 'owning' or 'moderating' the implementation of the strategy.

In this respect:

- A host or sponsoring organisation might 'own' or 'moderate' the development of an entire strategy and they may similarly 'own' or 'moderate' the implementation of an entire strategy.

- A single organisation may 'own' or 'moderate' the development of a single SubStrategy or group of SubStrategies and they may 'own' or 'moderate' the implementation of a single SubStrategy or group of SubStrategies.

- A single stakeholder might 'own' or 'moderate' the development of a single PRUB Item (Project or Result or Use or Benefit) and they may also 'own' or 'moderate' the implementation of a single PRUB Item.

The OpenStrategies philosophy recognises all these different levels of equality/ inequality and the OpenStrategies system enables each and every one of them to operate within the context of an overall strategy.

STAKEHOLDERS AS WILLING VOLUNTEERS

A psychologically important principle that should apply to all strategies and which underpins OpenStrategies is the perspective that stakeholders participating in a strategy should all be viewed as volunteers. While some stakeholders will in fact be paid to participate in strategy development, they all have many demands on their time, hence the concept of 'willing volunteers' helps promote ongoing effective stakeholder involvement.

A consequence of this principle is that the strategy processes and outcomes must *create at least some value for each and every stakeholder* so that they continue to be motivated to volunteer their time to attend strategy events and to get on with implementation.

STAKEHOLDERS AS KNOWLEDGEABLE CONTRIBUTORS

Another key OpenStrategies principle is to assume that stakeholders are knowledgeable contributors and that therefore they need a minimalist strategy system which does as little as possible and assumes (with good reason) that stakeholders can do the rest. Therefore, the OpenStrategies system does not attempt to do what people already do reasonably well (make good decisions when they are well informed), but instead it focuses on assembling information in a manner which makes it easier for as many stakeholders as possible to make those decisions.

This is analogous to the principles which apply to a flock of birds. Birds don't need to be told how to do many of the basic functions of day-to-day living (they each have their own personal rules for eating, flying, sleeping, procreating and feeding their chicks). However, when flying together, it helps if they observe simple *shared* rules (stay a minimum distance from your neighbours, turn when they do) and otherwise just 'get on with it'.

OpenStrategies 'rules' are like these minimalist flight rules. They assume that stakeholders know how to do most things and that all that is required are some basic information management and cluster behaviour rules and that they can work out the rest for themselves.

EARNING THE RIGHT TO LEAD

Strategies, whether traditional or OpenStrategies, can be led by stakeholders who either 'take control' or who 'earn the right to lead'. Given that most stakeholders are willing volunteers, they generally respond adversely to leaders who 'take control' and respond better to leaders who 'earn the right to lead' through their professional conduct.

The transparency of the OpenStrategies system provides stakeholders with opportunities to demonstrate their strategy development and implementation capabilities in such a professional manner that other stakeholders decide to let them 'get on with it' because they are demonstrably and transparently doing such a good job.

OpenStrategies calls this 'earning the right to lead'.

By transparently opening up strategy development to all stakeholders, it is found that many stakeholders are happy simply to view the strategy process and to then step back and let leaders who have demonstrated the ability to lead to get on with it. In effect, stakeholders insist on the *right to participate*, but, provided they have this right and can observe others participating and leading professionally and creating a healthy strategy, many stakeholders are happy to step back and let others lead – in effect to be *given* (not to *take*) control.

As a consequence those stakeholders who perform professionally when developing and implementing a SubStrategy will *build the trust* of their stakeholders' community and in doing so will 'earn the right to lead'. In our experience a leader who has earned the right to lead is more sustainably effective than a leader who attempts to lead by 'taking control'.

This transparency and mode of operation of the OpenStrategies system helps enable this form of earning the right to lead while simultaneously acknowledging that senior managers can, if they wish to, actually 'take control'. However, good leaders won't generally exercise the 'take control' option except in exceptional circumstances, such as conditions of 'chaos' where urgent leadership action and decision-making is required. Leaders who have previously 'earned the right to lead' will tend to be more effective and be more trusted in such chaotic situations.

A key side effect of leaders taking the approach of letting a strategy evolve transparently (such that the leaders end up earning the right to lead and effectively being 'in control') is that the strategy itself tends to take on a life of its own independent of the leaders. It becomes the multi-stakeholder group's strategy, rather than the leader's strategy, or a strategy which is perceived as being 'owned' by one or more of the larger stakeholders.

This has the advantage that any of the stakeholders can pick up the strategy and implement 'their' parts of it. It has a further advantage that the leaders can come and go but the strategy continues to exist with a life of its own. In effect the multi-stakeholder strategy becomes the 'group strategy and group memory' and can exist sustainably and independently of any single stakeholder. So in effect a well-structured multi-stakeholder OpenStrategy becomes a 'personality-free zone' focused on objective facts and strategies rather than relying on the personal charisma of a leader.

STAKEHOLDERS' FEARS OF PRUB AND OPENSTRATEGIES

Some stakeholders find the OpenStrategies transparency and non-hierarchical approach to be threatening. This fear appears to be based on two factors:

1.   a sense of a loss of control by 'senior' stakeholders;

2.   the fear that existing strategies may fail to survive objective public scrutiny.

As discussed in the section 'Earning the right to lead', stakeholders who control resources typically believe that they have an unequivocal right to control strategy development and implementation, even when the resources they control (such as ratepayers' and taxpayers' contributions) have been contributed by other stakeholders. This applies even when the resources have been supplied by the end-users, for example in the case of government agencies (providers) who are funded by taxpayers (end-users).

In particular, public sector resource-controllers (local and central government) frequently hold firmly to a cherished belief that it is their job to develop and 'deliver' public services to a passive, dumb public – the same public which is paying their salaries! Such 'controlling' stakeholders and their employees need to be coaxed and cajoled into accepting that *all* stakeholders have ideas to contribute to the development of strategies and that their ideas need to be treated with respect. It is a long, slow process to do this because the perception of 'the right to govern' is so strongly engrained in the minds and hearts of so many public sector stakeholders. In the private sector, a similar perception of 'the right and obligation to control' is equally engrained in the minds of many senior executives.

The second fear – that their existing strategies may not survive transparent and public scrutiny via a PRUB-Validate process – *is entirely valid*. Our experience shows that 15–40% of existing public sector strategies fail the PRUB-Validate test (see Chapter 6). As noted in Chapter 1, Professor Freek Vermeulen at the London Business School observes that the situation is similar in the private sector, where he believes that less than 10% of companies currently have effective strategies. Our clients in the public sector similarly comment that in their experience, 'definitely less than 10% and probably less than 5% of public sector strategies have any impact'.

In this respect the PRUB-Validate tool (see Chapter 6) is very effective at identifying Abandoned Orphan Results and hence identifying potential failures and/or savings in existing strategies. Such discoveries are seldom welcomed by those stakeholders who 'own' such failed strategies, so they will fight hard to avoid such discoveries being made (the metaphor comes to mind that 'turkeys seldom vote for Christmas ...').

This resistance to transparent strategy development/evaluation/ implementation is one of the strongest forces resisting the widespread introduction of PRUB thinking into existing multi-stakeholder groups, particularly where there are well-established groups who control a large percentage of the available resources and where these same groups (for example government departments or senior company executives) are neither the end-users nor are they the generators of the resources, which instead come from end-user taxpayers or customers.

To minimise this resistance the OpenStrategies team emphasises that PRUB thinking should be used as a strategy *validation* or refinement tool, not as an *invalidation* tool. The purpose of applying PRUB thinking and the PRUB-Validate tool to any strategic idea should be to use the PRUB-Validate concepts (SubStrategy + Evidence + Value) to guide the positive refinement and hence 'Validation' of each strategic idea.

So PRUB-Validate identifies where a strategy (represented as a SubStrategy) is *currently weakly Validated* rather than definitively saying that the strategy *cannot be Validated*. PRUB-Validate precisely identifies any sources of weakness in the existing strategy (such as a lack of Evidence or unconvincing Links from Results to Uses or limited information on the net Value of the strategy) and then provides guidance on strengthening the existing strategy so that it can be Validated (see Chapter 6 to learn about how PRUB-Validate does this).

5.2   Different Types of People

PEOPLE WHO PREFER TO WORK WITH DIFFERENT PARTS OF A STRATEGY

Figure 5.1 schematically displays a matrix of aspirational, guidance and operational SubStrategies and shows that there are a total of 12 'strategic thinking spaces' where different individual stakeholders will focus their attentions (that is, in one or more of the cells created by the three rows and four columns of strategy elements).

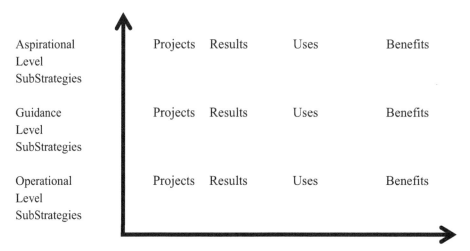

Figure 5.1   Matrix of strategy concepts

Referring to this matrix in any strategy development process, individual stakeholders generally prefer to operate with just one of the following:

- high-level strategies (aspirational SubStrategies – top level in Figure 5.1), *or*

- mid-level strategies (guidance SubStrategies – mid level in Figure 5.1), *or*

- grassroots-level strategies (operational SubStrategies – bottom level in Figure 5.1).

Similarly, some people prefer to focus on:

- Benefits and Uses, that is, the right-hand side of Figure 5.1, whereas

- others are more comfortable focusing on Projects and Results, that is, the left-hand side of Figure 5.1.

In our experience (and this does not imply the universality of these observations), doctors and surgeons appear most comfortable thinking strategically at aspirational and guidance levels about Projects and Results, whereas nurses and social workers appear most comfortable thinking strategically at operational or grassroots levels about Uses and Benefits (the observations and reasons for this would fill another book!).

Similarly, engineers tend to focus most on Projects and Results and have a desire to 'just get on with it'. Senior executives, directors and government ministers usually appear to be comfortable thinking about aspirational SubStrategies, whereas operational-level people are naturally more comfortable working with operational-level SubStrategies.

In the experience of the OpenStrategies team, individual stakeholders tend to be comfortable working in just one or two of the 'cells' in Figure 5.1 and to have a moderate level of comfort working with colleagues in perhaps four to five cells. This means that many stakeholders are uncomfortable working in over 50% of the strategy matrix in Figure 5.1.

It is therefore most important when working with multi-stakeholder groups to be explicitly clear exactly which part of the matrix in Figure 5.1 the stakeholders are addressing at any point in time. If this is not done openly and boldly, stakeholders will typically struggle to understand each other's perspectives as each stakeholder views the overall strategy matrix from their own limited (but nevertheless valid and valuable) perspective.

Each of these different preferences is valuable because they each identify detailed information relating to specific parts of a strategy matrix. Therefore, the people who are most comfortable with different aspects of the strategy all have something to offer.

In addition, different stakeholders will focus their attentions within an overall OpenStrategy on different themes, different demographic groups, different geographic areas, different provider organisations and so on.

In this respect the strengths of the OpenStrategies system are that:

- By encapsulating strategic information in PRUB-based SubStrategies, it becomes crystal clear that each type of information and contribution adds value to the overall strategy.

- Each type of strategic information has a logical 'home' within the overall OpenStrategy.

- Each type of information is linked via clear syntactical rules to all the other pieces of strategic information so as to constitute a complete OpenStrategy.

- The different stakeholders can see where their contributions fit and how they relate to the overall OpenStrategy.

SPLITTERS AND LUMPERS

In a similar vein, some people ('splitters') prefer to 'split' information by categorising it into its different component elements, whereas other people ('lumpers') are more comfortable 'lumping' information by clustering similar concepts under high-level headings.

Both splitting and lumping information are valuable processes, but it is important to know when and how to use each approach.

In terms of the management of strategic and operational information, the OpenStrategies system starts by lumping information at an appropriately 'high level' *because that is what most stakeholders want to know about*, especially if they need to work together. *Most* stakeholders want to start with an early indication of the overall parameters of a strategy before they get into the details of its component SubStrategies, hence why OpenStrategies usually start with 'lumped' high-level aspirational SubStrategies. Equally importantly, it is usually easier for stakeholders to agree on high-level aspirational strategies than it is to agree on guidance or operational level strategies which must necessarily get into more detail. It helps to achieve such high-level agreement to create an encouraging sense of everyone 'singing from the same song-sheet' before tackling the more difficult and contentious task of getting into the details.

We then recommend that stakeholders steadily increase the detail (splitting) of their strategies to create mid-level guidance strategies which include more specificity about exactly who the users are, what they want to do, where they want to do it and which stakeholder organisations are most likely to create the Results that the end-users need.

Finally, it is essential to split the strategic information into enough operational-level details so that strategies can actually be implemented. In this respect it may be feasible to provide operational-level groups with mid-level guidance strategies and leave it to them to create and implement operational-level strategies because it is likely that the operational-level people are the best positioned to understand what is actually possible at the operational level.

So the OpenStrategies system:

- starts by creating high-level aspirational SubStrategies (lumped information) which have the greatest chance of securing widespread stakeholder buy-in;

- then increases the level of detail by expanding these high-level SubStrategies into more detailed guidance-level SubStrategies (increasingly split information) before then;

- breaking the SubStrategies down into even more detail (more splitting) to create operational-level strategies which can actually be implemented;

- then within each Project, Result, Use and Benefit, more details are included (more splitting) to enable detailed operational management.

OpenStrategies thus enables the splitting of high-level information into whatever level of detail or categories each stakeholder wants *while still retaining the well-structured and interlinked overall strategy at all levels based on PRUB taxonomy, syntax and semantics.*

Similarly, this process can easily be reversed using the OpenStrategies approach by starting with individual, operational-level SubStrategies and progressively lumping them together into succinct, consolidated guidance or aspirational-level SubStrategies.

In doing this OpenStrategies enables all levels of information to use exactly the same information structure, that is, PRUB: it is just that they use it at different levels of detail. This means that high-level (lumped) information, guidance-level information (semi-split) and operational-level (split) information can be easily interlinked by using common sets of keywords based on OpenStrategies' four (or more) 'specificities' for all levels of information. (See Chapter 7 for more details on the aggregation and dis-aggregation of strategies.)

WHEN PEOPLE ARE 'PRODUCERS' AS WELL AS 'CONSUMERS/USERS'

Stakeholders can sometimes be users while simultaneously contributing to Projects. For example, members of the public may enjoy Using a restored wetland (as Users) while also contributing to actually restoring the wetland through weekend Projects to remove weeds and install fencing and board walks (Projects).

Therefore, it is important to distinguish between the *roles* of providers and Users and the *people* who perform those roles. As in the above example, the roles of providers and Users can be quite different even though exactly the same people perform the two different roles:

- in their roles as 'providers' people's primary function is to 'create/ restore/maintain' an asset;

- in their roles as 'Users' people's primary function is to Use an asset.

While this may at first glance appear to be a trivial distinction, we have found many strategies in which the lack of distinction between roles and people has led to considerable confusion within a strategy.

In some strategies it may be helpful to use the word 'citizen' to describe a member of the public who is contributing to a Project which is developing an asset and to use the word 'consumer' to describe someone who is Using an asset.

THE INTENSITY OF STAKEHOLDER FOCUS ON SUBSTRATEGIES

If there are many stakeholder organisations working together to create a large-scale strategy, we find that:

- Most stakeholders have some interest in *talking about* the overall strategy.

- A considerably smaller percentage are actually prepared to *contribute constructively to the design* of the overall strategy.

- Most stakeholders are not prepared to actively engage in *implementing* the overall strategy.

- Perhaps 80% of stakeholders are interested almost solely in their own specific area of work, that is, 80% of stakeholders are interested in just one or two SubStrategies.

- Perhaps 15% are interested in their own specific area of work as well as how it connects with other related areas of work, that is, 15% of stakeholders are interested in perhaps three to five SubStrategies.

- Perhaps 5% of stakeholders are interested in working with 'the big picture' of the entire strategy, that is, 5% of stakeholders are interested in all SubStrategies.

- *So about 95% of stakeholders are interested in working with single or small numbers of SubStrategies and only about 5% are motivated to work with (as distinct from just talk about) the big picture of strategies and OpenStrategies.*

- Most stakeholders will put their energy into creating and refining SubStrategies of specific interest to themselves and their own organisations.

OpenStrategy taps into the localised energy of this highly localised stakeholder focus on SubStrategies by enabling stakeholders to energetically and enthusiastically create their own SubStrategies and then enabling other stakeholders – who we call 'integrators' – to accumulate the SubStrategies into various combinations to create and monitor larger-scale OpenStrategies.

So:

- Many stakeholders want to *talk about* the overall strategy.

- Most stakeholders are prepared to *create and implement* SubStrategies of direct interest to them.

- A small number of integrators *accumulate and monitor* OpenStrategies.

THE EFFECTS OF TRANSPARENCY ON STAKEHOLDER ENGAGEMENT

Validated SubStrategies (see Chapter 6) make strategic ideas and their implementation transparently clear, especially in terms of identifying the roles of the different stakeholders *and* most importantly who will Benefit from the SubStrategies. The Beneficiaries will generally include customers, citizens, communities and the environment and frequently provider organisations will also receive Benefits. For example, the construction of a public asset such as a library will produce profits (Benefits) for the construction industry. Similarly, the construction of a convention centre will increase profits for nearby hotels and restaurants.

When *all* the Beneficiaries have been identified in a Validated SubStrategy, it becomes transparently clear why each stakeholder is lobbying for or supporting specific aspects of the SubStrategy. This transparency generally militates against stakeholders' behaviours which are self-serving because such behaviour becomes immediately obvious to all stakeholders.

WORKING WITH THE ENVIRONMENT

'The environment' is a special case topic because a 'healthy environment' can be a Result or a Benefit depending on how the Result/Benefit was achieved.

For example, a healthy environment as a result of citizens and organisations actively restoring something like a wetland is a Result. If people subsequently use the wetland sensitively, the consequence of this careful Use is a Benefit – but the consequence is still a 'healthy environment'.

The environment itself can be a key actor/stakeholder/provider. For example, a river may substantially alter itself (the asset) as a consequence of a major flood which clears out weeds. So the flood is a Project and the Result is a weed-free riverbed. If native species subsequently thrive in the riverbed (that is, they Use the riverbed) by keeping the riverbed free of weeds by eating the seedlings, the consequence of this Use is a Benefit.

So the strategic management of the environment highlights the distinction between creating an asset (restoring a wetland, a river flooding and removing weeds) to create a Result, and Using an asset (visiting a wetland, species maintaining the health of a riverbed through their Use of the riverbed) to create a Benefit.

So if something positive arises as a consequence of an action, it is a Result if the action was a deliberate development (Project) of an asset.

However, if something positive arises as a consequence of stakeholders Using an asset wisely, it is a Benefit.

WHEN EMPLOYEES ARE THE FOCUS OF A PROJECT

Many traditional strategies include actions which focus on 'capacity-building' or 'capability-building' in which employees within a provider organisation take part in training to build their skills. Because this training involves the development of an asset (trained staff), the training is a Project and the output of the training is a Result.

All too often this Result ends up being an Abandoned Orphan Result because the provider organisation has focused simply on 'building capacity' without any clear idea about how that capacity will enable Uses and hence lead to Benefits. In such situations, 'capacity-building' is seen as 'a good thing to do' so it is often done without any clear vision of how it will impact on Uses and Benefits.

The same applies to 'leadership development', a very popular concept in many private, public and third sector multi-stakeholder environments. Leadership development programmes repeatedly produce … leaders … which are just Abandoned Orphan Results unless these leaders have clear leadership roles (within Adopting Projects) to slot into. Far too often the freshly minted leaders return to their organisations into roles where they have few opportunities to lead. This isn't good enough!

Before *any* Project is started it should be a requirement that the Project be part of a start-to-finish SubStrategy which shows explicitly *how* any Project will contribute, eventually, to desired Benefits. Any 'capability-building' or 'leadership development' Project should be explicitly clear how the new capabilities and leadership skills will contribute to Uses (probably indirectly via Adopting Projects).

If the trained staff or new leaders directly engage with end-users (for example as front-line service staff), the new capabilities will be being Used to help end-users create Benefits.

However, if – as is frequently the case with newly skilled staff and leaders – the skills are Adopted into new Projects, these Projects should be required to produce better Results as a consequence of these new skills than they would otherwise have done.

So Projects which involve enhancing providers' capabilities frequently produce Orphan Results which need to be Adopted in order for end-user Benefits to ultimately be improved. Sadly, experience shows that traditionally and historically this is seldom the case, especially in the public sector.

USING SUBSTRATEGIES IN HUMAN RESOURCE MANAGEMENT

SubStrategies are generally designed to encapsulate the necessary and sufficient set of Projects, Results and Uses required to achieve desired Benefits.

Once such SubStrategies have been created, it is possible to distil related SubStrategies which are structured so as to represent the Projects that a particular stakeholder or staff member (in a provider organisation) contributes to or manages, thereby providing clarity to staff members relating to their roles, responsibilities and accountabilities.

For example, a stakeholder may contribute to a total of five Projects from three different SubStrategies. By first amalgamating the three SubStrategies and then distilling the Projects that the stakeholder is contributing to plus their related Results/Uses/Benefits, you can create a SubStrategy which uniquely defines the roles of the stakeholder (that is, their contributions within the Projects) and how the Projects they are contributing to ultimately lead to desirable Benefits.

Similarly, the performance measures within the SubStrategies which are specific to each Project, Result, Use and Benefit can be used to guide performance management for each stakeholder organisation, including the performance management of the stakeholder organisation's staff. To do this effectively requires that it first be determined exactly which indicators/targets relate to factors that the stakeholder or staff member can contribute to and to then define how the stakeholder's/staff member's role impacts on these indicators and targets.

Scaling this up, the performance management of organisations and multi-stakeholder groups also can be managed using the same, scalable OpenStrategies system.

5.3   Stakeholder Engagement Processes

DEFINITIONS

The International Association for Public Participation (IAP2) has defined a full spectrum of stakeholder engagement processes ranging from 'inform' through 'consult' and 'involve' to 'collaborate' and 'empower' (www.iap2.org/associations/4748/files/IAP2%20Spectrum_vertical.pdf).

For simplicity in this book we will use the terms:

- 'engagement' to mean the forms of participation appropriate for developing a strategy (generally 'inform, consult, involve');

- 'collaboration' to mean the forms of participation appropriate for implementing a strategy (generally 'involve, collaborate and empower').

COST BENEFITS OF ENGAGEMENT AND COLLABORATION

While the OpenStrategies team is enthusiastic about stakeholder participation in the development and implementation of strategies, we nevertheless caution against automatically assuming that any form of engagement and collaboration is better than no engagement and collaboration.

Large-scale stakeholder engagement and collaboration are generally difficult and expensive processes if they are to be effective and create greater value than the cost and effort involved.

Furthermore, there is a major risk with poorly facilitated engagement processes that stakeholders' expectations will be raised inappropriately and this subsequently leads to stakeholder dissatisfaction with both the strategy development and its implementation.

Practically everyone we listen to can tell us many stories of highly time consuming, feel-good but ineffective stakeholder engagement processes. This situation is so bad that it appears that a very large majority of stakeholder engagement processes are ineffective.

However, done well, engagement and collaboration can lead to excellent outcomes and an increased sense of community cohesion.

Given that there are hundreds of consultation and engagement tools available – see for example www.consultationinstitute.org/ and www.collaborate.com/ – why is engagement and collaboration so difficult to get right, especially in multi-stakeholder environments where there are many topics to be addressed?

Why is 'networking' so enjoyable yet seldom leads to objectively measurable changes?

Let's look at this mathematically by asking the following questions, which are reasonable questions to ask in situations such as local government, where many organisations need to work together on many topics (similar mathematics applies even in companies):

Question 1:

> How many discussions would be required for 100 stakeholders to discuss with each other 50 different topics just six times per year?

Answer:

> 1,500,000 discussions!

Even if the stakeholders decided to discuss just 10 topics twice per year, this would still require 50,000 discussions. Such engagement is unmanageable in most situations.

Question 2:

> In this situation, how would it be possible to:

> •   Record this huge number of discussions?

> •   Distil the key messages from all these discussions?

> •   Share the key messages with the relevant stakeholders who are interested in each topic?

- Develop strategies on each topic?

- Interlink related strategies into a combined strategy?

- Implement the strategies?

Answer:

We believe it is not humanly possible to do this.

So interconnecting or networking stakeholders via thousands of 'engagement' discussions simply isn't practical.

There has to be a better way.

The OpenStrategies approach is to network ideas rather than to network people.

Even in the most complex situations involving hundreds or thousands of stakeholders there is almost always a much smaller number of ideas than the number of stakeholders or the number of discussions required to address these ideas. Therefore the interlinking of ideas will be numerically less challenging than interlinking people.

Using the OpenStrategies approach to organise strategic ideas into interlinked collections of Validated SubStrategies enables stakeholders to rapidly identify the sub-set of strategic ideas of interest to them. This means they can focus their discussions on just these ideas and with just those stakeholders who are interested in the same sub-set of ideas, so the number of required discussions falls dramatically.

Transparent OpenStrategies enable the *self-organising* of stakeholders into clusters and so *optimises their discussions* and also provides a 'home' for the outputs of the discussions – that is, the newly evolving strategic information is put into refined SubStrategies which evolve and improve as each discussion generates additional information relevant to each SubStrategy.

So by networking ideas instead of networking people, the OpenStrategies system guides stakeholders to have fewer discussions as well as providing a repository (as SubStrategies) for capturing the evolving strategic thinking.

ENGAGEMENT WITH USER-STAKEHOLDERS FOR DEVELOPING STRATEGIES

As noted in all earlier chapters, understanding 'Uses' is crucially important for enabling the design of effective, implementable strategies which will enable 'organisations to create the right assets for people to use to generate benefits'.

This means *really* understanding what customers, communities and individuals will *actually do* if they are provided with the *right* assets/Results to enable them to create desirable Benefits.

The best way of learning what Users will actually do is to ask them the right questions.

As discussed in Chapter 4, learning about what Users *want* produces much less valuable and useful information than learning about what users are prepared to actually *do*.

So the most effective stakeholder engagement processes will first ask end-users what they are prepared to actually *do* and only after this question has been answered will end-users be asked what assets/Results they *want/need* in order to enable them to do what they want to do (Uses).

A word of caution is required here.

Many end-user stakeholders struggle to answer the question 'what do you want to do?' because:

- it requires them to think deeply about their own actions and how they fit into a strategy or SubStrategy;

- it requires them to take ownership of the Uses and Benefits components of a SubStrategy;

- it requires them to consider whether or not they are prepared to make any effort at all or to commit any resources to enable Benefits to be achieved;

- they are often so accustomed to being asked what they *want* that they struggle to comprehend that they actually have to be active participants in any process that will create Benefits because *only users can create Benefits*.

Asking stakeholders what they want to *do* provides stakeholders with the opportunity to come up with completely new concepts unconstrained by existing strategies.

For example (and this is a real example) an existing strategy included the construction of a swimming pool based on a belief by provider organisations that people in the community wanted to swim in a swimming pool. This was because stakeholders had been asked what they wanted and they responded by saying they wanted a swimming pool, partly because they wanted to go swimming and partly because they believed that it was a role for the local authority to provide swimming pools.

However, when people were asked what they wanted to *actually do*, many said that they did indeed want to swim but that their happiest memories of swimming were in clear mountain rivers, lakes and in the sea. Therefore, the Results that many of them wanted were in fact clean rivers, lakes and the sea to swim in rather than a swimming pool.

In a similar vein, when discussing transport options in a city many people will say that they *want* more cycle paths. However, when many of these same people are asked what they will *actually do* they admit, with some embarrassment, that actually they want to drive their cars because they hope that lots of other people will be using the cycle paths.

So asking people what they are prepared to *actually do* provides much more reliable information than asking people what they *want*.

Whereas many stakeholders struggle to define what they want to do, most stakeholders find it much easier to answer the question 'what do you want?' because:

- this frees the stakeholder to dream about what someone else can provide to them;

- it lets the stakeholder imagine all sorts of desirable Results without having to take responsibility for the costs or how they might be created and made available or what they personally might need to contribute.

Therefore, asking people what they *want* is an easy question and is easily answered – but the resulting answers are often 'wrong'. In this respect there may be multiple ways of enabling a Use by providing different assets/Results and it is often discovered that the most obvious Result is not in fact the best one.

Unfortunately many (probably most) engagement processes still ask stakeholders what they *want*. These processes can produce huge amounts of information which can be carefully analysed and apparently logical conclusions drawn and used to guide strategies. Unfortunately, for the reasons outlined above, the conclusions are often wrong, not as a consequence of poor analysis but because *the wrong questions were asked in the first place.*

Sadly, in many circumstances provider organisations believe that they know what customers and communities want so they don't even bother to ask the end-users. Often this is because provider organisations base their beliefs on what they are currently providing and on existing customer and community behaviours. The OpenStrategies approach of asking end-users what they want to be *doing* breaks this mind-set and opens up many more possibilities.

A further caution in this respect is to obtain compelling Evidence that providing end-users with what they *say* they will do and/or what they want will in fact lead to Uses and Benefits. Although end-users may genuinely believe the answers they give to questions such as 'what do you want to be doing?' and 'what do you want?' it is essential to back up their statements with hard Evidence that they will actually do what they say they will do. For example, many people say that they will exercise more and eat more healthily yet in fact few do so.

So in creating strategies with and for end-users it is essential to ground-truth what people are saying they want or want to do. There are many techniques for doing this and which are beyond the scope of this book (which focuses on the nature of the questions to be asked and the language and system used to encapsulate the strategy, rather than on promoting any particular technique for assessing the validity of end-users' answers). But the key point remains – that it is essential to identify, define and Validate end-users' answers.

Once you understand what people actually wish to be *doing* – the 'Use' in PRUB language – it becomes clearer what the ideal Projects are that will produce the *right* assets/Results that will enable end-users to do what they say they want to do.

ENGAGEMENT WITH NON-USER STAKEHOLDERS FOR DEVELOPING STRATEGIES

In addition to obtaining robust information about Uses and users as discussed above, it is also important to involve all key 'provider' and non-user stakeholders in the strategy development so that they take ownership of the process and the subsequent strategy implementation.

This means securing the active involvement of not only the end-users (the people who will be the prime 'actors' in Uses in order to generate Benefits) but also all the service providers (the organisations who will run Projects to produce Results), funders and potentially others such as regulators.

Effective engagement can benefit from involving as many brains as possible provided this is done in such a manner that it doesn't become just another talk-fest. Stakeholder engagement in the strategy development process needs to be balanced with the need to 'get on with it' so it must be done effectively and efficiently.

Such engagement with end-users and other stakeholders can take many forms (refer to the IAP2 website mentioned above for further information), so in this section I'll focus solely on aspects of this engagement that are unique to the OpenStrategies approach.

The first uniquely OpenStrategies component of stakeholder engagement is to introduce stakeholders to PRUB strategic thinking so that they become comfortable with the PRUB sequence for representing strategic ideas – which in turn represents what organisations actually *do*: they *create assets and enable people to use them to generate Benefits*. This can be achieved quite quickly using either an introductory brochure or a 15-minute introduction in a workshop setting.

The second step is to emphasise the importance of understanding Uses as discussed in the previous section.

Subsequent steps include all or some of the following:

1.   workshops (see below) using Projects, Results, Uses and Benefits thinking which use a 'sticky wall' or similar approach to guide people's thinking and capture their contributions to the development of SubStrategies and the overall OpenStrategy. This generally uses the strategy matrix shown in Figure 5.1 in order to

capture each piece of information from stakeholders and place it in
the appropriate part of the strategy matrix on the sticky wall;

2.   the establishment of a stakeholder group or individual (a 'strategy
        integrator') whose role is to oversee and facilitate the strategy
        development process to help it to remain coherent such that each
        SubStrategy blends into the overall OpenStrategy;

3.   the establishment of sub-groups of stakeholders whose focus
        is to develop specific SubStrategies based on selected themes,
        demographic groups, geographical areas, organisational
        responsibilities or other criteria;

4.   as these groups develop their SubStrategies, the 'strategy
        integrator' keeps advising the sub-groups as to whether or not the
        SubStrategies they are developing are consistent with and fit into
        the overall OpenStrategy;

5.   the evolution of the SubStrategies and the overall OpenStrategy
        as circumstances change, as more and more strategic information
        becomes available and as various components of the OpenStrategy
        are successfully implemented;

6.   the collaborative implementation of the SubStrategies (see next section);

7.   the effective performance management of the strategy implementation.

The ability to develop overall OpenStrategies in this modular way (by creating
and then interconnecting SubStrategies) must be done iteratively so that the
advantages of being able to create bite-sized chunks of strategy (SubStrategies) is
balanced by the need for the overall OpenStrategy to be integrated and coherent.

Ultimately it is individual SubStrategies which will actually get
implemented but both during the planning process and the implementation
process, stakeholders must remain acutely aware of, and manage, the
interconnections between SubStrategies.

Because individual stakeholders will have unique insights and perspectives
on the challenges facing the strategy and its implementation, they will
frequently see interconnections between SubStrategies that the 'strategy
integrator' doesn't initially identify.

An important feature of the OpenStrategies approach is that each of these stakeholders can create SubStrategies based on their perspectives and insights and these SubStrategies can then be 'offered' to the full group of stakeholders for integration (or not) into the overall OpenStrategy. Ideally, such SubStrategies will actually be developed in a way that they are integrated right from the start.

In this way stakeholder sub-groups and individuals can present their recommendations for action in the common format of Validated SubStrategies so that different groups' SubStrategies can then be compared like-with-like and they can also be readily interlinked into full OpenStrategies.

This freedom for sub-groups to create their own SubStrategies and offer them to the overall OpenStrategy is important because, as discussed earlier in this chapter, most stakeholders in a multi-stakeholder multi-themed strategy environment are interested in a relatively small set of issues. Therefore, they are energised to develop SubStrategies on this small set of issues even if they are not energised to work on the overall strategy.

The OpenStrategies approach enables them to do this, tapping into their localised energy while at the same time enabling the interlinking of all groups' SubStrategies into a cohesive OpenStrategy by the strategy integrator.

PRUB WORKSHOPS

Many strategy workshops consist of brainstorming/mind-leaking exercises which produce hundreds of Post-it notes™ plastered over walls – notes which someone has to make sense of after the workshop. Time and time again the resulting 'workshop report' is an Abandoned Orphan Result which few people read and practically no one acts on.

In contrast, by using PRUB strategic thinking as the underpinning knowledge management tool in strategy workshops, much more structured and hence useful information is collected and encapsulated in readily refined and implementable SubStrategies.

PRUB thinking is a powerful system for facilitating strategy analysis and development workshops.

At the practical level it works like this:

1. Create a 'sticky wall' made up of a 3–4-metre long by 1.5-metre wide strip of lightweight fabric that has been sprayed on one side with a 'repositionable adhesive'.

2. Attach this sticky wall to a physical wall (sticky side out) using masking tape and attach the four 'Projects, Results, Uses and Benefits' headings across the top of the sticky wall.

3. Invite stakeholders to generate ideas for their SubStrategies, write them on A5 or A6 pieces of paper and attach them to the sticky wall under the appropriate PRUB heading. It is likely you will initially need to edit stakeholders' statements so that they clearly define Project, Results, Uses and Benefits.

4. If the starting point for the workshop is a blank strategy, start by identifying and defining the high-level Benefits that the implementation of any new strategy is expected to create and then work to the left to identify Uses, Results and Projects.

5. If the starting point for the workshop is an existing strategy, start by taking each existing strategic idea and distilling Projects, Results, Uses and Benefits from this idea.

6. As Projects, Results, Uses and Benefits get added to the sticky wall, make a decision about what level of strategy is being developed:

    – high-level aspirational strategy,
    – mid-level guidance strategy,
    – grassroots-level operational strategy.

7. Continue to build the strategy at the desired level while retaining any other ideas which may be appropriate to other levels of the strategy.

By focusing tightly on the concepts of Projects, Results, Uses and Benefits, you will find that your strategy will come together very fast. Typically gaps appear in the SubStrategies as information is identified as missing, usually relating to Uses. There will generally be a shortage of convincing Evidence that Results will in fact be Used at a level to justify the Projects that produce the Results.

If stakeholders propose ideas which don't appear to be a Project or a Result or a Use or a Benefit, it is quite likely that the idea is a 'value statement' such as 'we see water as sacred'. At this point it is helpful to ask questions such as 'how would you know if water was being treated sacredly?' The answers to this question are likely to be Projects, Results, Uses and Benefits.

COLLABORATION FOR IMPLEMENTING STRATEGIES

As well as securing psychological and practical buy-in to strategies from stakeholders via the collaborative OpenStrategies approach, it is often possible to tap into the substantial resources of end-users to help implement a strategy.

For example, in a New Zealand situation where self-sown wilding pine trees were spreading uncontrolled into pristine mountain areas, the walkers, climbers and skiers who frequented the area (end-users) volunteered their time to cut down the trees on the condition that the regional authorities would provide tools and transport to the area. The nearby farmers provided a barbeque at the end of the day because the removal of the wilding trees also prevented them from spreading on to the farmers' land. So the primary cost (labour) of implementing the SubStrategy to remove the wilding trees was actually provided free of charge by the end-users.

This effective solution arose because the end-users were involved in the development of the strategy and were able to offer their resources to complement the resources of the traditional service providers.

There are many situations where such end-user involvement can enable SubStrategies to be implemented better than would otherwise have happened, or to be implemented in circumstances where provider organisations don't have the resources to enable the implementation.

Defining strategic ideas as SubStrategies clarifies for all stakeholders exactly what needs to be done and who will benefit. This makes it easier for end-users to step forward and offer their services and resources to enable end-user-desirable SubStrategies to be implemented.

Unfortunately few traditional strategies tap into the resources of the end-users because the service providers are so locked in to their concepts of 'deliver' and 'provide' (see Chapters 3 and 4) that they are unable to acknowledge that end-users may have many resources that they can, and willingly will, contribute to the implementation of strategies.

Some of the key challenges of collaborative strategy implementation are discussed below, together with information on how the OpenStrategies approach addresses these challenges.

SILO WORKING

'Silo working' describes a situation in which stakeholder organisations work in isolation rather than collaboratively. One of the main reasons why organisations prefer to work in silos is that they are generally held accountable as organisations for performing defined activities to produce defined outputs with defined budgets. Therefore they fear that working collaboratively will make it difficult for them to retain clarity on their exact contributions to activities and outputs and to control their budgets.

Silo working is effective for achieving organisation-by-organisation accountability. In contrast, joined-up working is effective for implementing multi-stakeholder strategies.

People wishing to collaborate frequently bemoan the silo mentality of their collaborators so they try to 'break down' the silos.

In contrast, the OpenStrategies approach is to 'join up the silos'. In this way each organisational silo can retain its independence and accountabilities while still collaborating effectively.

The OpenStrategies approach enables this joined-up working by defining the SubStrategies that need to be implemented in such a manner that different service providers can identify actions they can take and be accountable through their own silos within an overall context of an OpenStrategy that interlinks their actions with those of all the other service providers.

This in turn leads to the concept of 'joined-up budgets' as distinct from 'pooled budgets'.

'Pooled budgets' are where all stakeholders' budgets are contributed to a pool of funds and resources and the stakeholders collectively determine how these funds and resources are allocated. This approach directly confronts the independence and accountability of each existing silo of operation.

In contrast, 'joined-up budgets' are where each organisational silo retains full control of its budgets but does so in full cognition of other stakeholders' strategies and budgets and so increasingly runs their own Projects alongside these other stakeholders to produce better Results collaboratively.

So the OpenStrategies approach of 'joined-up budgets' works by each organisation identifying their own contributions to an agreed SubStrategy and managing those contributions alongside similar contributions being managed independently but in parallel by other service providers.

By encapsulating each organisation's strategies as SubStrategies it becomes possible to interlink strategies across organisations to achieve effective collaboration while still retaining silo-based organisational responsibility and accountability.

This means that each organisation retains full accountability for its budgets and contributions to the strategy while at the same time being able to see how their SubStrategies fit into the big picture of an overall OpenStrategy. This helps them to work collaboratively alongside other service providers and reinforces the principle of 'joined-up working' or 'joining up silos' rather than 'breaking down silos'.

IMPLEMENTING SUBSTRATEGIES

While the *development* of large OpenStrategies will ideally involve all affected stakeholders, in general many of the SubStrategies will be *implemented* by sub-groups of service providers rather than by all the stakeholders working collaboratively to implement all SubStrategies.

So the scale of engagement for developing a strategy may differ significantly from the scale of collaboration for implementing the strategy.

Most implementable SubStrategies contain multiple Projects, Results, Uses and Benefits which need to be implemented collaboratively. Therefore it is seldom beneficial to implement individual Projects and, instead, it is generally much more effective to implement entire SubStrategies and clusters of interlinked SubStrategies.

Given that many SubStrategies involve multiple stakeholders, collaboration becomes almost essential. By defining all the interlinked steps that need to be taken from an initial set of Projects through to a final set of Benefits, the OpenStrategies approach clarifies for all the stakeholders exactly what needs to be done. This means that stakeholders can select those actions where they can make a worthwhile contribution and, subject to other stakeholders similarly identifying the actions they will take in parallel, the service providers can then get on with implementing their components of each SubStrategy knowing how their contributions fit collaboratively with other service providers' contributions.

Typically, not only is there collaboration within SubStrategies (groups of stakeholders working alongside each other to implement individual SubStrategies), but there is also collaboration across SubStrategies (stakeholder groups implementing individual SubStrategies working alongside other stakeholder groups implementing other complementary SubStrategies).

OpenStrategies enable groups to continue to work within and be accountable for their own silos of activity while simultaneously being aware of and working alongside other silos of activity.

OpenStrategy explicitly recognises and enables this reality through its focus on implementable small-group SubStrategies while retaining the OpenStrategy view of the big picture.

As noted earlier, it is important to contract someone with the role of 'strategy integrator' to retain the overview of the overall OpenStrategy so that, as the SubStrategies are implemented, they do in fact stay interlinked with other related SubStrategies.

Therefore, the OpenStrategies system helps enable *scalable* collaboration ranging from collaboration within single SubStrategies to collaboration across an entire OpenStrategy.

PART II
Creating and Validating Strategies

Chapter 6

PRUB-Validate

PRUB-Validate is an OpenStrategies tool which uses the Projects, Results, Uses and Benefits sequence plus 'Evidence' and 'Value' to guide the development and validation of strategies.

In Chapters 1–5 we reviewed the challenges of multi-stakeholder strategy development and implementation through the lenses of PRUB thinking and OpenStrategies. However, PRUB thinking is much more than just a strategy diagnosis tool. PRUB-Validate underpins strategy development and also guides strategy validation, implementation and performance management.

PRUB-Validate does this for any size of strategy, ranging from a single small SubStrategy up to an OpenStrategy consisting of many interlinked SubStrategies.

6.1 The PRUB-Validate Process

Anyone can come up with an idea and claim that it is strategic and that it should be implemented. It is a very different matter to identify, define *and Validate* a strategic idea so that:

- there is compelling cause-and-effect Evidence that the strategic idea genuinely should and can be implemented;

- there is convincing information that it will be worthwhile implementing the strategic idea.

The PRUB-Validate process distinguishes between:

- 'Validated' strategies which can be implemented, and

- 'non-Validated' strategies which must either be improved before implementation or not implemented at all.

It does this objectively and simply by addressing four questions for each strategic idea:

1. What desired outcomes should the strategic idea lead to?

    – Action: define the idea in a 1:1:1:1 PRUB sequence.

2. Exactly what needs to be done to make the strategic idea successful?

    – Action: expand the idea into a theoretical SubStrategy.

3. What Evidence do we have that the strategic idea will definitely lead to the desired outcomes?

    – Action: partially Validate the SubStrategy with compelling cause-and-effect Evidence for each Link.

4. Is it worth it?

    – Action: complete the Validation by determining the strategic ideas' net Value.

This four-step process is 'PRUB-Validate'.

- Each one of the above steps *must* be completed before it is even possible to take the subsequent steps.

- Each of the above steps is easier than the subsequent steps.

- This means that the easiest steps can quickly eliminate or improve those strategic ideas which fail each step.

- Eliminated strategic ideas don't need to be processed through the subsequent, more challenging Validation steps.

The following section describes how to do this efficiently and effectively.

6.2   How?

STEP I: CLARIFY THE STRATEGIC IDEA

The first step in Validating each strategic idea is to define it rigorously in a 1:1:1:1 Projects, Results, Uses and Benefits sequence, as shown in Figure 6.1.

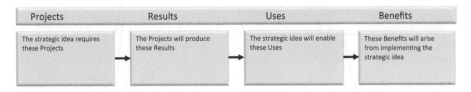

Projects	Results	Uses	Benefits
The strategic idea requires these Projects	The Projects will produce these Results	The strategic idea will enable these Uses	These Benefits will arise from implementing the strategic idea

Figure 6.1   A simple high-level 1:1:1:1 SubStrategy

If it is not possible to describe the strategic idea using PRUB thinking like this, improve it or eliminate it.

This PRUB sequence is not yet sufficient to Validate the strategic idea. We still need to know details of all the actions that are required to support the strategic idea, whether the Results will actually be Used by customers and citizens and whether it is sufficiently valuable to be worthwhile. This leads to step 2 in the PRUB-Validate process.

STEP 2: EXPAND THE STRATEGIC IDEA INTO A SUBSTRATEGY

To Validate each strategic idea, it must be expanded into a 'SubStrategy' that contains all the Linked Projects, Results and Uses which are both *necessary and sufficient to generate the desired Benefits*. This is shown in Figure 6.2.

There are no shortcuts from Projects to Benefits. To be validated, a Project must lead to Results which must lead to Uses which must lead to Benefits. If it is not possible to convert the strategic idea into a necessary and sufficient SubStrategy like this, do not continue with the strategic idea. Improve it or eliminate it.

Remember that Projects often produce 'Orphan Results' *which cannot be directly Used by communities.*

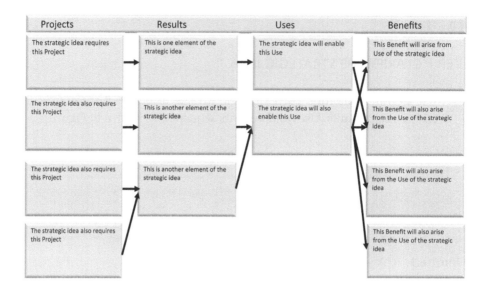

Figure 6.2   A SubStrategy that defines and Links all the necessary and sufficient things needed for a strategic idea to be effective

Orphan Results have been discussed already but they are a vitally important concept, which is why we review them here.

There are two types of Orphan Results:

1.   Adopted Orphan Results.

2.   Abandoned Orphan Results.

Adopted Orphan Results

If an Orphan Result is Adopted by another Project run by another organisation or elsewhere in the same organisation, we say that the Orphan Result has been 'Adopted' – it is an 'Adopted Orphan Result', as shown in Figure 6.3.

Both Projects in Figure 6.3 have been successfully PRUB-Linked so they can proceed to the next step in the Validation process.

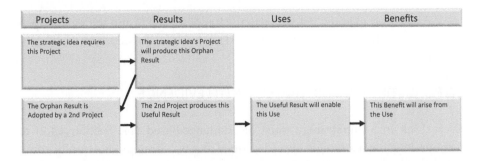

**Figure 6.3   A SubStrategy that shows the sequence in which an Orphan
             Result can be Adopted by another Project**

Abandoned Orphan Results

If an Orphan Result is not 'Adopted' by another organisation, we define it as an
'Abandoned Orphan Result', as shown in Figure 6.4.

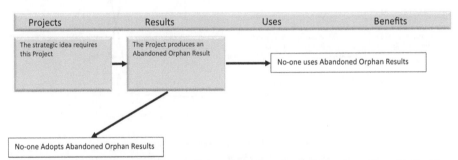

**Figure 6.4   A Project that produces an Abandoned Orphan Result that is
             not Used and not Adopted**

If a Project produces an Abandoned Orphan Result, do not continue with
the strategic idea. Improve it or eliminate it.

A SubStrategy in which all the Results are either Used or Adopted is still not
enough to Validate a strategic idea because at this stage it is merely a theoretical
map of strategic possibilities.

We still need to know if it will actually happen (step 3) and if it will happen at a level which is worthwhile (step 4). This leads us to step 3 of the PRUB-Validate process.

STEP 3: JUSTIFY THE SUBSTRATEGY WITH EVIDENCE

Every Link in a SubStrategy must be Evidence-based (see Section 4.1.2) to demonstrate that a strategic idea (described as a SubStrategy) is actually going to be used by customers or citizens and will lead to the desired Benefits.

This cause-and-effect Evidence is precisely located in the Links (pointed to by vertical arrows) in the SubStrategy figure of each Strategic Option, as shown in Figure 6.5.

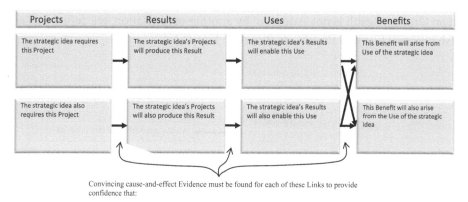

Figure 6.5   **Where Evidence fits into the OpenStrategies syntax**

Some Evidence is easier to find than other Evidence. For example, it is usually straightforward to find cause-and-effect Evidence that a Project will lead to a Result.

It is usually more difficult (yet vital) to determine objectively and quantitatively if Results will actually be Used, to what extent, and whether these Uses will genuinely lead to the desired Benefits. Justifying an Evidence-based SubStrategy requires convincing cause-and-effect Evidence that Results will actually be Used.

Experience shows that the most useful Validation Evidence is the Evidence which confirms that Results will actually be Used. If such Evidence is lacking, do not continue with the SubStrategy. Improve it or eliminate it.

Even if a strategic idea has been successfully defined, mapped into a SubStrategy and fully Evidenced (steps 1–3), this is still not enough to Validate a strategic idea. We still need to know 'is it worth it?' This is determined in step 4 of PRUB-Validate.

STEP 4: ASSESS THE VALUE OF THE STRATEGIC IDEA

If a strategic idea has been successfully defined, mapped into a SubStrategy and fully Evidenced (steps 1–3 of PRUB-Validate), this is still not enough to Validate it.

We still need to know if the net value (economic, social, environmental and cultural values) of the Benefits exceeds the net costs of creating those values. Specifically:

> *Does the value of the Benefits exceed the sum of the costs of the Projects plus the costs of the Uses?*

Determining the value of Benefits is often very challenging. This fact alone is a powerful reason why, *before* attempting to determine the net value of the Benefits which might arise from a strategic idea, it is easier to conduct steps 1–3 above to screen out:

- all strategic ideas which cannot be defined as a basic PRUB sequence;

- all strategic ideas which cannot be succinctly described in a SubStrategy;

- all SubStrategies which cannot be effectively Evidenced.

It is precisely because economic, social, environmental and cultural valuations are so challenging that steps 1–3 above are so powerful for rapidly assessing strategic ideas.

Having screened out strategic ideas which fail the first three steps, we now have a smaller set of strategic options to 'Value' and hence to Validate.

The second step (translating the strategic idea into a SubStrategy) identifies *exactly which costs will be incurred to achieve which Benefits. This is important because it is simply impossible to determine the net value of a SubStrategy unless it is crystal clear exactly which costs need to be correlated with the value of exactly which Benefits.*

So it is impossible to determine 'is it worth it?' without first completing steps 1–3 above, which are necessary to determine exactly which Benefit-values should be evaluated relative to exactly which Project-costs and Use-costs.

Frequently the Users' costs exceed the Project's costs so they *must* be included in the value calculations. For example, it might make good economic sense from a government's perspective to amalgamate many local community hospitals into a central hospital. However, doing so will increase the costs to the users because instead of attending their local hospital, they will now incur the added cost of travel to the central hospital plus possibly accommodation costs.

So crucially, the net value of a strategic idea must take into account all three factors:

1.   the value of the Benefits;

2.   the cost of the Projects;

3.   the cost to Users of using the Results to achieve the Benefits;

and then determine whether the value of the Benefits outweighs the costs of *the sum of* the Project costs and the Use costs:

Mathematically, is $\Sigma V_B > \Sigma C_P + \Sigma C_U$

where ΣV_B = *Sum of the Values of the Benefits*

ΣC_P = *Sum of the Costs of the Projects*

ΣC_U = *Sum of the Costs of the Uses*

There are many articles, papers and books on determining the value of outcomes/Benefits and this book will not attempt to describe them. A keen reader is invited to start with these articles:

www.ncvo-vol.org.uk/psd/commissioning/social_value2

www.siaassociation.org/wp-content/uploads/2012/05/NAVCA-report-on-measuring-social-value-social-outcomes-and-impact.pdf

www.sciencedirect.com/science/article/pii/S0022435901000410

http://en.wikipedia.org/wiki/Predicted_outcome_value_theory

The key point here is that the PRUB-Validate approach precisely identifies *which* costs and the value of *which* Benefits need to be correlated and compared in order to determine if it is worth implementing a SubStrategy.

Also, if it proves to be challenging to determine the values of the Benefits, this 4th step in the PRUB-Validate process identifies the *minimum value that these Benefits must have* if the SubStrategy is to be fully Validated. This minimum value must exceed the combined costs of the Projects plus the Uses.

6.3   Summary of the PRUB-Validate Process

PRUB-Validate asks four questions and recommends four actions to Validate each strategic idea:

1.   What desired outcomes should the strategic idea lead to?

   – Action: define the idea in a 1:1:1:1 PRUB sequence.

2.   Exactly what needs to be done to make the strategic idea successful?

   – Action: expand the idea into a theoretical SubStrategy.

3.   What Evidence do we have that the strategic idea will definitely lead to the desired outcomes?

   – Action: partly Validate the SubStrategy with compelling cause-and-effect Evidence.

4.   Is it worth it?

   – Action: complete the Validation by determining the strategic ideas' net Value.

The first three steps simply and succinctly describe and, where appropriate, retain or eliminate strategic ideas without having to speculate on the actual Values of the Benefits to arise from each SubStrategy.

The fourth step, which can only be completed *after* the first three steps have been completed, uses the SubStrategy from step 2 to precisely identify those costs and values which must feed into the value assessment to complete the strategic idea validation process.

All four steps are essential to justify implementing a strategic idea.

There are no shortcuts.

You can confidently proceed to implement a SubStrategy when is has been fully PRUB-Validated.

Let us now look at an example of the application of the PRUB-Validate process to the strategic idea of an inner-city public swimming pool.

6.4   An Example of how to Create a Validated SubStrategy

The following example takes the concept of 'we need a public inner-city swimming pool' through the four PRUB-Validate stages. This same PRUB-Validate process works for all public, private and voluntary sector strategies.

STEP 1: CLARIFY THE STRATEGIC IDEA – EXAMPLE

The basic strategic idea relating to 'we need an inner-city swimming pool' is straightforward and identifies that the pool will be used by both adults and children and is intended to lead to both health and happiness Benefits, as shown in Figure 6.6.

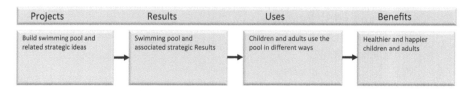

Projects	Results	Uses	Benefits
Build swimming pool and related strategic ideas	Swimming pool and associated strategic Results	Children and adults use the pool in different ways	Healthier and happier children and adults

Figure 6.6   The basic strategic idea: 'we need a public inner-city swimming pool'

STEP 2: EXPAND THE STRATEGIC IDEA INTO A SUBSTRATEGY – EXAMPLE

The strategic idea relating to 'we need a public inner-city swimming pool' is subsequently expanded into a succinct cause-and-effect SubStrategy so as to identify in detail exactly who will use the pool and why (Benefits). Once these Uses and Benefits have been identified, it will be possible to determine what Results and Projects are *both necessary and sufficient* to enable the desired Uses.

In the simplified example in Figure 6.7, adults will primarily Use the swimming pool for 'aquacise' classes and young people will use it primarily for formal swimming programmes. In reality there will be many more and different Uses – we are just showing an indicative example here.

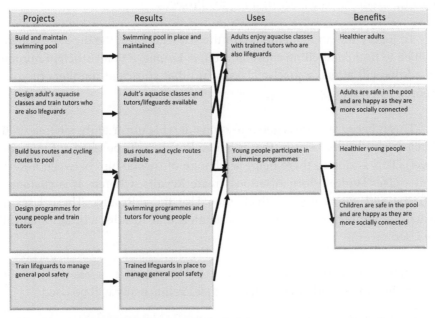

Figure 6.7   **A simplistic but realistic SubStrategy representing the main steps needed to address the aspirational-level strategic idea: 'we need a public inner-city swimming pool'**

For the swimming pool strategic idea to be effective, there is as a minimum the need for effective bus and cycling options to enable people to access the pool plus lifeguards, aquacise classes and young people's swimming programmes. A full PRUB-Validate analysis of this swimming pool strategic idea would undoubtedly identify further necessary Projects and Results.

This SubStrategy defines a *theoretical* sequence of interlinked Projects, Results, Uses and Benefits relating to the proposed public swimming pool. This defines what will ideally happen, but it has not yet been Validated by adding Evidence ('will this SubStrategy *really* happen?') and assessing its net Value ('will it be *worth it*?').

We therefore need to proceed to steps 3 and 4 of the PRUB-Validate process.

STEP 3: JUSTIFY THE SUBSTRATEGY WITH CAUSE-AND-EFFECT EVIDENCE – EXAMPLE

It will be relatively easy to find Evidence that the proposed Projects will create Results. This is because the creation of the Results will be under the control of the organisations which are running the Projects.

To justify the implementation of the strategic idea, the biggest challenge will be to find compelling cause-and-effect Evidence that sufficient numbers of adults will attend aquacise classes and that sufficient numbers of young people will attend swimming programmes.

This is because there is generally considerable uncertainty inherent in the Links from Results to Uses (that is, will a Result *really* be Used at the desired level). This is due to there being a 'change of ownership' between a Result and a Use. Typically organisations create Results, whereas it is customers, citizens and communities which then Use these Results. These Uses are usually voluntary so it cannot be assumed that Results will automatically be Used.

Therefore, in order to Validate a SubStrategy, it is essential to find compelling cause-and-effect Evidence that Results really will be Used.

It will also be challenging to find Evidence that the Uses will definitely lead to Benefits but frequently it will be found that similar Uses have previously been studied and documented elsewhere in the world.

Figure 6.8 indicates that the key convincing Evidence required will be on the links from Results to Uses and may be along the lines of:

1.   What Evidence do we have that sufficient numbers of adults will definitely be sufficiently attracted by the swimming pool to actually Use it?

2.   What Evidence do we have that the aquacise classes, bus/cycling options and lifeguards will be sufficient to attract enough of these adults to Use the pool?

3.   What Evidence do we have that sufficient numbers of young people will definitely be sufficiently attracted by the swimming pool to actually Use it?

4.   What Evidence do we have that the swimming programmes, bus/cycling options and lifeguards will be sufficient to attract enough of these young people to Use the pool?

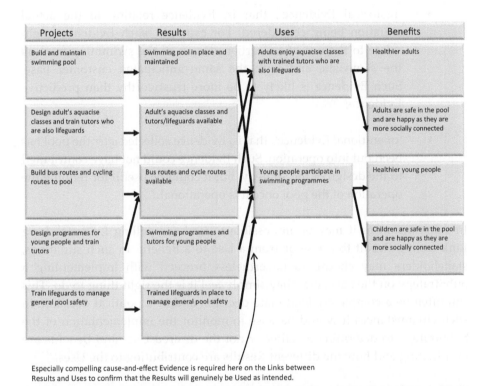

Especially compelling cause-and-effect Evidence is required here on the Links between Results and Uses to confirm that the Results will genuinely be Used as intended.

Figure 6.8   Identifying the Links where compelling Evidence is needed to show that intended Results will be Used

Note that this Evidence may be only indirectly related to the particular swimming pool being proposed. For example, relevant Evidence may come from the use of a similar swimming pool in a similar town. So Evidence can be:

- 'predictive Evidence', that is, Evidence which predicts what is likely to happen and is often based on what has happened elsewhere or on what stakeholders say they want. Predictive Evidence needs to be treated with great care because it is often difficult to prove that this Evidence is valid and true when applied to the specific strategic idea that is being developed;

- 'historical Evidence', that is, Evidence relating to the actual situation being considered. For example, such Evidence might relate to the use of an earlier version of the swimming pool on the same site and with the same anticipated customer base. Such Evidence is likely to be more trustworthy than predictive Evidence;

- 'operational Evidence', that is, Evidence collected *after* the pool has been put into operation. Such Evidence could not have contributed to the design of the strategy, but it could be useful for refining the operation of the pool once it is operational.

In some instances it may be impossible to find compelling Evidence for a Link from a Result to a Use or from a Use to a Benefit. In such situations, stakeholders may choose to nevertheless proceed with implementing a SubStrategy on the basis that they simply feel it is the right thing to do. This can often be a completely legitimate decision and/or a political decision. In such circumstances it would be wise to monitor the implementation of the SubStrategy to determine whether or not the desired Uses and Benefits are eventuating and how the different Results are contributing to the Uses.

STEP 4: ASSESS THE VALUE OF THE SUBSTRATEGY – EXAMPLE

The Evidenced SubStrategy from step 3 above identified five Projects and two Uses, all of which will have costs associated with them.

The Strategic Option also identified four Benefits, all of which will have a Value.

In order to justify continuing with the swimming pool strategic idea, the Value of these four Benefits must exceed the net costs of the five Projects *plus* the net costs of the two Uses.

Mathematically, ΣV_B must be greater than $\Sigma C_P + \Sigma C_U$

where ΣV_B = Sum of the Values of the Benefits

ΣC_P = Sum of the Costs of the Projects

ΣC_U = Sum of the Costs of the Uses

The costs of the Projects will generally be straightforward to determine.

The costs to the Users will be more difficult but not impossible to determine and will probably be primarily the travel and parking costs for Users. Any fees that Users pay to use the pool will simply offset any Project costs such as pool maintenance so they have no net effect on the total costs of achieving the desired Benefits.

The value of the Benefits will be more challenging to determine. Fortunately for the swimming pool strategic idea, there is a great deal of documented research about the value of citizens being healthy. There is less quantitative information on the value of the social/happiness Benefits arising from Users using the swimming pool.

Therefore, the swimming pool 'Value question' is likely to be something like:

Is the annual health Value (estimated at £1.9 million/year for 1,000 people/ day using the pool) plus the likely social/happiness Benefit Value (this could be a subjective 'value' because it is difficult to determine financially, but perhaps it can be speculated as being £0.5–1 million per year)

greater than

the amortised capital costs plus annual running costs of the pool (construction and maintenance), aquacise programmes (development and running), lifeguards (training and maintenance), young people's swimming programmes (development and running) and bus/cycle strategic ideas (development and maintenance) plus the costs to the users of getting to, and using, the pool?

6.5   Using PRUB-Validate to Assess and Refine Existing Strategies

It is frequently useful to review existing, traditionally documented strategies in order to determine how successfully they have been implemented and/or to refine them to improve their implementation. This involves translating the existing strategy into SubStrategies so that each SubStrategy and the overall OpenStrategy can be PRUB-Validated.

This translation is a four-step process:

STEP 1: DISTIL

This involves distilling from the existing strategy all statements that naturally fit into Projects, Results, Uses and Benefits. Provided that the existing strategy is of reasonably high quality, this step can usually be completed with minimal engagement with the stakeholders associated with the strategy. Our experience indicates that only a small percentage of traditional strategies can be easily distilled into meaningful and Validated SubStrategies.

STEP 2: REFINE

This involves editing and refining existing strategic statements into Projects, Results, Uses and Benefits and can usually be done with a small amount of guidance from the strategy's stakeholders.

STEP 3: INFER

This involves inferring logically likely Projects, Results, Uses and Benefits from the existing strategy and adding these inferred concepts to the SubStrategies. This step requires significantly more involvement with stakeholders, who will need to confirm that the inferred ideas are in fact logically correct and are wanted by the stakeholders.

STEP 4: CREATE

This involves creating new Projects, Results, Uses and Benefits in order to create a complete OpenStrategy. This step will ideally be undertaken by the strategy's stakeholders under the guidance of a facilitator familiar with the OpenStrategies taxonomy, syntax and semantics.

Once SubStrategies have been edited or created, you can then apply steps 3 and 4 of the PRUB-Validate process to add cause-and-effect Evidence and to determine the net Value of the SubStrategies. Given that so few existing strategies use well-defined strategy taxonomy, syntax and semantics and even fewer existing strategies clearly identify Uses, Evidence and Value, even step 1 above is often very challenging and steps 2–3 are frequently impossible using existing strategic information.

In these circumstances you may be better to start from scratch and create new SubStrategies (aspirational-level, guidance-level and operational-level) and the corresponding interlinked OpenStrategy rather than to attempt to work with seriously flawed existing 'strategic' information.

When translating existing strategies into SubStrategies and attempting to Validate them, it is important to be aware that many existing strategies simply cannot be successfully Validated. This is because they are insufficiently well written to enable the development of sensible SubStrategies and because, most commonly, they don't have compelling cause-and-effect Evidence that Results will in fact be Used and/or that the Uses will in fact generate enough of the desired Benefits to be worthwhile. The loose use of words in such 'strategies' often reveals the quality of the thinking that went into developing the strategies.

In such circumstances stakeholders are likely to become quite resistant to the in-depth assessment and redevelopment of their strategies into SubStrategies because they will find that their existing strategies cannot in fact be modified so as to become successfully PRUB-Validated.

In these circumstances some stakeholders may feel threatened and become uncooperative, so it will be important for the facilitator of this assessment and PRUB-Validation process to find ways to keep these stakeholders engaged and to guide them to refine their strategies so that they can in fact be PRUB-Validated.

Help them to 'Validate' their strategies by improving them rather than focusing on the fact that their existing strategies are unable to be PRUB-Validated.

Chapter 7

Creating and Integrating SubStrategies into OpenStrategies

This chapter provides guidance on how to set up and Validate an OpenStrategy and how to aggregate and disaggregate OpenStrategies.

7.1 Starting an OpenStrategy

Many traditional strategy documents are rambling affairs which cannot be easily understood, let alone implemented. Quite apart from the other factors already discussed in this book, one of the reasons why these strategies cannot be implemented is because they were created without enough clarity on what level the strategy was, who it was for, what the main themes were and what format the strategy should be in.

Before establishing a strategy or OpenStrategy (that is, a suite of interlinked SubStrategies), it is important to establish a few fundamental parameters about the strategy. These are identified and discussed below.

THEMES, DEMOGRAPHICS, GEOGRAPHY AND ORGANISATIONS

It is essential to identify the key themes, demographic groups, geographical areas and provider organisations that the strategy will address. While these parameters may evolve during the development and implementation of the strategy, it is nevertheless important to be clear what the starting point is.

For example, if the overall theme of the strategy is 'transport', does this relate to all forms of transport or just to public transport or just to land transport or some other sub-set of transport?

Similarly, it is important to identify who the end-users are. So, for example, with a transport strategy that is focusing on public transport, is it expected that everyone in the community will use the public transport or is the public transport strategy intending to target a specific sub-set of the community such as elderly people?

So when establishing a new strategy and acknowledging that it will evolve over time, we recommend that as a minimum you establish:

- the main theme and any sub-themes for the strategy;

- the main demographic group of end-users and any sub-groups;

- the main geographic area and sub-areas that the strategy will address;

- the likely main service providers.

BOUNDARY CONDITIONS AND HANDOVER

Once the above specificities have been defined, it is then necessary to establish the 'boundary conditions' and the 'handover' for the strategy. This is necessary so that all stakeholders are clear about the start and end points of the strategy (that is, the 'boundary conditions') and the nature of the 'handover' from service providers to end-users (that is, from Results to Uses).

The real world is more complex than a simple Projects, Results, Uses and Benefits sequence and in fact is more like PRPRPRUBUBUB. A PRUB-based strategy could potentially be developed that represents any of the combinations of PRPR or PRUB or UBUB.

However, for most strategies it is relatively clear who the main service providers and end-users are and hence the 'location' of the handover from Results to Uses. This handover point establishes the 'centre' of the SubStrategies and OpenStrategy.

Similarly, for the above service providers and end-users, there are usually relatively straightforward start and finish points for the strategy.

For example, an 'education strategy' is likely to have a start point relating to the identification and development of courses (Projects) and an end point of 'educated students'. In this instance the 'handover' would be between the course providers and the students.

This strategy might nest within a larger 'economic strategy' in which the educated students are then employed, thereby earning money for themselves, creating products and services for customers and creating wealth (or other values) for their employers.

This economic strategy may reasonably have the same start point as the education strategy, but its end point (that is, Benefits) will be one or two steps beyond the education strategy. This could be accommodated by using compound Uses (see section 4.7) such as 'students attend courses, learn, secure qualifications, obtain jobs and work for employers'.

For the economic strategy the handover point would be the same as for the education strategy, that is, between the Results created by the education providers and the students.

Alternatively, the economic development strategy could define the Projects and Results as consisting of developing courses to produce courses (Orphan Result) followed by an Adopting Project of students attending courses, thereby producing a Result of trained students.

The Use would then be the trained students working in companies to generate personal wealth, happy customers and profitable employers.

So the end point of the economic strategy would relate to the wealth of employees, happy customers and profitable employers. In this instance, the 'handover' would be between the trained students (as Results) and the employers (as Users).

So the boundaries (start and finish points) of the strategy and the handover from providers to end-users both need to be carefully defined so that all stakeholders understand and appreciate how strategic ideas will be organised in the strategy, that is, in the SubStrategies and OpenStrategy.

LEVEL OF STRATEGY/SPECIFICITIES

As discussed throughout this book, OpenStrategies has identified three main levels of strategies:

- high-level **aspirational** strategies;

- mid-level **guidance** strategies;

- grassroots-level **operational** strategies.

When developing a new strategy it is important to decide which level of strategy is to be developed, whether it will be developed at just one of the three levels or whether it will be developed for two or for all three levels.

For example, if a government minister has asked for a strategy, it is likely that a high-level aspirational strategy will be appropriate.

If instead the management within a company wants clarity on the company's strategic Projects, it is likely to be appropriate to develop a mid-level guidance strategy for managers.

If stakeholders want a strategy that they can directly implement, they need to work at the grassroots level to create an operational strategy.

In some instances a high-level aspirational strategy will be 'imposed' on stakeholders and their task may be to create a mid-level guidance strategy which they can forward to grassroots-level people, who in turn will create the operational-level strategy and implement it, guided by the two higher-level strategies.

Alternatively, grassroots-level stakeholders (for example end-users) may be clamouring for local action so they may create local, operational-level strategies which they intend to implement. However, before they can do so they may need to secure resources from service providers (for example a local council), so their operational-level strategy may then require the development of higher-level strategies to slot into the council's strategic plan.

The crucial issue is for stakeholders to be 100% clear about what level(s) of strategy they are trying to create so that there is consistency in people's strategic thinking and in the evolution of the desired strategy/SubStrategies/OpenStrategy.

LEVELS OF DETAILS WITHIN SUBSTRATEGIES

Once you have established the overall level of the desired strategy, you should also establish a few more parameters to guide the development of the strategy.

These include but are not limited to:

- the nominal size of Projects, Results, Uses and Benefits. For example, will the size of Projects and Uses be restricted to:

  - Projects over a certain size (for example costing over £50,000) and/or;
  - Projects that are small but are nevertheless essential, such as getting permission to implement a key Project;
  - Uses which will affect more than 10% of the end-user group and/or;
  - Uses which strongly affect selected sub-groups and/or;
  - Other criteria?

- Which SubStrategies will be included:

  - SubStrategies which are already under way;
  - SubStrategies which are not yet under way but have been scoped and/or received funding;
  - SubStrategies which are still at the 'idea' stage;
  - SubStrategies which are ongoing and/or SubStrategies which have a fixed lifespan;
  - Validated SubStrategies which contain compelling Evidence and convincing Value statements or less-well-Validated SubStrategies?

LEVELS OF DETAIL WITHIN EACH PROJECT, RESULT, USE AND BENEFIT

The question of how much information to include within each Project, Result, Use and Benefit is related to the overall level of the strategy (aspirational, guidance or operational). However, even within these levels it is helpful to decide at the start of the process just how much detail to include.

OpenStrategies recommends that as a minimum each Project, Result, Use and Benefit (Item) should include the following information:

- a summary of the Item in the form of a short, one-sentence title;

- a more detailed description of the Item, ideally with embedded references or hyperlinks to more detailed information;

- a timescale for the Item (start dates, end dates and whether it is part of an ongoing SubStrategy);

- a budget (finance and other resources required);

- an indication of whether the Item is already happening, has been scoped and costed and is seeking resources or if it is just an idea which is still evolving;

- for Projects and Results: which end-users are likely to Use the Results;

- for Uses and Benefits: which organisations are likely to be involved in creating the related Results.

Note that it will not be possible to include all the above information within the PRUB boxes in a SubStrategy. Therefore the boxes need to include the summary statement and the more detailed information needs to be captured in an associated table.

7.2 Strategy Integration

We have yet to discover any viable strategic idea which cannot be succinctly represented as a Validated SubStrategy. This applies whether the strategic idea is at an aspirational level, a guidance level or at an operational level.

Once each strategic idea is in the form of a Validated SubStrategy, it can be interlinked with other similarly Validated SubStrategies in three main ways:

1. vertically (aspirational-level strategy linked to guidance-level strategy linked to operational-level strategy);

2. horizontally (strategies interlinked across themes, demographic groups, geographical areas and across organisations);

3. sequentially (where a strategy follows the implementation of an earlier strategy).

Each Validated SubStrategy is a building block within a larger interlinked OpenStrategy.

In a similar way in which Validated SubStrategies can be aggregated into larger SubStrategies and OpenStrategies, so such larger SubStrategies can be disaggregated into smaller SubStrategies, often on different themes, as described below.

VERTICAL STRATEGY INTEGRATION

The OpenStrategies team has identified that there are three broad levels of strategies:

- high-level aspirational strategies;

- mid-level guidance strategies;

- grassroots-level operational strategies.

High-level aspirational strategies are brief documents which capture the general principles and desired outcomes of a strategy. Aspirational strategies are typically valuable to politicians and business leaders who are focused primarily on 'the big picture' or 'vision' for a strategy.

Mid-level guidance strategies are more substantial documents which flesh out the aspirational strategy in sufficient detail so that people understand broadly what needs to be done, but they don't provide enough detail to enable implementation. Typically they outline what will be done and provide limited information on who it is being done for, where it will be done and who will implement the strategy. Guidance strategies are valuable to senior operational managers to enable high-level budgeting, planning and inter-organisational collaboration.

Grassroots-level operational strategies are comprehensive and detailed action plans which specify exactly what will be done, who it is being done for, where it will be done and who will implement the strategy. They are valuable to the people who actually make things happen.

Aspirational strategies contain broad statements with limited specificity in terms of:

- themes (what will be done);

- demography (who it is being done for);

- geography (where it is being done);

- organisations (who will do it).

Guidance strategies provide more information on these four specificities without getting into the operational details. Operational strategies provide sufficiently detailed information on each of the four specificities so that anyone reading the operational strategy would know exactly what to do to implement it. Ideally aspirational, guidance and operational strategies (and their respective stakeholders) should be intimately interlinked, but traditionally this is seldom the case.

The OpenStrategies system explicitly enables such interlinking of different levels of strategies. This is achieved by writing each level of strategy using the same PRUB taxonomy, syntax and semantics so that each level has Projects, Results, Uses and Benefits as well as Links, Evidence and Performance Measurement parameters. In this way, an aspirational-level 'Project' (for example 'Improve ecosystem health in Exmoor National Park') can be disaggregated and linked with guidance-level 'Projects' (for example 'Improve the management of Exmoor National Park fauna' and 'Improve the management of Exmoor National Park flora' and 'Develop eco-friendly activities for visitors to Exmoor National Park').

Then each guidance-level 'Project' (for example 'Improve the management of Exmoor National Park flora') can be further disaggregated and linked with detailed operational-level SubStrategies such as 'Exmoor National Park management to remove noxious weeds from within 10 metres of each public walkway' and 'Exmoor National Park management to stop the removal of fallen trees and let them rot to provide micro-climates for emerging tree seedlings'.

Each of the above Projects can be expanded into a full SubStrategy appropriate to aspirational-level, guidance-level and operational-level strategies. In the OpenStrategies system, the three levels of SubStrategies are interlinked by ensuring that each Project, Result, Use and Benefit contains one or more keywords relating to each of the four specificities (thematic, demographic, geographic and organisational).

So in the above example, the Projects at all three levels would include (as a minimum) keywords along the following lines:

Thematic – ecosystem health

Demographic – flora

Geographic – Exmoor National Park

Organisational – Exmoor National Park management

Figure 7.1 shows an example of a high-level aspirational regional water management strategy.

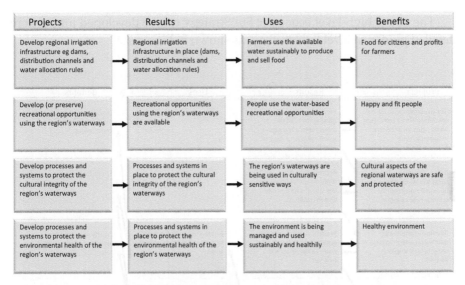

Figure 7.1   A high-level aspirational water management strategy containing four SubStrategies which address the four well-beings

This high-level aspirational strategy identifies that regional water management will address the 'four well-beings' (economic, social, cultural and environmental). It does not provide any details as to *how* these four well-beings will be achieved, but nevertheless it is a worthwhile high-level strategy because, as a minimum, it acknowledges that all four well-beings need to be addressed.

The descriptions of each Project, Result, Use and Benefit provide some indication of the theme being addressed (in this case the four well-beings) as well as indicating that it is likely that 'processes and systems' will need to be developed.

However, this high-level aspirational strategy provides almost no guidance as to *how* these well-beings will be addressed and it certainly does not provide any details about specific Projects.

So let us now look at a guidance-level SubStrategy that might evolve
from the first of the four SubStrategies ('Develop regional irrigation
infrastructure ...') in the above high-level aspirational strategy.

The above high-level economic SubStrategy can be developed into a more
detailed guidance-level SubStrategy, as shown in Figure 7.2.

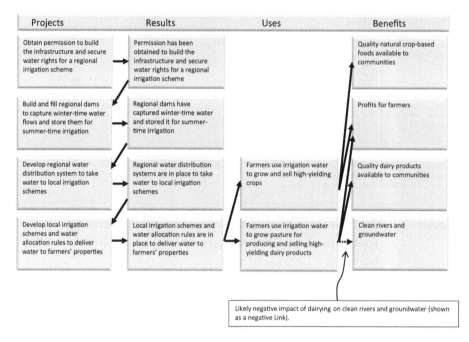

**Figure 7.2   Guidance-level economic SubStrategy as a sub-set of the
overall water management strategy**

In this guidance-level SubStrategy more detailed strategic concepts have been
identified together with how they are interconnected into a SubStrategy. There
is still insufficient detail to enable the implementation of this SubStrategy, but it
nevertheless provides some level of guidance as to how the economic SubStrategy
of the high-level regional water management OpenStrategy will evolve.

In particular, this guidance-level SubStrategy identifies the fact that
permissions and water rights need to be obtained, dams need to be built and
filled, that water from the dams needs to be distributed to local irrigation
schemes and that these schemes need to further distribute the water to local
farmers based on an agreed water allocation system and rules.

The SubStrategy notes that a dam full of water on its own is no use to farmers (it is an Orphan Result) because the water has to actually be distributed to the farmers to be useful. However, a dam full of water could nevertheless be directly useful for fishing, boating and swimming to create social Benefits. The guidance-level economic SubStrategy also identifies that there is a logical time sequence for implementing the strategy:

- first secure permissions and water rights;

- *then* build the dams;

- *then* fill them;

- *then* distribute water to the local schemes;

- *then* distribute water to the individual farmers;

- *then* use the water to grow and sell crops and produce dairy products for customers, thereby producing profits for the farmers.

The SubStrategy also disaggregates the concept of 'Farmers use the available water sustainably to produce food' into two more detailed Uses:

- 'Farmers use irrigation water to grow and sell high-yielding crops';

- 'Farmers use irrigation water to grow pasture for producing and selling high-yielding dairy products'.

Through this disaggregation of the Use, the SubStrategy also identifies the possible negative impact of intense dairy farming on the quality of surface and ground water. Therefore this economic theme of the water management strategy necessarily needs to interlink with the environmental theme of the water management strategy.

Also, the fact that rivers are going to be dammed implies that the economic theme of the water management strategy needs to interlink with recreational uses of the water (fishing and white-water rafting in the previously undammed rivers; fishing and flat-water boating on the new lakes).

By getting into more detail, this guidance-level SubStrategy has now identified more of the stakeholders who need to be involved in fine-tuning an implementable operational-level strategy, including:

- the farmers who wish to grow crops (and their potential customers);

- the farmers who wish to produce dairy products;

- the builders of dams;

- the builders of regional-level water distribution infrastructure;

- the builders of local-level irrigation schemes;

- the organisations that are required to give legal approval to the development of the irrigation scheme, to grant water rights and to monitor and manage the implementation of those water rights;

- recreational users of the water and people who represent the interests of the environment (especially ground and surface water quality).

In summary, the above guidance-level SubStrategy has identified a number of factors which now need to be analysed in even more detail in order to produce an implementable operational-level SubStrategy. It has also identified at least some of the key stakeholders who need to be involved in refining the SubStrategy.

This then leads to the development of operational-level SubStrategies. So let us look more closely at the fourth Project from the guidance-level SubStrategy:

Develop local irrigation schemes and water allocation rules to deliver water to farmers' properties.

To translate this guidance-level strategy into an implementable strategy we need to be more specific about:

- the theme – that is, exactly what will be done?

- the demographics – that is, exactly who are the end-users and what do they want to do?

- the geographics – that is, exactly where will the irrigation schemes and farming take place?

- the organisations – that is, exactly who will implement the Projects and performance-manage the Results, Uses and Benefits?

So for example: the Theme is already reasonably well developed, that is, to develop and use irrigation water to sustainably grow crops and dairy products for the benefit of customers. This theme would be captured by one or more keywords attached to each aspirational-, guidance- and operational-level SubStrategy.

The demographics are also reasonably well defined, that is, crop farmers and dairy farmers. As above, these demographics would be captured in the OpenStrategies system by attaching one or more demographic keywords to each aspirational-, guidance- and operational-level SubStrategy

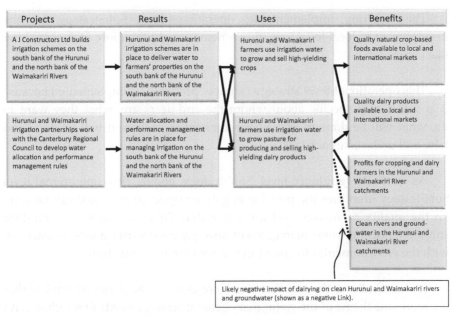

Figure 7.3   Operational-level economic SubStrategy within the overall water management OpenStrategy

The geographics is not yet well defined because it simply refers to 'regional' and 'local' irrigation schemes. So to be implementable, more specific statements are required on exactly which 'regional' and 'local' areas are going to have irrigation schemes and irrigated farms. For example, this geographic specificity might be as shown in the example in Figure 7.3.

Geographic keywords such as 'Canterbury' and 'Hurunui River south bank' and 'Waimakariri River north bank' would be attached to each level of SubStrategy to link the different levels together.

Organisationally it will be necessary to specify for example that 'A J Constructors Company Ltd' will build the local irrigation schemes to deliver water to the farmers' properties and that the 'Canterbury Regional Council in partnership with irrigation groups in the Hurunui and Waimakariri River catchments' will develop the water allocation and performance management rules. Keywords would again be used to interlink the organisational aspects of the aspirational, guidance and operational SubStrategies.

The resulting implementable, operational-level SubStrategy for the development of local-level irrigation schemes might therefore look something like Figure 7.3.

This operational-level strategy can now probably be implemented because it is sufficiently specific about whom the end-users are, what they want to do, what will be done to implement the strategy, where it will be done and who will undertake each task.

As with the guidance-level SubStrategy above, this operational-level SubStrategy identifies the possible negative impact of intense dairy farming on the quality of surface and ground water. Therefore, this dam-building sub-theme of the water management strategy necessarily needs to interlink with the environmental theme of the water management strategy.

As noted above, the fact that rivers are going to be dammed implies that the economic theme of the water management strategy needs to interlink with recreational uses of the water.

To have confidence that the above operational-level strategy is viable, it would now be necessary to add in compelling Evidence that:

•   each Project will in fact produce the intended Result;

- each Result will in fact be Used as intended;

- each such Use will in fact produce the desired Benefits.

It would also be necessary to quantify the net value of the Benefits and check that it exceeds the net costs of the Projects' costs *plus* the costs of the Uses.

In the OpenStrategies system each of the above boxes of information on Projects, Results, Uses and Benefits would also be supported by detailed information on such things as start and finish dates, financial and resource requirements, performance indicators, targets and actual measurements. However, these are secondary pieces of information which are of significant value to the stakeholders who need to implement each part of the strategy but are of less value to other stakeholders.

The key point of the above discussion is that the same PRUB taxonomy, syntax and semantics applies for high-level aspirational strategies, mid-level guidance strategies and grassroots-level operational strategies and also that these three levels of strategies can easily be intimately interlinked when they all use this common PRUB system.

HORIZONTAL STRATEGY INTEGRATION

Horizontal integration of OpenStrategies describes the interlinking of strategies which are all at the same level, that is, when they all are aspirational-level, or all guidance-level, or all operational-level strategies.

The four main forms of horizontal strategy integration are:

1. thematic integration – when SubStrategies on multiple related themes are interlinked;

2. demographic integration – when SubStrategies relating to different demographic end-user groups are interlinked;

3. geographic integration – when SubStrategies relating to the same geographic area are interlinked;

4. organisational integration – when multiple SubStrategies each being led by the same organisation are interlinked into an overall organisational OpenStrategy.

SubStrategies frequently overlap even when they are on different themes, for different demographic groups, for different geographical areas and led by different organisations.

For example, a cycling SubStrategy will almost invariably overlap a car strategy, which in turn is likely to overlap heavy transport and/or public transport SubStrategies (thematic overlap).

Similarly, a physical fitness strategy is likely to overlap with a recreational strategy, which is likely to overlap with an environmental strategy (thematic overlap).

In the same vein a swimming SubStrategy for young people will often overlap with a swimming SubStrategy for older people (demographic overlap), or a transport SubStrategy for one district will overlap the transport SubStrategy for a neighbouring district (geographic overlap).

Traditionally such discrete strategies have each been created using their own strategy taxonomy, syntax and semantics and it has been very difficult to interlink different strategies in a meaningful way.

In contrast, if all such SubStrategies are created using the PRUB taxonomy, syntax and semantics, the different SubStrategies can be readily interlinked.

The hypothetical example in Figures 7.4a–7.4c (all within Figure 7.4) illustrates this point with three guidance-level thematic SubStrategies on 'fitness', 'recreation' and 'the environment'.

Imagine a physical fitness SubStrategy, a recreational SubStrategy and an environmental SubStrategy along the following lines (these three guidance-level SubStrategies are deliberately simplistic to help delineate their interlinking).

These three thematic SubStrategies overlap in that different groups will be using the same regional park, the users will have an impact on the ecosystems and users will use the park for several different reasons.

This leads to the following hypothetical combined fitness, recreational and environmental SubStrategy in Figure 7.5.

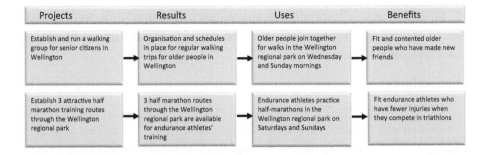

Figure 7.4.a   Guidance-level fitness SubStrategy

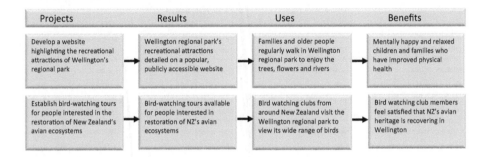

Figure 7.4.b   Guidance-level recreational SubStrategy

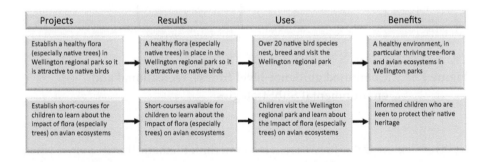

Figure 7.4.c   Guidance-level environmental SubStrategy

Figure 7.5 shows some of the more obvious links amongst the hypothetical fitness, recreational and environmental thematic SubStrategies resulting in a possible combined SubStrategy.

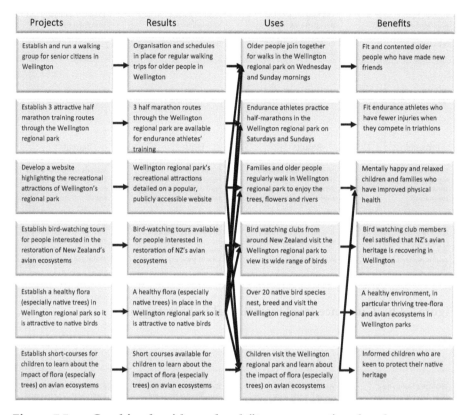

Figure 7.5   Combined guidance-level fitness, recreational and environmental SubStrategies

This demonstrates how easy it is to interlink thematic SubStrategies when they each use the same PRUB taxonomy, syntax and semantics.

In exactly the same way as the thematic SubStrategies have been interlinked above, it is equally simple to interlink strategies based on different demographic groups, different geographic areas and different organisational responsibilities.

Once the above interlinks have been made between the three thematic SubStrategies, it is possible to distil new thematic, demographic, geographic or organisational SubStrategies.

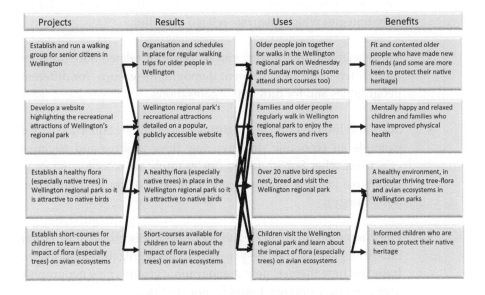

Projects	Results	Uses	Benefits
Establish and run a walking group for senior citizens in Wellington	Organisation and schedules in place for regular walking trips for older people in Wellington	Older people join together for walks in the Wellington regional park on Wednesday and Sunday mornings (some attend short courses too)	Fit and contented older people who have made new friends (and some are more keen to protect their native heritage)
Develop a website highlighting the recreational attractions of Wellington's regional park	Wellington regional park's recreational attractions detailed on a popular, publicly accessible website	Families and older people regularly walk in Wellington regional park to enjoy the trees, flowers and rivers	Mentally happy and relaxed children and families who have improved physical health
Establish a healthy flora (especially native trees) in Wellington regional park so it is attractive to native birds	A healthy flora (especially native trees) in place in the Wellington regional park so it is attractive to native birds	Over 20 native bird species nest, breed and visit the Wellington regional park	A healthy environment, in particular thriving tree-flora and avian ecosystems in Wellington parks
Establish short-courses for children to learn about the impact of flora (especially trees) on avian ecosystems	Short-courses available for children to learn about the impact of flora (especially trees) on avian ecosystems	Children visit the Wellington regional park and learn about the impact of flora (especially trees) on avian ecosystems	Informed children who are keen to protect their native heritage

Figure 7.6   A possible 'children's, families' and older people's SubStrategy' distilled from Figure 7.5

For example, Figure 7.6 shows a SubStrategy on a selected demographic of 'children, families and older people' that has been distilled from the integrated fitness+recreation+environment SubStrategy.

In the process of 'distilling' this new SubStrategy, a decision was made to open up the short courses (initially intended solely for children) to older people because it was recognised that they too would benefit from the courses and that there would be minimal extra cost in permitting them to attend the courses. In the process, the children and older people would get to know each other and it was expected that this would enhance community cohesion.

This distilled 'demographic' SubStrategy demonstrates that not only can thematic (and demographic and geographic and organisational) SubStrategies be interlinked, but also that new SubStrategies can be distilled based on other criteria, such as the above SubStrategy based on the end-user demographic of 'children, families and older people'.

Summarising the horizontal interlinking and distillation of SubStrategies:

- Once strategic concepts have each been described in the form of Validated SubStrategies, they can be easily interlinked horizontally (that is, all at the same level of strategy) to create new, larger SubStrategies which integrate related activities.

- This horizontal interlinking can be done for related SubStrategies with different themes, different demographic groups, for different geographies and for different organisations.

- Such interlinking often highlights the fact that one SubStrategy (for example an economic strategy) may have positive and negative effects on other SubStrategies (for example an economic strategy may have positive and/or negative impacts on an environmental SubStrategy).

- Once integrated SubStrategies have been assembled into larger SubStrategies, it is then easy to distil or disaggregate SubStrategies based on new themes, new demographic groups, new geographic areas and new organisational responsibilities

SEQUENTIAL STRATEGY INTEGRATION

Sequential integration of OpenStrategies describes the interlinking of strategies which are all at the same level but which occur in a time sequence in which one OpenStrategy overlaps a subsequent OpenStrategy. For example, an 'educational SubStrategy' might consist broadly of the SubStrategy shown in Figure 7.7.

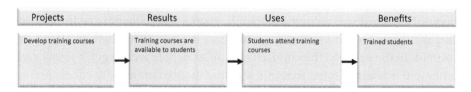

Figure 7.7   High-level aspirational educational SubStrategy

This is an educational SubStrategy because the final Benefit (trained students) represents an educational achievement.

Such an educational SubStrategy might then be followed by an overlapping 'economic SubStrategy', as shown in Figure 7.8.

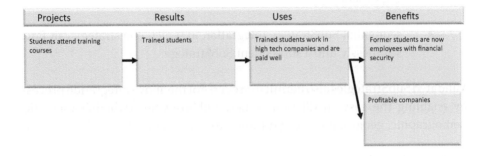

Figure 7.8   High-level aspirational economic SubStrategy

In this example the Uses and Benefits from the educational SubStrategy become the Projects and Results for the economic SubStrategy. Because both SubStrategies use the same PRUB taxonomy, syntax and semantics, they can readily be interlinked by overlapping the Uses and Benefits from the educational SubStrategy with the Projects and Results of the economic SubStrategy.

This concept of sequential OpenStrategies recognises that the real-world sequence of strategies is in fact more like PRPRPRPRPRUBUBUB rather than just a single simple PRUB sequence. However, despite this reality, many strategies work well with a single PRUB sequence because they are focused on predefined start and finish points (defined Projects leading through Results and Uses to predefined Benefits) and predefined 'handover' points (from Results to Uses) which perfectly fit the single-stage PRUB model.

SUMMARY OF STRATEGY INTEGRATION

Validated SubStrategies are uniquely defined building blocks which enable three main categories of strategy integration:

- vertical SubStrategy integration in which high-level aspirational strategies are interlinked with mid-level guidance strategies which in turn are interlinked with grassroots-level operational strategies;

- horizontal SubStrategy integration in which strategies which are at the same level can be interlinked across different themes, different demographic groups, different geographies and different organisations;

- sequential SubStrategy integration in which one strategy can flow seamlessly into a subsequent SubStrategy.

Validated SubStrategies also permit the reverse of the above integration process by enabling the easy distillation of new SubStrategies (whether thematic, demographic, geographic or organisational) from single large SubStrategies.

This means that a multi-stakeholder group can create a suite of Validated SubStrategies and then interlink them and/or re-distil them into a wide range of different strategies based on themes, demographics, geographies and organisational responsibilities.

Therefore it is no longer necessary to write a separate strategy on each and every theme, demographic grouping, geographical area or organisational responsibility but instead to write a single large OpenStrategy or set of SubStrategies and distil from it whatever classification of SubStrategy may be required from time to time by different stakeholders.

7.3   A Master Library of SubStrategies/OpenStrategies

Validated SubStrategies have value beyond their immediate multi-stakeholder group. For example, an effective Validated SubStrategy on cycling in London would be of direct interest to cycling groups and local authorities in any large (Western) city. Similarly, an effective Validated SubStrategy on protecting a threatened bird species in the mountains of Ecuador would be of interest to bird conservationists in many other countries.

Therefore there would be considerable merit in accumulating effective Validated SubStrategies into an online accessible library of SubStrategies. Such SubStrategies could be 'rated' by how useful different groups found these SubStrategies. Then over time the library of SubStrategies would contain a graduated library of Validated and less-well-Validated SubStrategies.

This concept is under development, so if you would like to get involved please email me at: phil@openstrategies.com.

Chapter 8

Summary of the Projects, Results, Uses and Benefits Sequence and OpenStrategies

This chapter summarises the key factors relating to the diagnosis, development, validation and implementation of strategies.

Key Points

- Most strategies, perhaps as many as 90%, have very little impact.

- A key reason is that the taxonomy (the classification of strategic concepts), syntax (the logical sequencing of strategic concepts) and semantics (the meaning of strategies) of most strategies is flawed.

- Typically strategies need to be understood and implemented by many and diverse stakeholders with wide-ranging skills and experience.

- Humans are cognitively limited to holding 7 +/– 2 ideas in their heads at one time.

- OpenStrategies estimates that people can work with only about 15 +/– 5 ideas when those ideas are displayed in a simple logic map.

- So strategies must be simple and clear if large numbers of stakeholders are to understand and implement them.

- Strategies must focus on improving the core functions of organisations.

- The core functions of organisations in the private, public and voluntary sectors are to *create assets (products, services, infrastructure) and enable people to use them to create benefits.*

- OpenStrategies encapsulates these core functions in the logical sequence represented by the acronym 'PRUB'.

- PRUB represents the sequence: 'Organisations run **P**rojects which produce **R**esults which people **U**se to create **B**enefits'.

- PRUB represents *'the smallest amount of strategic information that has the highest value to the most stakeholders'.*

- Projects are what organisations do to create assets.

- Results are the assets created by the Projects.

- Uses define how people and the 'environment' Use the Results.

- Benefits are the positive outcomes for people and the environment derived from Using the Results.

- Links are the logical connections from Projects to Results, from Results to Uses and from Uses to Benefits. Note that if a Use has a negative impact on a desirable Benefit, this negativity is encapsulated within a 'negative Link'.

- Evidence is the cause-and-effect evidence that a Project really will create the intended Result, that a Result really will be Used as intended and that the Use really will create the desired Benefit.

- Value is the net value arising from implementing a SubStrategy and equates to the sum of the values of all the Benefits minus all the costs of the Projects and the costs of the Uses:

  Mathematically Net Value = $\Sigma V_B - (\Sigma C_P + \Sigma C_U)$

  where ΣV_B *= Sum of the Values of the Benefits*

ΣC_p = *Sum of the Costs of the Projects*

ΣC_U = *Sum of the Costs of the Uses*

- Performance management:

  1. Indicators are the key parameters or measures of each Project, Result, Use and Benefit and which, when measured, provide useful 'indications' of whether or not the Project, Result, Use or Benefit is being implemented as desired.

  2. Targets are the desired levels of indicators.

  3. Measurements are the actual measures of indicators.

  4. If a measurement of an indicator shows that the indicator is not meeting its desired target, the place to fix this failure is one step to the left in the PRUB sequence, that is, if a Benefit is not hitting its target, it will be necessary to 'fix' the Use. If a Use is not hitting its target, it will be necessary to 'fix' the Result. If a Result is not hitting its target, it will be necessary to 'fix' the Project.

- Use the BURP sequence for guiding the development of a strategy and use PRUB for implementing strategies.

- Once strategies have been developed they also need to be 'Validated' in order to build confidence that they are the right strategy and that they really will work.

- PRUB-Validate is a four-step process for developing and validating strategies:

  1. Define the strategy as a 1:1:1:1 PRUB sequence.

  2. Develop a SubStrategy to define the logical sequence from input Projects to outcome Benefits.

  3. Partially 'Validate' the strategy by adding convincing cause-and-effect 'Evidence' on all Links, especially on the Links from Results to Uses.

4.   Complete the 'Validation' of the strategy by determining the net Value of the strategy or SubStrategy ['Net Value' $= \Sigma V_B - (\Sigma C_P + \Sigma C_U)$].

• When establishing a strategy, it is essential to establish:

1.   The 'boundary conditions' for an OpenStrategy, that is, its start and finish points.

2.   The point of the 'handover' from 'providers' to 'Users'.

3.   What level of strategy is to be developed:

– aspirational;
– guidance;
– operational.

• Almost without exception it is impossible to 'deliver' services/products/infrastructure. Such assets can only be 'made available' and then it is up to Users to come and Use these assets, usually voluntarily.

• In every single strategy it is essential to fully understand Uses (that is, what users will actually *do*), otherwise there is a great risk that the wrong Results (Orphan Results) will be created.

• There are two types of Orphan Results:

1.   Adopted Orphan Results – these are Results which cannot be directly Used by end-Users but they can be Adopted by other Projects.

2.   Abandoned Orphan Results – these are Results that no one ever Uses and they are also not 'Adopted' by other Projects. Projects which produce Abandoned Orphan Results should either be modified so they create Useful Results or Results which will be Adopted by other Projects or they should be stopped and resources saved.

• OpenStrategies Ltd estimates that 15–25% of all public sector actions produce Abandoned Orphan Results.

- The standardised OpenStrategies system of PRUB-based SubStrategies enables strategies to be aggregated and disaggregated in several ways:

  1. Vertical aggregation and disaggregation – once strategies have been translated into PRUB-based SubStrategies, they can be aggregated and disaggregated:

     - through different strategy levels (aspirational level, guidance level and operational level);
     - through different operational levels (national, regional, county, district, local).

  2. Horizontal aggregation and disaggregation – once strategies have been translated into PRUB-based SubStrategies, they can be aggregated and disaggregated:

     - across strategic themes;
     - across demographic end-User groups;
     - across provider organisations;
     - across geographic areas.

  3. Sequential – once strategies have been translated into PRUB-based SubStrategies they can be aggregated and disaggregated:

     - in sequence – the real world actually consists of logical strategy sequences represented by PRPRPRUBUBUB and the OpenStrategies system enables SubStrategies to be created, interlinked and implemented anywhere along this sequence.

- OpenStrategies uses the terms:

  1. 'Stakeholder engagement' to refer to the process of collectively developing strategies with stakeholders.

  2. 'Stakeholder collaboration' to refer to the process of collectively implementing strategies with stakeholders.

- Existing strategies can be 'translated' into SubStrategies and OpenStrategies in the following sequence:

1.   Distil – this step distils existing strategy concepts directly into Projects, Results, Uses and Benefits. This is a straightforward process which can usually be completed independently of providers and users.

2.   Refine – this step takes existing strategy concepts and refines them a small amount so that they can be meaningfully represented as Projects, Results, Uses and Benefits. This is also a relatively straightforward process which needs some input from providers and end-users to check that the refinements still convey the intended strategic concepts.

3.   Infer – this steps addresses gaps in the distilled and refined SubStrategies and infers likely Projects, Results, Uses and Benefits to fill in the gaps. This step is somewhat more challenging and should be completed in consultation with providers and end-users to check that the inferences encapsulate the intended strategic concepts.

4.   Create – this step involves the creation of new Projects, Results, Uses and Benefits in order to complete the strategy. This step can only be undertaken in conjunction with providers and end-users because only they can decide what new strategies and SubStrategies need to be created.

- Projects, Results, Uses and Benefits should always be worded as positive or neutral concepts. Any negativity in a SubStrategy is encapsulated within the Links in the SubStrategy.

- Fundamental principles and values – when strategies are being developed stakeholders frequently define concepts which do not fit the PRUB sequence. Generally these statements will be in the form of 'values' or 'principles'. These values and principles are important and must not be lost. However, values and principles cannot be implemented, so when values and principles have been defined it is important to take the next step of precisely defining what these values and principles will look like *in practice*. PRUB provides an excellent information structure for encapsulating these *in-practice* definitions.

- Philosophy/psychology:

1. Equality/inequality of stakeholders – stakeholders are equal when it comes to generating ideas and creating strategies and SubStrategies but they generally have unequal abilities and resources to implement the strategies. They are also unequal in terms of the ability to Use assets and create Benefits. Typically providers control the creation of assets and users Use the assets to generate Benefits. It therefore makes sense for Users to play a major role in deciding what Results they need for them to Use to create Benefits.

2. Stakeholders as willing volunteers – it is helpful to consider most stakeholders in most strategies to be 'willing volunteers' in that they generally cannot be compelled to do anything (with some exceptions, for example in the justice sector). Therefore the strategy development (engagement) and implementation (collaboration) processes must necessarily be attractive to them.

3. Stakeholders, especially Users, are knowledgeable volunteers – most stakeholders have at least some knowledge and wisdom to contribute to the development and implementation of strategies. Given that Users are generally the main participants in the implementation of any strategy and also that generally the Users are the ones who are ultimately paying for the implementation of the strategy, it is imperative that Users play a major role in developing and implementing strategies.

4. Earning the right to lead, not taking control – if stakeholders attempt to 'take control' of a strategy, they will often fail to achieve sufficient 'buy-in' from other stakeholders to enable the strategy to be effectively implemented. The OpenStrategies approach helps leaders to 'earn the right to lead' rather than to 'take control'.

5. Stakeholders' fears of PRUB-Validate – PRUB-Validate can equally be 'PRUB-InValidate', thereby identifying SubStrategies which won't lead to desired Benefits and Projects which will produce Abandoned Orphan Results.

Some stakeholders will not want their pet SubStrategies and Projects to be 'PRUB-InValidated' so they will resist the OpenStrategies process. In such situations it is important to use the PRUB-Validate approach to identify how potentially invalid Projects and SubStrategies can be improved so that they can in fact be PRUB-Validated.

6.   Different types of people – stakeholders in many strategies have different skills, experiences and preferences. These differences need to be recognised and managed in order to optimise the quality of strategies and their implementation. Differences include:

  – preferences for working on different parts of a strategy (for example preferences for working with Projects and Results rather than with Uses and Benefits and *vice versa*);
  – preferences for working at different levels of a strategy (for example at aspirational, guidance and operational levels);
  – preferences for splitting ideas into their component parts ('splitters') in contrast to lumping ideas into chunks ('lumpers');
  – preferences to work on selected themes within an OpenStrategy;
  – preferences for working in secret (as may be required in companies operating in a competitive environment) or openly.

• Performance management for organisations and staff – Validated SubStrategies based on PRUB provide a robust structure for encapsulating indicators, targets and performance measurements for both organisations and individual stakeholders. In addition, if a particular target is not being met, the PRUB sequence identifies where action needs to be taken to increase the chances of the target being met in future.

• Strategy words – many traditional 'strategy words' actually mean very little when it comes to implementation. OpenStrategies provides guidance on the use of strategy words (taxonomy), the sequencing and relationships between strategy words (syntax) and their subsequent meanings (semantics).

Your Strategy Checklist

When developing a strategy it is essential to be clear about a number of factors, including the taxonomy, syntax and semantics of the documented strategy.

In summary, it is essential to:

- be clear about what level the strategy is (aspirational? guidance? operational?);

- clearly define the desired Benefits;

- clearly define the intended Uses which will lead to those Benefits;

- clearly define the necessary and sufficient Results to enable those Uses;

- clearly define the Projects required to produce the desired Results;

- clearly define the sequence from inputs (Projects) through Results and Uses to outcomes (Benefits);

- be clear about exactly who are the intended Users (demographic specificity);

- be clear about exactly what will be done (PR) and why (UB) (thematic specificity);

- be clear about exactly who will implement the Projects (organisational specificity);

- be clear about what geographic area is covered by the strategy (geographic specificity);

- include convincing cause-and-effect Evidence on each Link and especially on the Links from Results to Uses;

- include a convincing Value estimate (value of the Benefits minus the combined costs of the Projects and Uses);

- include a small number of simple and relevant indicators and targets;

- exclude any Projects that will produce Abandoned Orphan Results;

- positively and definitely phrase all Projects, Results, Uses and Benefits;

- capture any negativity in the Links between Projects and Results, Results and Uses and between Uses and Benefits;

- where appropriate, be clear about what resources will be required and who will provide them.

Appendix I

Projects, Results, Uses and Benefits and OpenStrategies Glossary

This chapter defines the words and concepts use in the OpenStrategies system.

Active/Passive

Uses can be written as active or passive Use. OpenStrategies strongly recommends that all Uses are written as active Uses in order to confirm that it is the actions of end-users which make a strategy successful.

Aspirational Strategies

These are the highest-level strategies and describe what stakeholders aspire to. They typically describe desired outcomes without defining how these outcomes will be achieved.

High-level aspirational strategies are brief documents which capture the general principles and desired outcomes of a strategy. Aspirational strategies are typically valuable to politicians and business leaders, who are focused primarily on 'the big picture' or 'vision' for a strategy. Aspirational strategies can be defined as SubStrategies but they don't contain enough detail to enable them to be Validated or implemented.

In essence, aspirational strategies are generally broad statements of purpose with limited specificity in terms of:

- themes (what will be done);

- demography (who it is being done for);

- geography (where it is being done);

- organisations (who will do it).

Benefits

Benefits are the desired consequences of Uses or actions or activities done by *citizens, customers* or *the community.* They are the final goal within any strategy and are sometimes called 'outcomes' in other strategy documents.

Budget

The budget identifies the resources (especially financial resources) that will be required to enable a Project to proceed.

BURP

This acronym is used to denote the four types of OpenStrategies Items *in reverse order*: Benefits, Uses, Results and Projects. Items are often recorded in this order when the focus is first and foremost on defining the actual desired Benefits for a community or when the focus is more on developing strategy and less on recording existing activities.

Collaboration

In this book we use the term collaboration to refer to the involvement of stakeholders during the *implementation* of a strategy.

Compound Uses

Every Use involves multiple steps. These steps can be written as a 'simple Use' (for example 'students learn new information during classes') or as multiple steps in a 'compound Use' (for example 'students listen to their tutors, complete exercises and do homework in order to learn new information').

Effectiveness

In the OpenStrategies system 'effectiveness' is defined as 'doing the right things' as distinct from 'doing things right' (which is 'efficiency').

Efficiency

In the OpenStrategies system 'efficiency' is defined as 'doing things right' as distinct from 'doing the right things' (which is 'effectiveness').

End-point PRUB Item

'End-point' Items are 'one-off' completed Items with a fixed point of completion (or application or availability). They can be quantified or measured. For example, an 'end-point' Result could be 'a cycle-track' as this would be the end point of a Project to 'build a cycle-track'. Hopefully it would not be the end point of a SubStrategy involving a cycle-track because such a SubStrategy should include the *Use* of the cycleway as well as the Benefits to be derived from that Use.

End-users

In the OpenStrategies system end-users are the people, communities and organisations who Use the Results (assets) created by service providers.

Engagement

In this book we use the term engagement to refer to the involvement of stakeholders during the *development* of a strategy.

Evidence

In the OpenStrategies system the term Evidence refers to information which provides confidence that the Links in an OpenStrategy are in fact true and will happen in practice.

A SubStrategy or OpenStrategy only has real value if there is compelling cause-and-effect Evidence that the statements it contains are true or very likely to be true. This is particularly so in relation to having solid Evidence that Results will in fact be Used by customers/communities/citizens *and* that such Uses will generate worthwhile Benefits. It is also crucially important to have firm Evidence that adoptable Orphan Results are in fact going to be Adopted.

Evidence 'resides' in the Links in a SubStrategy.

Cause-and-effect Evidence is not the same as performance measurement data (see section 2.10). Cause-and-effect Evidence provides information on the impact a Project has on a Result or a Result has on a Use or a Use has on a Benefit. In contrast performance measurement simply measures parameters *within* each Project, Result, Use and Benefit and does not contain cause-and-effect information.

This information is not Evidence of cause and effect – it is simply a measure of the 'effect'.

When seeking compelling Evidence to help validate a strategy, it is essential to know 'what caused what' to happen (that is, Evidence) rather than to merely measure the 'consequences of what happened' (performance measurement data).

Understanding cause-and-effect Evidence is a key component of effective risk management.

Evolving PRUB Item

An evolving Item implies the prospect of continuing change and improvement; the focus is on changes that happen over a (sometimes specified) period of time. An example of an evolving Use could be: 'Each year a further 1% of the local population attends the health clinic'.

Fundamental Principles

Fundamental principles are core concepts which apply to all actions and consequences in a strategy. For example, they may relate to a 'commitment to public participation' in a strategy or a 'commitment to ecological sustainability'. As such they are not actions or consequences.

Guidance Strategies

Mid-level guidance strategies are documents which flesh out an aspirational strategy in sufficient detail so that people understand broadly what needs to be done but they don't provide enough detail to enable implementation. Typically they outline what will be done and provide limited information on who it is being done for, where it's being done and who will implement the strategy.

Guidance strategies are valuable to senior operational managers to enable high-level budgeting, planning and inter-organisational collaboration. Guidance strategies can be created as SubStrategies but they do not contain enough details to enable them to be Validated.

Guidance strategies provide more information on the four key 'specificities' (thematic, demographic, geographic and organisational) than do aspirational strategies but they still do not get into operational details so they cannot be directly implemented.

Issues

Issues are themes or topics which are the focus of SubStrategies or an OpenStrategy. They typically generate a number of different PRUB Items and sometimes entire SubStrategies or sequences of PRUBs.

Items

An Item is one of the four elements making up the PRUB structure and is a Project, a Result, a Use or a Benefit.

Links, Positive and Negative

In the PRUB structure, when one Item contributes to another a Link is formed as indicated by arrows. The Link between two Items may be positive, negative or neutral.

A positive Link indicates that the first Item will *increase the likelihood of the second Item occurring or increase the extent to which it occurs.*

A negative Link indicates that the first Item will *decrease the likelihood of the second Item occurring or reduce the extent to which it occurs.*

If it is not possible to establish Links between Items in a SubStrategy, this provides an indication that something is wrong with the SubStrategy and needs investigation.

Ongoing PRUB Item

Ongoing Items have no fixed 'end point' of availability or application. Such Items are not or cannot easily be quantified or measured and may continue indefinitely. A typical ongoing Use could be: 'people continue to visit the museum'.

Operational Strategies

Operational strategies are comprehensive and detailed action plans which specify exactly what will be done, who it is being done for, where it is being done and who will implement the strategy. They are valuable to the people who actually make things happen. Operational strategies can be created as SubStrategies and they contain enough detail to enable them to be Validated and implemented.

Operational strategies provide sufficiently detailed information on each of the four specificities (thematic, demographic, geographic and organisational) so that anyone reading the operational strategy would know exactly what to do to implement it.

OpenStrategy

An OpenStrategy is a strategy that has been translated into PRUB items in the form of an interlinked suite of SubStrategies, audited for gaps, repetition, lack of clarity, and so on, and then Validated using the PRUB-Validate process (see Chapter 6). There is no strict dividing line between a SubStrategy and an OpenStrategy other than that a SubStrategy is usually smaller and is focused on a single issue, whereas an OpenStrategy is more likely to address many interlinked themes.

OpenStrategy Diagnosis

An OpenStrategy diagnosis is the audit of strategies to assess whether they satisfy the rules of SubStrategies, OpenStrategies and PRUB-Validate.

OpenStrategy Matrix

An OpenStrategy Matrix consists of several layers of OpenStrategies, such as an interlinked set of national, regional and local OpenStrategies or an interlinked set of aspirational-, guidance- and operational-level OpenStrategies.

Performance Measurement and Management

In the OpenStrategies system performance indicators, targets and measurements reside within each PRUB Item (see Chapter 2):

- indicators define the performance parameters that are to be measured;

- targets define the desired performance for each indicator;

- measurements are the actual measurements of each indicator.

Placeholder PRUB Item

A placeholder Item is used when creating a SubStrategy and you are not yet clear about the exact wording of a Project, Result, Use or Benefit. A placeholder Item captures the fact that a Project, Result, Use or Benefit needs to be defined and in so doing it captures an idea without needing it to be fully defined.

Pooled Budgets vs. Joined-up Budgets

This book distinguishes between pooled budgets and joined-up budgets as follows:

- Pooled budgets are where stakeholders' budgets are consolidated into a central pool of resources which are then allocated to SubStrategies by a committee of stakeholders. Stakeholders then have no direct accountability for where their own specific resources are allocated.

- Joined-up budgets are where stakeholders selected SubStrategies or parts of SubStrategies to which they will supply their own resources in collaboration with other stakeholders who are similarly selecting and implementing SubStrategies. Stakeholders retain direct accountability for where their resources are allocated while still working collaboratively.

Projects

Projects are actions or activities undertaken by organisations to create and/or maintain assets. They can appear in many different shapes or forms depending on the organisations involved.

PRUB

The PRUB acronym denotes the four types of OpenStrategies Item: Projects, Results, Uses and Benefits. Items are often recorded in this order when, prior to developing SubStrategies, a record of existing Projects and activities is desired. This order is also useful when the focus is on implementing a strategy or SubStrategies.

PRUB-Validate

PRUB-Validate (see Chapter 6) is a four-step process for creating Validated SubStrategies. It can also be used to evaluate existing strategies to determine whether or not they can be Validated.

PRUB-Validate Diagnosis

A PRUB-Validate Diagnosis is a Project-by-Project diagnosis of real Projects that are ready and able to be implemented in order to assess whether they will genuinely lead via Results and Uses to Benefits and whether or not this sequence will be worth doing.

Results

Results are the consequences of Projects and are in place to be 'handed over' to the end-users (customers, citizens and communities) to Use and Benefit from.

There are basically two main categories of Result:

- a usable Result that is able to be used directly and immediately by end-users;

- an unusable Result that is not able to be used directly and immediately (Orphan Result).

There are some powerful subtleties relating to the types of Results (both usable and unusable), as follows:

- A **usable** Result is one that is ready to be handed over and used by end-users; it is sufficient, it may or may not be necessary, and it may or may not be wanted.

- An **unusable** Result is one where there are obstacles to its use and where some sort of modification needs to be made before it can become a usable Result.

- A **necessary** Result is one which must be present in order to achieve the desired Use and Benefit. A necessary Result is both usable and wanted (valued).

- An **unnecessary Result** is one where something sufficiently similar already exists or where the unnecessary Result is simply not required.

- A **sufficient** Result has everything ready for handover to the end-users: nothing is missing and no further steps are needed before the handover can occur.

- An **insufficient Result** is one that is not currently being used but which could be used once it has been modified or further developed in some way or where, if accompanied by other Results, it could be part of a sufficient set of Results.

- A **wanted** Result is one which the community sees as having value and thus something they want to Use. A wanted Result should be usable, may or may not be necessary and should be sufficient.

- An **unwanted Result** is one which lacks any Evidence of community need or desire and where subsequently there is no pick-up or Use by the community.

- An **Abandoned Orphan Result** is one which cannot or will not be used in any way whatsoever, either internally by the organisation or by clients or the community.

- An **Adopted Orphan Result** is one which cannot be directly used by end-users but which contributes to other Projects and so is used internally by service provider organisations.

- An **internal** Result refers to the use of Adopted Orphan Results which are used internally to contribute to another Project (note that no capital letter is used for 'internal use'; 'Use' with a capital letter refers only to 'Use' by end-users).

Scalability

Scalability refers to the ability of a process to operate at multiple levels. The OpenStrategies system is scalable in a number of ways, including:

- being effective for multiple levels of strategies (aspirational, guidance and operational);

- being effective for strategies ranging from small single-issue SubStrategies up to large multi-stakeholder, multi-themed strategies affecting many categories of people;

- enabling collaboration at the level of small single-issue SubStrategies up to large multi-stakeholder, multi-themed strategies affecting many categories of people.

Service Providers

In the OpenStrategies system service providers are the organisations and individuals who run Projects to produce Results (assets). Service providers can be companies, government departments, local government agencies, voluntary agencies, individual citizens and anyone else who creates assets which are to be Used.

Strategy

A strategy is a plan and an Evidence-based rationale for that plan.

Strategy Environment Diagnosis

A Strategy Environment Diagnosis consists of identifying all strategy requirements for a stakeholder group, defining how they do or should interlink, clarifying the quality of these strategies and interlinks and recommending actions for creating an effective OpenStrategy.

A Strategy Environment Diagnosis will also identify the key characteristics of a strategy environment, for example, whether the strategic environment is predominantly simple, complicated, complex or chaotic. A Strategy Environment Diagnosis should be performed before any strategies are created.

SubStrategies

In the OpenStrategies system a SubStrategy is a small-scale strategy usually on a single theme or for a single demographic group of end-users or for a single geographic area. An interlinked suite of multiple SubStrategies constitutes an OpenStrategy.

SubStrategies are small sets of up to about 20 PRUBs which typically focus on a specific topic or demographic group. If they are at an aspirational or guidance level, they cannot be directly implemented. If they are at an operational level, they can be directly implemented.

SubStrategies may be created in their own right or they may be distilled from larger broad-themed OpenStrategies in order to focus attention on specific topics. SubStrategies can be created from other strategy documents by applying the PRUB translation principles of distilling, refining and inferring.

Translate: Distil + Refine + Infer + Create

When working with existing strategy documents or material with a view to translating the text into PRUB Items (and possibly forming SubStrategies), you apply the skills of **distilling** and **refining** PRUB Items and **inferring** meaning from those parts of the strategy document where the meaning is unclear, ambiguous or incomplete.

- **Distil** – this involves taking apart and breaking down existing text into PRUB Items.

- **Refine** – this task involves modifying existing text in order to turn it into PRUB Items.

- **Infer** – this step becomes necessary when the existing text is ambiguous, imprecise or has gaps in meaning. Inferring may also take place when existing text has been omitted to 'spell out the obvious'.

- **Create** – this step involves the creation of new Projects, Results, Uses and Benefits in order to complete the strategy.

Transparency

In the OpenStrategies system the term transparency refers to the ease with which stakeholders can *access* and *understand* a strategy.

Uses

Uses are *actions or activities* done by individuals or groups of individuals or even companies who are Using an asset created by a service provider. Generally they will be undertaking these Uses for their own Benefit, but often other people (or for example the environment) will also Benefit.

The main categories of Uses (see Chapter 4 for more details) are:

- An **ongoing** Use is one which continues unchanged over a period of time.

- An **evolving** Use is one which is changing over time.

- An **emergent** Use may initially not exist and people may not be aware of it as a possibility but which becomes apparent over time.

- An **end-point** Use is one which is completed at a particular point in time.

- A **one-off** Use is one which only happens once.

- An **intermittent** Use is one which happens from time to time.

- An **optional** Use (representing most Uses) is one where the Users can choose to either Use or not Use one or more Results.

- A **non-optional** Use is one where Users are forced to Use a Result.

- An **automatic or unconscious** Use is one where the Users have not consciously decided to Use a particular Result or Results and they may be completely unaware that they are using a new Result.

- An **opt-out** Use is one where people choose to Use a different Result from the ones provided for in a SubStrategy or OpenStrategy.

- An **invisible** Use is one which many stakeholders might totally overlook but which is nevertheless very important to some people.

- An **exclusive** Use is one where the Use of a Result or Results prevents other people from using the same Result(s).

- A **non-exclusive** Use is one where the Use of a Result or Results do not prevent other people from using the same Result(s).

- An **abstractive** Use is one which irreversibly consumes resources.

- A **non-abstractive** Use is one which does not consume resources.

Validate

In the OpenStrategies system the term Validate means to create a SubStrategy which:

- encapsulates a logical sequence of actions and consequences from Projects through Results and Uses to Benefits;

- confirms that this logical sequence is very likely to happen by adding compelling cause-and-effect Evidence;

- confirms that it is worth implementing this local sequence by demonstrating that the SubStrategy has a net positive Value.

Value

In the OpenStrategies system the term Value refers to the net value of a SubStrategy, which is determined by calculating (the total value of all the Benefits) minus (the costs of all the Projects plus the costs of all the Uses).

Appendix 2

Analysis and Specification for an Integrated Strategic Information Management System

Strategies come in many different shapes and sizes, as outlined in Table A1.

Table A2.1   A selection of different categories of strategies which have been needed by different stakeholder groups

---

Type 1: Thematic strategies – strategies on particular topics

Type 2: Demographic strategies – strategies on all themes relevant to a particular demographic group

Type 3: Geographic strategies – national, regional, district and local strategies

Type 4: Organisational strategies – that is, single strategies which address the requirements of a single organization

Type 5: Partnership strategies – strategies which focus on a sub-set of activities all of which require multi-stakeholder collaboration

Type 6: Aspirational strategies – strategies which define high-level outcomes but which usually provide minimal guidance on how the strategies will actually be implemented

Type 7: Guidance strategies – mid-level strategies which provide indications of how outcomes will be achieved but are nevertheless insufficiently detailed to be implemented

Type 8: Operational strategies – grassroots-level strategies which provide details on how a strategy will be implemented to achieve its desired outcomes

Type 9: Hierarchical strategies – strategies which interlink high-level aspirational strategies with mid-level guidance strategies with operational-level implementable strategies

Type 10: Micro-strategies – strategies which address a single, relatively small issue

Type 11: Layered organisational or demographic strategies – strategies which combine two or more 'layers' of strategy, for example combined national and regional strategies, or combined organisational and departmental strategies

Type 12: 'Quick wins' strategies – strategies which address a small sub-set of issues and which are expected to produce results quickly

Type 13: Cross-cutting strategies – strategies which address two or more inter-related thematic issues

Type 14: Integrated strategies – strategies which address combinations of two or more of the first 13 categories

An ideal Integrated Strategic Information Management System (ISIMS) will be able to guide the creation of any and all of these different types of strategies as well as any other types of strategies which may be required by stakeholder groups.

This Appendix disaggregates different, real and observed stakeholder groups' strategy requirements into themes and sub-topics, analyses them and then distils functional specifications for an idealised Integrated Strategy Information Management System (ISIMS) which will meet each and every one of these requirements. Each sub-topic would justify several pages of analysis. However, given that there are about 60 sub-topics to address, each analysis will necessarily be much more succinct.

While many of these requirements have been distilled from thousands of conversations in the central and local government sectors, most requirements are equally relevant in small and large non-government organisations and in private and public companies.

The OpenStrategies system directly addresses each and every one of these requirements.

This Appendix now analyses stakeholders' requirements for an effective ISIMS under the following themes:

1.   Development and evolution.

2.   Clarity.

3.   Validation.

4.   Prioritisation.

5.   Implementation.

6.   Performance management.

7.   Outcomes focus.

8.   Stakeholder engagement (planning together).

9.   Stakeholder collaboration (working together).

10.   Interlinking.

11.   Governance.

12.   Libraries of validated strategies.

13.   Integrated strategy development.

Theme 1: Development and Evolution

Sub-topic 1.1: Defining Strategy Using Specific Language

Stakeholders' requirement

Stakeholders want strategies which are clear about exactly what needs to be done.

In this respect many of the words which appear in strategy documents, including in so-called plans, are actually of limited value.

The problem with the language used around strategy seems to be that:

- There are simply too many 'strategy words and phrases' in circulation altogether!

- Many of those words are too close in meaning – to some people they are interchangeable while other people perceive slight but important differences. For example, for some people 'goals' and 'objectives' are interchangeable; for other people there are subtle but important differences in meaning between the two words and they are not interchangeable – and this widely observed inconsistency of perception applies both within and across organisations.

- Where people have a different understanding of the same words there are endless opportunities for confusion, misunderstanding and frustration. Working to develop and implement strategy is difficult enough without this adding to the challenge!

- Words and phrases go in and out of fashion (those 'buzz' words!). No sooner do you become comfortable with the latest 'correct' expressions than you discover that those phrases are now out of date and have been replaced by others.

The inconsistent and excessive use of jargon in most strategy documents causes confusion and unnecessary complexity.

For this reason, if information is to be shared and strategies are to be integrated, it is necessary that a simple and consistent language is used across all strategies and across organisations – and this is where PRUB helps.

For example, words such as 'protect', 'encourage', 'conserve', 'ensure', 'deliver' and 'optimise' all sound like ideal words to appear within implementable projects, whereas in reality they are only useful as part of very high-level aspirational statements. Such words do not actually describe actions which can be implemented (see also sub-topic 10.1 below on the integration of high-level aspirations with operational-level implementable strategies).

Another popular strategy word, especially in the public sector, is the term 'collaborate'. Many strategies contain projects 'to collaborate ...'. Collaborate is a *way* of undertaking an action; it is not an action itself. It's not possible to go out there and 'collaborate' – it is only possible to go out there and do things *in a collaborative manner*.

Further challenges arise with traditional strategy words such as 'objectives' and 'goals' and 'outcomes' and 'outputs'. Despite the public sector in many Western democracies saying they are 'outcomes focused', it is rare to find a public servant who can give a clear definition of an 'outcome'. The same applies to many other traditional strategy words.

For example, consider the building of a swimming pool. The builder's *objective* is likely to be 'a completed swimming pool', whereas the swimming coach's *objective* may be 'to have at least 50 children per day attending swimming lessons'. The Ministry of Health's *objective* might be 'healthy children because they are swimming more'. So the word 'objective' has no unique meaning in most traditional strategies.

In a similar vein, many strategies contain actions along the lines of 'increase profits by 15%' or 'reduce costs by 10%'. These are not implementable actions. Certainly it is possible to take an action of 'buy cheaper raw materials' which might result in an output of 'lower costs', but there is no such action as 'reduce costs'. Equally there is no such action as 'increase profits'. It may be possible to have an action to sell products and services at a higher price and thereby lead to increased profits, but the action is to 'sell products and services at a higher price' – it is *not* and *cannot be* to 'increase profits'.

Therefore, when creating a multi-stakeholder strategy, it is essential to use an explicit strategy language taxonomy which unequivocally defines components of the strategy as grounded in reality and independent of the perspective of each stakeholder.

Functional specification 1.1 for an ISIMS to address this requirement

A concise and rigorously defined 'strategy language taxonomy' which encapsulates and defines actions that can actually be implemented.

Sub-topic 1.2: Defining Strategy Using a Common Language

Stakeholders' requirement

Stakeholders are often involved in many different strategies. Major confusion arises because each strategy uses different words (for example objectives, goals, outcomes, outputs, targets and so on) and even where they use the same words, stakeholders often give them different meanings. For example some stakeholders believe that goals are sub-sets of or precursors to objectives. Other stakeholders believe that objectives are sub-sets of or precursors to goals.

So not only must the strategy language be concise and rigorous (sub-topic 1.1), it must also be *commonly understood* by all stakeholders.

Functional specification 1.2 for an ISIMS to address this requirement

A rigorous 'strategy language taxonomy' which is easily and fully understood by all stakeholders.

Sub-topic 1.3: Mapping Strategies in a Common Format

Stakeholders' requirement

Stakeholders are often involved in many different strategies. Major confusion arises because each strategy uses a different layout for strategic information.

For example, many strategies use LogFrame (Logic Framework) mapping. LogFrame is a powerful approach which is very flexible, allowing many different types of strategy maps to be created. However, this flexibility means that each strategy looks different and so it becomes very challenging to interlink related strategies, such as, for example, linking a cycling strategy with a road strategy with a safety strategy.

Functional specification 1.3 for an ISIMS to address this requirement

A single, concise and rigorously defined 'strategy format' which lays out strategic information in a consistent format which all stakeholders can follow and fully understand.

Sub-topic 1.4: It Must Actually be a Strategy

Stakeholders' requirement

Stakeholders want strategies that are actually strategies. This seemingly obvious statement apparently is not obvious to many people who create strategies. There are tens of thousands of strategies in this world, but only a small percentage actually focus on what needs to be done and why.

Far too often 'strategies' consist primarily of important information such as organisational history, the status of an organisation, descriptions of customers and their needs, environmental scanning, strategy scenarios and other information, all of which should *feed into and inform a strategy but which are not in themselves 'strategy'*.

Functional specification 1.4 for an ISIMS to address this requirement

A clear plan of what needs to be done and why.

Sub-topic 1.5: Mapping What's Already Happening

Stakeholders' requirement

Stakeholders are frequently unclear about what is already happening in their strategy environment so they need a strategy system which enables them to concisely map what is already happening. Indeed, experience demonstrates that when current activities are clearly defined in an effective strategy system, many stakeholders comment that it is the first time they have had a clear idea of what is going on.

Quality control theory and practice has confirmed that for any system it is essential to understand the existing system explicitly before making any changes to it. The same applies to organisational systems and strategies.

Functional specification 1.5 for an ISIMS to address this requirement

The ability to rapidly and concisely map existing strategic activities as the basis for both refining/deleting existing activities and for adding new and validated strategic activities.

Sub-topic 1.6: Mapping What Needs to be Done

Stakeholders' requirement

Stakeholders need to determine what needs to be done and why and to display this information in a concise format to guide decision-making and inform stakeholders.

Functional specification 1.6 for an ISIMS to address this requirement

The ability to rapidly and concisely map new strategic activities.

Sub-topic 1.7: Necessary and Sufficient Actions to Lead to the Desired Outcomes

Stakeholders' requirement

Too often strategies are created which encapsulate many worthwhile actions which are insufficient to enable the desired outcomes to be achieved. For example, a strategy may include the building of a swimming pool for children but omit to include the employment of lifeguards. Other strategies have been found which ineffectively and unnecessarily duplicate resources and services.

So stakeholders want strategies which contain all those actions which are both *necessary and sufficient* to lead to the desired outcomes.

Functional specification 1.7 for an ISIMS to address this requirement

The ability to guide and enable the development of strategies which contain all those actions which are both necessary and sufficient to lead to the desired outcomes.

Sub-topic 1.8: Effective and Efficient Strategy Development

Stakeholders' requirement

Stakeholders, particularly complex multi-stakeholder groups, require the process of strategy development to be both effective and efficient so as to produce high-quality strategies with minimal time and effort. They often need to balance the need for widespread stakeholder engagement with an urgency to complete the strategy and start implementing it. They do not want endless discussion forums, brainstorms, conversations and workshops but they also do not want top-down diktats from a small number of senior stakeholders telling them what to do.

If 100 stakeholder organisations want to work together on a large strategy (for example a children's strategy for an English county), with perhaps 100 topics within the strategy, and for each stakeholder to meet in groups of 10 with other stakeholders for a day just four times per year per topic to plan how they will collaborate on these 100 topics, that amounts to 4,000 topic meetings involving 40,000 person-days and tens of thousands of conversations. So 'networking' in this way to achieve collaboration with such strategies is mathematically unrealistic. There has to be a better way to enable many stakeholders to work together without having to have hundreds of thousands of conversations.

Functional specification 1.8 for an ISIMS to address this requirement

The ability to guide and enable stakeholders to efficiently create effective strategies.

Sub-topic 1.9: Capture All Possible Strategic Ideas even if they are not Immediately Implemented

Stakeholders' requirement

Many multi-stakeholder groups have more strategic ideas than can be immediately supported with existing resources. Some of the currently unsupported ideas may be very much worth supporting at some stage by sub-groups of stakeholders, so it is important that such ideas are captured and displayed as sub-strategies which are waiting for resources.

Functional specification 1.9 for an ISIMS to address this requirement

The ability to encapsulate strategic ideas which can be supported in the future as well as ideas which will be supported immediately.

Sub-topic 1.10: Easily Update and Refine Strategies

Stakeholders' requirement

The world is changing fast, so strategies must also change fast as the strategic environment changes and as new information becomes available.

Functional specification 1.10 for an ISIMS to address this requirement

Must be flexible and enable easy, rapid and frequent updating.

Sub-topic 1.11: Scalability

Stakeholders' requirement

Strategies sometimes start small with a limited number of topics, stakeholders and end-users. Over time they may evolve to include more topics, more stakeholders and more end-users. An ISIMS must enable this scalable evolution.

Also, some stakeholders will be 'splitters' and some will be 'lumpers'. Splitters want to break strategic ideas down into their component parts, whereas lumpers prefer to work with the big picture. An ISIMS must enable stakeholders to move seamlessly from 'lumped' big picture ideas down to 'split' small strategic concepts and vice versa.

Functional specification 1.11 for an ISIMS to address this requirement

Must enable the scalable evolution of larger and larger strategies, ideally made up of smaller modules (sub-strategies) which fit together to create a larger overall strategy.

Sub-topic 1.12: Access and Use Strategic Information over Extended Periods of Time even as Individuals and Organisations Change

Stakeholders' requirement

Organisations typically continue for decades even as the members and employees of the organisations come and go. Therefore, it is imperative that strategy and operations have continuity and are not dependent on individuals to continue to make them work.

Functional specification 1.12 for an ISIMS to address this requirement

Must have an ongoing life of its own independent of each organisation's individual members and employees.

Theme 2: Clarity

Sub-topic 2.1: Smallest Amount of Strategic Information

Stakeholders' requirement

Cognitive research has demonstrated that humans can hold 7 +/– 2 interlinked ideas in their heads at any one time (http://library.mpib-berlin.mpg.de/ft/rh/RH_More_2003.pdf). Our experience further suggests that humans can comprehend about 15–20 interlinked ideas when they are displayed in a clear graphical format.

Therefore, strategic information needs to be succinct and to be 'chunked' into digestible sized quantities.

Functional specification 2.1 for an ISIMS to address this requirement

Must use the *smallest* possible amount of strategic information to convey its messages and must enable this information to be 'chunked' into digestible sized chunks.

Sub-topic 2.2: Most Valuable/Useful Strategic Information

Stakeholders' requirement

A complete strategy for even quite small organisations can contain an enormous amount of information. Given that humans have limited cognitive ability to absorb large amounts of information, it is therefore important for effective strategies to contain the *most valuable* strategic information. This minimalist set of most valuable information will also be the most useful information, ideally able to be used for many different purposes.

Functional specification 2.2 for an ISIMS to address this requirement

Must contain the smallest amount of *most valuable* strategic information.

Sub-topic 2.3: Strategic Information of Most Value to the Most Stakeholders

Stakeholders' requirement

Most strategies need to engage with many stakeholders, whether customers, citizens, employees, suppliers, managers, regulators and others. Therefore, strategic information needs to be meaningful and valuable to all these stakeholders and not just to a select few in the 'strategy department'.

Functional specification 2.3 for an ISIMS to address this requirement

Must contain the smallest amount of information that is the most valuable to the *most stakeholders*.

Sub-topic 2.4: Clear Cause-and-Effect Links from Inputs through to Outcomes

Stakeholders' requirement

In order for stakeholders to effectively implement a strategy so as to achieve the desired outcomes, they need and want explicit information on the cause-and-effect sequences of all the necessary and sufficient actions required by the strategy, including how actions impact on each other.

In general a project or activity run by an organisation will not directly cause a desired outcome.

For example, a company may run a project to produce better widgets but it then requires customers to buy the widgets before the company's final desired outcome of 'a profitable and sustainable company' is achieved.

Similarly, a public sector project such as 'make obesity counselling services readily available' won't directly impact on obesity. Only when obese people eat less and exercise more will obesity levels fall.

In both these cases it is essential to understand the full cause-and-effect sequence from the initial project ('build better widgets' and 'make obesity counselling services readily available') via the ways in which customers and citizens engage with the results of these projects to eventually create the desired outcomes.

Functional specification 2.4 for an ISIMS to address this requirement

Must explicitly show all the cause-and-effect linkages from actions through to the desired outcomes.

Sub-topic 2.5: Clarity about the Resources and Funding Required

Stakeholders' requirement

Stakeholders invariably want to know the costs/resources required to implement projects. Increasingly stakeholders also want to know the costs to the end-users of using the services and products created by organisational stakeholders.

Functional specification 2.5 for an ISIMS to address this requirement

Must be explicitly clear about the costs/resources required both for the implementation of projects and for the use of products and services created by 'provider-stakeholders'.

Sub-topic 2.6: Strategic Information in the Right Place

Stakeholders' requirement

We frequently hear from stakeholders who struggle to find the actionable information they are looking for in strategies. Experience suggests that a key reason is because strategy documents are so often cluttered up with pages and pages of 'status reports' and 'environmental scanning reports' and 'scenarios', all of which are important but are not actually the strategy.

Many strategy documents appear to have minimal logic in the way the strategic information is presented, that is, how it is 'chunked', interlinked and sequenced. This makes it very difficult for stakeholders to identify key information within a strategy and to distinguish the different types of information (external factors, internal factors and the strategy itself).

Functional specification 2.6 for an ISIMS to address this requirement

Must be clear on the distinction between information which *informs* the strategy and information which *constitutes* the strategy.

Sub-topic 2.7: Transparency to Help Build Inter-stakeholder Trust

Stakeholders' requirement

A common message from stakeholders is that they feel excluded from strategy development processes as they have often been presented with near-final strategies as a fait accompli. They also discover that their responses to such draft strategies have been largely ignored in the final version of the strategy.

A constant request is for a strategy system that is sufficiently transparent that stakeholders can see at any time during the strategy development and implementation process what is being proposed by which stakeholders. In this way all stakeholders can choose when and whether or not to engage. They may simply be happy with the transparent process or they may identify all or parts of the strategy where they wish to contribute.

To achieve transparency, strategies need to be both:

- clearly and succinctly presented (the clarity of the strategic information);

- made visible (the availability of the strategic information).

Functional specification 2.7 for an ISIMS to address this requirement

Must be sufficiently transparent (both clear and available) so that all stakeholders can see what is going on with both the development and the implementation of the strategy.

Sub-topic 2.8: Distilling Simple Actions from Complicated, Complex and Chaotic Strategic Environments

Stakeholders' requirement

Much of the world is complicated, complex or chaotic. In contrast, each and every action is, and can only be, a simple step. There might be many steps in parallel or in sequence and the outcomes of the steps might be uncertain, but nevertheless all actions consist of simple steps.

In complex situations it may not be clear what actions will definitely lead to the desired outcomes. However, unless stakeholders are happy to sit back and do nothing, they will instead take those simple actions which they believe at the time to be most likely to lead to the desired outcomes. They may subsequently modify these actions as they learn more and more about the complexity of their environment and how this environment responds to their actions. Despite this uncertainty and complexity, their individual actions will always be simple steps.

So strategic environments are often complex and evolving but strategic actions always and necessarily consist solely of simple actions.

Functional specification 2.8 for an ISIMS to address this requirement

The ISIMS must enable the distillation of simple strategic actions from the analysis of the simple, complicated, complex and chaotic world.

Sub-topic 2.9: Positivity and Negativity

Stakeholders' requirement

Most strategic actions have both positive and negative impacts. For example, cutting down trees for timber may have a positive impact on the economy but a negative impact on the environment. Building a swimming pool may have a positive impact on children's health but a negative impact on local traffic congestion. Strategies need to take into account all the positive and negative effects of any action.

Functional specification 2.9 for an ISIMS to address this requirement

Must capture both positive and negative effects of actions.

Theme 3: Validation

Sub-topic 3.1: Confidence in 'Doing the Right Things' as well as 'Doing Things Right'

Stakeholders' requirement

In many organisations too much focus is placed on 'efficiency', that is, 'doing things right' and not enough focus is put on 'effectiveness', that is, 'doing the right things'. Often as a result the wrong things get done really well.

So the strategy must specify what needs to be done: 'doing the right things' and not just be primarily an analysis of the strategic environment that the organisation(s) is/are operating in or a list of efficiency improvements (such as 'cut costs by 5% and increase sales by 10%').

Functional specification 3.1 for an ISIMS to address this requirement

Must focus on effectiveness (doing the right thing) first before efficiency (doing things right).

Sub-topic 3.2: Confidence that the Strategy can Genuinely be Implemented

Stakeholders' requirement

Stakeholders want confidence that a strategy is 'doable', so that if they invest the required resources, the desired outcomes can genuinely be achieved. Therefore, each and every action, its required resources and how it contributes to the achievement of outcomes must all be explicitly defined.

Functional specification 3.2 for an ISIMS to address this requirement

Must contain information and evidence that the strategy can be implemented.

Sub-topic 3.3: Risk and Uncertainty Management

Stakeholders' requirement

Strategies and their implementation involve risks. Stakeholders say they want a strategy system which explicitly identifies where risks and uncertainties may lie and hence exactly where to search for more information and evidence to help guide decisions for managing and minimising the impacts of the risks and uncertainties.

Functional specification 3.3 for an ISIMS to address this requirement

Must identify exactly where risk and uncertainty lie within a strategy and hence provide guidance on where more information and evidence may be required to fully validate the rationale of the strategy.

Sub-topic 3.4: Effective Ways for Stakeholders to Contribute

Stakeholders' requirement

In most strategic environments it will not be possible for a single individual to fully understand and validate the strategy.

Stakeholders have therefore asked for a strategy system in which all stakeholders (or, as a minimum, a group of key stakeholders) can view the strategy and add their wisdom and knowledge via comments and suggestions or even edit the strategy under appropriate authority.

Functional specification 3.4 for an ISIMS to address this requirement

Must enable key (or all) stakeholders to view, comment on and edit the strategy so it benefits from their collective wisdom and knowledge.

Theme 4: Prioritisation

Sub-topic 4.1: Straightforward Prioritisation

Stakeholders' requirement

Strategies, particularly in the public sector, generally involve trade-offs and comparisons amongst multiple competing ideas. It is therefore essential for an ideal strategy system to enable the like-with-like comparison of strategic ideas in a manner which enables both qualitative and quantitative comparison of ideas so that they can be prioritised.

So each strategic idea needs to be presented as a complete sequence from 'inputs' through to 'outcomes' together with hard evidence that this sequence is doable, together with financial information that confirms that it is worth proceeding with the strategic idea.

Then, once this information is assembled for each strategic idea, it will be possible to compare and prioritise them.

Functional specification 4.1 for an ISIMS to address this requirement

Must display each strategic idea in the same format, including a full cause-and-effect sequence from inputs to outcomes plus compelling evidence that this sequence is viable plus compelling evidence that the idea is worth implementing.

Sub-topic 4.2: Stakeholders Clustering into Sub-groups to Support Sub-group Ideas

Stakeholders' requirement

When prioritising strategic ideas with multi-stakeholder groups, if strategic ideas are prioritised on the basis of popularity (for example by voting) amongst stakeholders, most of the time the least controversial ideas become the top priorities. But the least controversial ideas are not necessarily the ideas which should actually be implemented.

So a voting process often results in strategic ideas that are crucially important to sub-groups being allocated low priority and hence they don't get implemented. This upsets the sub-groups, some of whom are big enough to implement the ideas on their own. In other cases the sub-groups may not be able to implement these ideas but the ideas may nevertheless be crucially important to a sub-group and therefore deserving of being made high priorities.

Functional specification 4.2 for an ISIMS to address this requirement

Must enable strategic issue prioritisation based on both the issue's popularity (to select the issues which are the least controversial to the whole group) as well as on issues which are crucial to sub-groups.

Theme 5: Implementation

Sub-topic 5.1: Implementation

Stakeholders' requirement

As outlined in Chapter 1, experience shows that many strategies don't get implemented, so they don't make any difference to anyone. In a sense, this entire Appendix is about identifying and defining the many reasons why strategies don't get implemented.

Therefore, this theme focuses on the need for strategies to be explicit about exactly what needs to be done and to describe such actions in a manner that makes sense to those who are tasked with implementing the strategy.

There is seldom much point in high-level executives creating a high-level 'aspirational strategy' and then asking operational-level people to create an implementable 'action plan' from this strategy, yet this is so often what happens. We hear many stories of executives saying 'I do the high-level thinking, I don't do details'. This is a cop-out because anyone can come up with high-level aspirational statements ('we'll increase profits by 10% and decrease costs by 5%', 'we'll expand into overseas markets' and so on). The hard work of making a strategy work is in the detail of the action plans, so a strategy must link aspirations to actions.

Similarly, high-level strategies often have so-called projects to 'increase collaboration'. Collaboration is not a project. Collaboration is a way of doing a task; it is not a task itself. So setting out to 'collaborate' is like setting out to 'drive fast' without knowing what you are driving, where you are driving to, or why.

Along similar lines, many strategies have projects to 'improve leadership' or 'develop capabilities' without any clarity about what strategic tasks such leadership and capabilities will contribute to in order to achieve the desired outcomes.

Functional specification 5.1 for an ISIMS to address this requirement

Must create strategies that link the high-level aspirations directly to actions which can be directly implemented.

Sub-topic 5.2: Delivery

Stakeholders' requirement

One of the most misused terms when it comes to the implementation of strategies is the concept of the 'delivery' of strategies and the concept of the 'delivery' of products and services, whether in the private or public sectors.

It is not actually possible to 'deliver' services or to 'deliver outcomes'. Certainly it's possible to make services *available* to the public, but the public then need to come and use the services in order to create the desired outcomes.

A classic example would be the statement that a particular health service is being 'delivered' to young mothers. It is not possible to 'deliver' a health service to young mothers. Certainly it is possible to make the health service *available* to young mothers, but it is *only* when the young mothers come along and use the service that the service has been completed.

Given that any one service is likely to have hundreds if not thousands of such users, the key actors are the users, not the service providers. So if improvements are to be made, they need to be such as to achieve greater *uptake* of the service, not more intense *delivery* of the service.

This is crucially important. If a service could in fact be 'delivered', it would imply that the service providers were in control of the process of 'delivering' services 'to or at or for' citizens. In contrast, the concept of making services *available* to citizens highlights the active role which must be played by citizens (who far outnumber the service providers). Citizens need to actively come and use the service.

Therefore, citizens have a huge degree of control over whether or not a service will be used. This puts the onus back on the service providers to design and develop services that the public actually want, rather than providers 'delivering' to/at/for citizens what the providers believe are good for citizens.

This particular concept relating to the term 'deliver' is core to the OpenStrategies system. It is frequently debated intensely by OpenStrategies users but, to date, all such debates have ended with an acknowledgement from those present that services cannot be 'delivered' – providers can only 'make them available' (exceptions being aspects of the criminal justice and defence systems).

Functional specification 5.2 for an ISIMS to address this requirement

Must create strategies which make crystal clear what can be achieved by service providers and what must also be done by end-users of a strategy if it is to be successfully implemented.

Theme 6: Performance Management

Sub-topic 6.1: Indicators for Effective Performance Management

Stakeholders' requirement

Once a strategy is being implemented, stakeholders want continual reassurance that everything is on track. This means they want to monitor factors which indicate if the projects are producing results, if end-users are using the results and if genuine outcomes are being achieved.

This calls for the identification of which parameters to measure that will give early indications of whether or not everything is on track (lead indicators) as well as to provide subsequent measures of actual success in achieving outcomes (lag indicators).

Functional specification 6.1 for an ISIMS to address this requirement

Must encapsulate clear information about what needs to be measured and monitored so as to confirm whether or not the strategy implementation is 'on track'.

Sub-topic 6.2: Targets for Effective Performance Management

Stakeholders' requirement

As noted in 6.1, stakeholders need to know *what* to measure but they also need to know what *target* value of each measurement is desirable. In addition, they also need to know if it is desirable to have targets for lead indicators to give early indications of whether final outcomes are likely to be achieved.

For example, a company may aspire to 'increase sales and profit margins in our Asian markets', but this is somewhat meaningless unless there is some appreciation of what will constitute success. In this instance the company may set a target outcome of 'additional net profits of $325,000/year by the end of 2015', which may require a sales target of: 'Asian customers buy and use $3.5 million per year of our products by the end of 2015.' These two targets may then indicate a need for a new target company output of '$4.2 million worth of our products is shipped to Asia each year by the end of 2015', which naturally would lead to a need for a clear manufacturing target.

Functional specification 6.2 for an ISIMS to address this requirement

Must be clear about performance targets.

Sub-topic 6.3: Actual Measurements for Effective Performance Management

Stakeholders' requirement

As noted in 6.1 and 6.2, stakeholders need to know *what* to measure and the desired *target* value of each measurement plus they need actual measurements over time so they can compare them with the desired targets.

So each indicator (what is to be measured) and target (the desired value of each indicator) needs to be regularly compared with the actual measurements of performance and actions taken if actual measurements do not appear to be moving appropriately towards the target values.

In this respect it is important to measure 'upstream' activities as soon as possible; for example, in the example in 6.2 above of new sales into an Asian market, it would be essential to make early measurements on manufacturing and the transport of new products to the Asian market in order to ensure that sufficient product was arriving in Asia to satisfy the anticipated market demand. As soon as the new products arrived in Asia, it would be essential to immediately measure early sales to give the earliest possible indication of whether longer-term sales and profit targets were likely to be met.

So it is essential to be crystal clear about what to measure, what the desired values of those measurements are and what the actual measurements are so as to be able to make management decisions to maintain or improve performance.

Functional specification 6.3 for an ISIMS to address this requirement

Must clearly encapsulate and collate actual performance measurements and enable their comparison with targets.

Sub-topic 6.4: Where to Take Action to Improve Performance

Stakeholders' requirement

Performance measurements on their own are of minimal value: to justify the cost of collecting them they must be used to improve the performance of processes. For example, it is clear that if the desired outcome is 'a fat pig', simply measuring the pig won't make it any fatter. Stakeholders want to be able to respond to performance measurements by taking the right actions in the right places to improve the performance of their strategies. Therefore, any strategy and performance management tool *must* make it clear where action needs to be taken whenever targets are not being met.

Functional specification 6.4 for an ISIMS to address this requirement

Must make it explicitly clear where actions need to be taken in response to any measurement which demonstrates that targets are not being met.

Sub-topic 6.5: Reporting, Audit and Scrutiny

Stakeholders' requirement

Strategic performance frequently needs to be reported to third parties, for example to a board of directors, to government, to citizens, to regulatory authorities and others.

Functional specification 6.5 for an ISIMS to address this requirement

Must enable simple and clear reporting on performance and progress towards desired outcomes.

Sub-topic 6.6: Defending a Strategy through Audit and Scrutiny

Stakeholders' requirement

Stakeholders need to not only manage the performance of their strategies and report to all parties, they often also need to objectively defend their decisions relating to priorities, performance, resource allocation and the modifying of actions which currently aren't living up to expectations. This is particularly important in the public sector where otherwise good strategic decisions may be politically damaging to the parties in power. They therefore need to be able to objectively demonstrate that their decisions are soundly based.

Functional specification 6.6 for an ISIMS to address this requirement

Must encapsulate the reasons for each strategic decision and back them up with a compelling rationale and evidence

Sub-topic 6.7: Linking the Performance of Individuals, Stakeholders and Organisations to the Performance Management of the Strategy

Stakeholders' requirement

Too often strategies are almost completely disconnected from the performances of organisations and individuals, yet it is the performance of individuals, stakeholders and organisations which is required to ensure the successful implementation of a strategy.

As a result individuals are often insufficiently engaged with and motivated towards the successful achievement of the desired outcomes. In contrast, experience shows that if people are crystal clear about their roles and how their roles contribute to the 'big picture' strategy, their motivation and commitment increase.

Functional specification 6.7 for an ISIMS to address this requirement

Must enable the distillation from the strategy of the roles and related performance measurements of individuals, stakeholders and organisations as they contribute to the implementation of the strategy.

Theme 7: Outcomes Focus

Sub-topic 7.1: Outcomes which are Customer, Citizen, Community and Environment-centric

Stakeholders' requirement

Practically all strategies are created by organisations that intend to create assets and services to be used by customers, citizens, communities and the environment. Ideally these strategy-creation processes engage effectively with end-users to co-design the strategies to produce outcomes which will be of value to the end users, but such in-depth engagement is rare.

Irrespective of the level of engagement, every *successful* strategy must create assets and services which end-users will actually use and in so using will create value (outcomes) for themselves and others. Therefore, every successful strategy must fully understand and address the needs and wants of end-users and why they have these needs and wants.

Functional specification 7.1 for an ISIMS to address this requirement

Must reflect and encapsulate an in-depth understanding of end-users' needs and wants.

Sub-topic 7.2: Improvements in the 'Four Well-beings' (Economic, Social, Environmental and Cultural)

Stakeholders' requirement

The implementation of most strategies is expected to generate a range of outcomes which encapsulate what have become known as the 'four well-beings': financial, social, cultural and environmental (in some countries the 'cultural' well-being is not explicitly addressed).

For example, the implementation of a public sector strategy relating to parks and recreation may generate revenue for the providers from the hire of recreational facilities (financial well-being/outcome), increased community cohesion from users playing sport and attending outdoor concerts together in the parks (social well-being), increased cultural activities through ethnic groups using the facilities (cultural well-being) and an enhanced environment (environmental outcome).

Functional specification 7.2 for an ISIMS to address this requirement

Must enable the encapsulation of the four well-beings as desired outcomes.

Sub-topic 7.3: High Levels of Uptake by End-users of Services and Products

Stakeholders' requirement

Sub-topics 7.1 and 7.2 define the types of outcome that a strategy needs to achieve. However, not only must the 'right types' of outcome be achieved, but these outcomes must be achieved at sufficient levels – through sufficient levels of uses – to justify the resources which are committed to the strategy development and implementation.

In this respect, achieving a high level of uptake or use of a product or service may require more than just a good product or service. It may also require effective new marketing methods (for example via social media) of the new product/service to customers or citizens of communities. It may also require new distribution arrangements or new sales processes, for example franchising or enabling purchasing of the products and services through the Internet.

This sub-topic of 'high levels of uptake by end-users' is perhaps *the* most crucial aspect of the development and implementation of any strategy because it is typically the area of action which is most difficult for a provider organisation to influence, let alone control. Therefore, an effective ISIMS *must* have a very strong focus on encapsulating all the strategic information required to achieve high levels of end-user uptake and use of the outputs from provider organisations.

Functional specification 7.3 for an ISIMS to address this requirement

Must create strategies which lead to sufficiently high levels of end-user uptake and hence generation of benefits to justify the resources which are committed to the strategy development and implementation.

Sub-topic 7.4: Vision

Stakeholders' requirement

Many stakeholders involved in strategies like to have a 'vision' which, within one or two sentences, encapsulates key aspects of what their strategy is trying to achieve.

Functional specification 7.4 for an ISIMS to address this requirement

Must encapsulate a 'vision' for the strategy.

Notes on Themes 8 and 9

The majority of strategies involve two quite distinct 'groups' of stakeholders:

- 'providers': those organisations and individuals who create services and products

- 'users': people and organisations who (buy and) use the services and products.

Typically a relatively small group of providers (for example a single company or a small cluster of public service organisations) creates services and products for a very much larger group of uses (customers or citizens).

So with the majority of strategies there is a crucially important 'handover' of products and services from a small provider group to a large user group. This handover is where many strategies fall apart because the end-users do not want the products and services on offer or they are not aware of them or they cannot access them or they cannot afford them.

Therefore, it is essential to understand this handover from providers to end-users and this understanding is achieved through 'engagement' between providers and end-users.

Themes 8 and 9 (below) relating to stakeholder engagement and collaboration make an important distinction between 'engagement' (providers and users *planning together* – Theme 8) and 'collaboration' (providers and users *working together* – Theme 9).

The sub-topics under each of these two themes have been disaggregated into quite fine detail because, when it comes to engaging and collaborating with stakeholders for strategy development and implementation, the subtle details really do matter.

For a more detailed exposé of the multiple facets of effective stakeholder engagement, it is well worth viewing the comprehensive information and engagement standards displayed on the website of the International Association for Public Participation (www.iap2.org/).

Theme 8: Stakeholder Engagement (Planning Together)

Sub-topic 8.1: When Developing Strategies, to Engage Easily and Sustainably with Provider Organisations

Stakeholders' requirement

In developing multi-stakeholder strategies, whether within companies and organisations or involving multiple organisations, stakeholders generally operate within their own organisational silos and tend to defend their 'patch'. Such silo behaviour is usually very understandable – stakeholders are generally held accountable for the performance of their own silos of operation – but it is unhelpful for collectively developing successful strategies.

One option could be to 'break down the silos', but this is usually fiercely resisted as each organisation rightly argues that it must remain accountable for its own performance and hence must operate within its own silo.

Another option is to 'join up the silos' so that they can plan together while retaining their silo-based accountabilities.

In either case, it is important that it be easy for all stakeholders, whether providers or users, to engage with the strategy development process if, when, where and how it suits them without threatening their own organisation's accountabilities.

Functional specification 8.1 for an ISIMS to address this requirement

Must make it easy for stakeholders to plan together while at the same time enabling them to be held accountable for their silo-based actions.

Sub-topic 8.2: When Developing Strategies, to Engage Easily and Sustainably with End-users

Stakeholders' requirement

Practically all strategies are created by organisations who intend to create assets and services to be used by end-user customers, citizens, communities and the environment. Ideally these strategy-creation processes engage effectively with end-users to co-design the strategies to produce outcomes which will be of value to the end-users, but such in-depth engagement is rare.

More typically organisational stakeholders appear to believe it is appropriate for them to create and implement strategies *for* end-users rather than *with* end-users. Sadly this is particularly prevalent in central and local government sectors.

The IAP2 standards for stakeholder and end-user engagement spell out the full spectrum of types of engagement and are a practical guide to effective end-user engagement.

Functional specification 8.2 for an ISIMS to address this requirement

Must make it easy for end-users to engage with the strategy development process, ideally at all levels of engagement as defined by the IAP2 standard.

Sub-topic 8.3: When Developing Strategies, to Engage with All Levels and Types of Stakeholder, Irrespective of Their Education and Own Agendas

Stakeholders' requirement

Strategy development and implementation is not solely the domain of pin-stripe-suited executives. It should ideally involve all affected stakeholders, whether provider organisations, end-users or the environment (which needs to be represented by 'environmentalists').

Such stakeholders typically have widely varying skill sets, experience, interests, enthusiasms and time and these variations need to be taken into account when designing strategy engagement processes.

A subtle but important variation is the need for stakeholders at all levels within delivery organisations to be able to communicate effectively with each other so that top executives' high-level aspirational strategies are as well understood by operational-level people as the operational-level strategies are understood by the top executives. Too often this is not the case. Typically strategies are written in 'aspirational management jargon', which avoids details, whereas operational-level action plans are written in pragmatic operational language, which often ignores the overarching strategic imperatives. The gaps between these two types of strategy and action documents must be effectively bridged.

Functional specification 8.3 for an ISIMS to address this requirement

Must enable stakeholders with widely varying skills, experience, interests, enthusiasms and time to engage effectively in strategy development.

Sub-topic 8.4: When Developing Strategies, to Enable Stakeholders to Achieve Clarity about Their Roles and How Their Roles Contribute to the 'Big Picture'

Stakeholders' requirement

When a strategy is implemented, it is seldom implemented by a single player – it is almost invariably implemented by stakeholders or groups of stakeholders. Therefore, a strategy is generally implemented in 'chunks', each of which contributes in some way to the 'big picture'.

It is therefore imperative that each chunk of implementation connects seamlessly with other chunks of implementation and that stakeholders can see at any time how their contributions fit into the big picture.

Experience shows that stakeholders' motivation and energy lifts when they are clear about what their roles are *and* how their contributions fit into the big picture.

Functional specification 8.4 for an ISIMS to address this requirement

Must explicitly show how each organisation's and stakeholder's actions contribute to the big picture defined by the overall strategy.

Sub-topic 8.5: When Developing Strategies, to Enable Stakeholders to Understand and Appreciate Other Stakeholders' Roles and How They Fit into the 'Big Picture'

Stakeholders' requirement

A subtle but important extension of sub-topic 8.4 is that as well as understanding how their own actions contribute to the big picture, stakeholders also need to understand how other stakeholders' contributions contribute to the big picture.

Functional specification 8.5 for an ISIMS to address this requirement

Must explicitly show how each organisation's and stakeholder's actions join with other stakeholders' actions to contribute to the big picture defined by the overall strategy.

Sub-topic 8.6: When Developing Strategies, to Enable Stakeholder to Easily Scan a Strategy so They Can Quickly Decide If, Where, When and How to Contribute to the Process of Strategy Development

Stakeholders' requirement

Stakeholders often tell us that they are over-consulted about strategies, particularly in the public sector. They tell us that they want a strategy system where they can search all the strategies under development and select just those topics which interest them and where they can make contributions.

Then they want to be able to contribute when, where and how it suits them, perhaps online, perhaps by email, perhaps in public meetings or perhaps in face-to-face meetings with the leaders of the strategy.

Functional specification 8.6 for an ISIMS to address this requirement

Must enable stakeholders to easily identify areas of direct interest to them and then to contribute in ways that suit them.

Sub-topic 8.7: When Developing Strategies, to Share Sub-strategies' Ideas in a Controlled Manner

Stakeholders' requirement

Stakeholders frequently have their own clear ideas about what needs doing. They therefore want channels for presenting these ideas and having them encapsulated, either in the strategy which subsequently gets implemented or at least in a 'future strategy' document for possible implementation at a later date.

They therefore want somewhere that they can insert their ideas in the same format as the official strategy and to do this in stages. Initially they want to be able to privately insert relatively un-formed ideas for their own viewing only and then as they refine their ideas to be able to open them up to wider viewing by some or all stakeholders.

Functional specification 8.7 for an ISIMS to address this requirement

Must enable ideas to be kept confidential to a submitter until such time as the submitter is happy for them to be more widely shared (such confidential ideas may or may not be part of the overall strategy).

Theme 9: Stakeholder Collaboration (Working Together)

Sub-topic 9.1: When Implementing Strategies, to Enable Stakeholders to Collaborate 'across Silos' while Retaining Organisational Accountability

Stakeholders' requirement

As with planning together, so with strategy implementation, stakeholders need to work across silos to achieve desired outcomes.

In particular many stakeholder organisations are reluctant to 'pool budgets' and then allow a committee made up of multi-stakeholder groups to spend their resources. Instead, organisations need ways of 'aligning their budgets' with those of other organisations ('joining up budgets, not pooling budgets').

Functional specification 9.1 for an ISIMS to address this requirement

Must enable stakeholders to implement and resource a strategy together while at the same time enabling them to be held accountable for their silo-based actions and budgets.

Sub-topic 9.2: When Implementing Strategies, to Enable End-users to be Actively Involved in the Implementation of Sub-strategies

Stakeholders' requirement

In many instances end-users can make active contributions to the implementation of strategies, for example they can contribute to the development of an asset such as a public park as well as be an end-user of that park.

In this respect stakeholders' and users' motivation can be maintained or even improved by starting with actions which lead to 'quick wins'.

Functional specification 9.2 for an ISIMS to address this requirement

Must enable end-users to contribute to the implementation of a strategy and not just be passive end-users of assets and services created by others.

Sub-topic 9.3: When Implementing Strategies, to Enable Stakeholders to Work Collaboratively, Irrespective of People's Different Personality Types, Skill Sets and Agendas

Stakeholders' requirement

As with planning together, so with strategy implementation, stakeholders with different skill sets, different personalities and different agendas need to work together to jointly achieve the outcomes desired by the stakeholders.

Functional specification 9.3 for an ISIMS to address this requirement

Must enable stakeholders to work around personal and organisational differences by, if possible, being as objective as possible and by being crystal clear on how outcomes will be achieved and who will benefit from them.

Sub-topic 9.4: When Implementing Strategies, to Enable Stakeholders to Easily Plan Collaboratively but Nevertheless Implement Sub-strategies Individually and/or in Small Groups

Stakeholders' requirement

The implementation of multi-stakeholder strategies invariably involves large and small sub-groups implementing different parts of the strategy. Frequently the sub-groups which contributed to the development of the strategy will be the same sub-groups which implement components of the strategy which are relevant to them. However, also frequently, different groups implement the components of the strategy from those that developed them.

Functional specification 9.5 for an ISIMS to address this requirement

Must integrate the contributions of each stakeholder group to the implementation of a strategy so that the overall strategy implementation is cohesive and achieves the desired outcomes.

Sub-topic 9.5: When Implementing Strategies, to Enable Stakeholders to Easily Scan a Strategy so They Can Quickly Decide If, Where, When and How to Contribute to the Process of Strategy Implementation

Stakeholders' requirement

As with sub-topic 8.7 on the joint development of strategies, the collaborative implementation of strategies also requires a system which enables stakeholders to regularly scan the strategy and monitor its implementation so that they can decide if, where, when and how to contribute to the process of strategy implementation.

Functional specification 9.6 for an ISIMS to address this requirement

Must be structured so as to enable stakeholders to identify areas of direct interest to them (including performance management) and then to contribute in ways that suit them.

Theme 10: Interlinking

Sub-topic 10.1: Interlink High-level Aspirational Strategies with Grassroots Operational-level Strategies and Everything in between

Stakeholders' requirement

Strategies are written at many different levels, yet it is only at the operational level that they can actually be implemented. This is not to imply that higher-level strategies have no value. They do have value in terms of informing lower and lower levels of strategy until the operational level is reached.

The advantage of a high-level strategy is that it can address many themes within a relatively concise document, but it is unable to include enough detail to actually be implemented. In contrast, an operational-level strategy addressing the details of every action that needs to be taken will be a substantial 'document' or archive of actions, which will be overwhelming for many people.

As discussed in section 1.6 in Chapter 1, there are three main levels of strategies:

- high-level aspirational strategies;

- mid-level guidance strategies;

- grassroots-level operational strategies.

For example, a high-level aspirational strategy may include overarching statements such as 'Improve the transport system in the city' and this may then filter down through more and more detailed levels of strategy. A mid-level guidance strategy may include a statement such as 'Develop a mix of public and private transport to improve the transport system in the city' and a grassroots-level operational strategy may contain a statement such as 'Build a cycle path from the central city through Clearwater Park to the university'.

Functional specification 10.1 for an ISIMS to address this requirement

Must enable the seamless integration or interlinking of strategies from high-level aspirational strategies down through mid-level guidance strategies to grassroots-level operational strategies so that it is crystal clear which high-level strategies each operational-level strategy is contributing to.

Sub-topic 10.2: Interlink Strategies across Multiple Themes

Stakeholders' requirement

Frequently strategic actions impact on or depend on each other. For example, a strategy to 'build a swimming pool' needs to be linked with other strategies such as 'employ and train lifeguards' and 'provide parking for swimming pool users'. Similarly, a transport strategy needs to interlink with strategies on motor vehicles, bicycles, walking and perhaps horse riding.

Functional specification 10.2 for an ISIMS to address this requirement

Must enable the seamless interlinking of strategies on related themes.

Sub-topic 10.3: Interlink Strategies across Multiple Organisations

Stakeholders' requirement

Frequently several organisations will implement similar strategies or strategies which impact on each other. For example, a local body, a police agency and the fire service may all implement strategies relating to crowds attending football games, so it is important that these strategies work together.

Functional specification 10.3 for an ISIMS to address this requirement

Must enable strategies from different organisations to be seamlessly interlinked in order to optimise outcomes.

Sub-topic 10.4: Interlink Strategies across Multiple Demographics (User Groups)

Stakeholders' requirement

Strategies are often developed for a single demographic group of end-users, for example the elderly. However, it sometimes becomes clear that the assets and services being created for such a group can be meaningfully used by other groups, perhaps at different times of the day. It is therefore important that strategies which have been designed for different demographic groups of end-users can be easily interlinked to other end-user groups.

Functional specification 10.4 for an ISIMS to address this requirement

Must enable strategies which have been initially developed for specific end-user groups to be seamlessly interlinked with strategies for other end-user groups.

Sub-topic 10.5: Interlink Strategies Sequentially

Stakeholders' requirement

Frequently the implementation of strategies by one group of stakeholders requires the subsequent implementation of further strategies by the same or other groups. For example, the building of a swimming pool may be followed by the development of swim-training programmes for young people.

Functional specification 10.5 for an ISIMS to address this requirement

Must seamlessly interlink strategies which are implemented in sequence.

Theme 11: Governance

Sub-topic 11.1: Clear Governance for the Development, Implementation, Performance Management and Reporting of Strategies

Stakeholders' requirement

Almost all strategies involve multiple stakeholders, even within quite small organisations and companies. Experience shows that for a strategy development and implementation process to be effective, it is crucially important for all stakeholders to be crystal clear about who is responsible for what actions.

This is particularly important in those situations in which one sub-group of stakeholders may want a particular action to be taken (they may be the beneficiaries of the action), but the action may need to be undertaken by other stakeholders (the providers).

For example, a cluster of sporting clubs may strongly desire the construction of a new stadium, but it will be a cluster of sponsors, the city council and contractors who actually build the stadium. In this instance it will be essential for the sports clubs to fully engage with the sponsors and city council as they collectively develop the stadium strategy. It is likely to be appropriate that the sports clubs have a governance role during this strategy development process. In contrast, governance is most likely to shift to the sponsors, the city council and contractors for the implementation of the stadium strategy.

Functional specification 11.1 for an ISIMS to address this requirement

Must be explicitly clear about who is responsible for which actions during both the strategy development and strategy implementation phases.

Sub-topic 11.2: Clear Organisational Sovereignty

Stakeholders' requirement

As noted under Themes 8 and 9, stakeholders frequently want to or need to work together while retaining their organisational sovereignty, that is, their organisational authority and responsibility. In some circumstances organisations may be perfectly happy to surrender some of their sovereignty to a multi-stakeholder group, whereas under other circumstances they may wish to retain full sovereignty or control over issues.

Interestingly, experience shows that when some organisations participate transparently and professionally in a multi-stakeholder group, other stakeholders are more likely to let these organisations lead the group by 'earning the right to lead, not taking control'.

Functional specification 11.2 for an ISIMS to address this requirement

Must explicitly enable stakeholders and organisations to manage their own sovereignty as they see fit and to enable leaders to 'earn the right to lead, not take control'.

Theme 12: Libraries of Validated Strategies

Sub-topic 12.1: Master Library of Validated Strategies

Stakeholders' requirement

Billions of dollars are spent every year creating strategies, yet it would be hard to argue that all the created strategies contain mostly new concepts. For example, almost all local governments in the Western world will have strategies on cycling, roads, waste collection, environmental management and so on. While there will be local variations in these strategies, there will also be many similarities given the thousands of local authorities in existence. It therefore appears extremely wasteful for every organisation to spend resources creating and re-creating strategies when thousands of proven strategies exist and could be readily edited and adopted by other organisations.

It would make good sense if each *successful* strategy and its component parts (sub-strategies) could be archived and displayed in a readily accessible format so that they could be copied, edited and implemented by others interested in the same topics.

Functional specification 2.1 for an ISIMS to address this requirement

Will ideally enable successful public strategies and their sub-strategies to be made visible to others interested in the same topics, perhaps in the form of an international library of proven successful sub-strategies.

Theme 13: Integrated Strategy Development

Sub-topic 13.1: A Single Simple System so Stakeholders can Improve Their Organisation, Meet Stakeholders' and End-users' Expectations and Make the World a Better Place

Stakeholders' requirement

Stakeholders frequently report frustration at having to use many different tools for strategy development, action planning, risk management, performance management and for stakeholder and end-user engagement.

They also report that the different tools are too complex for most of their needs. They repeatedly tell us that they use only a small part of the functionality of each tool and that, frequently, they collect a lot of information, it does not get well used and the tool eventually falls into disuse.

Instead they would prefer a single, simple (minimalist) integrated and rigorous system to enable them to robustly but minimally manage every aspect of their strategy development and implementation.

Functional specification 13.1 for an ISIMS to address this requirement

Will ideally be a single simple and robust system which enables all strategy-related actions to be seamlessly integrated.

Checklist of Requirements for an Integrated Strategic Information Management System

A fully Integrated Strategic Information Management System must meet the following functional specifications:

Theme 1: Development and Evolution

1.1   Specific Language

A concise and rigorously defined 'strategy language taxonomy' which encapsulates and defines actions that can actually be implemented.

1.2   Common Language

A rigorous 'strategy language taxonomy' which is easily and fully understood by all stakeholders.

1.3   Common Format

A single, concise and rigorously defined 'strategy format' which lays out strategic information in a consistent way which all stakeholders can follow and fully understand.

1.4   Must Actually be a Strategy

A clear plan of what needs to be done.

1.5   Mapping What is Already Happening

The ability to rapidly and concisely map existing strategic activities as the basis for both refining/deleting existing activities and for adding new and validated strategic activities.

1.6   Mapping What Needs to be Done

The ability to rapidly and concisely map new strategic activities.

1.7   Necessary and Sufficient Actions to Lead to the Desired Outcomes

The ability to guide and enable the development of strategies which contain all those actions which are both necessary and sufficient to lead to the desired outcomes.

1.8   Effective and Efficient Strategy Development

The ability to guide and enable stakeholders to efficiently create effective strategies.

1.9   Capture all Possible Strategic Ideas Even If They Aren't Immediately Implemented

The ability to encapsulate strategic ideas which can be supported in the future as well as ideas which will be supported immediately.

1.10   Easily Update and Refine Strategies

Must be flexible and enable easy, rapid and frequent updating.

1.11   Scalability

Must enable the scalable evolution of larger and larger strategies, ideally made up of smaller modules (sub-strategies) which fit together to create a larger overall strategy.

1.12   Access and Use Strategic Information over Extended Periods of Time even as Individuals and Organisations Change

Must have an ongoing life of its own independent of an organisation's individual members and employees.

Theme 2: Clarity

2.1   Smallest Amount of Strategic Information

Must use the *smallest* possible amount of strategic information to convey its messages and must enable this information to be 'chunked' into digestible sized chunks.

2.2   Most Valuable/Useful Strategic Information

Must contain the smallest amount of *most valuable* strategic information.

2.3   Strategic Information of Most Value to Most Stakeholders

Must contain the smallest amount of information that is the most valuable to the *most stakeholders*.

2.4   Clear Cause-and-Effect Links from Inputs through to Outcomes

Must explicitly show all cause-and-effect linkages from actions through to the desired outcomes.

2.5   Clarity about the Resources and Funding Required

Must be explicitly clear about the costs/resources required both for the implementation of projects and for the use of products and services created by stakeholders.

2.6   Strategic Information in the Right Place at the Right Time

Must be clear on the distinction between information which *informs* the strategy and information which *constitutes* the strategy.

2.7   Transparency to Help Build Inter-stakeholder Trust

Must be sufficiently transparent (both clear and available) so that all stakeholders can see what's going on with both the development and the implementation of the strategy.

2.8   Distilling Simple Actions from Complicated, Complex and Chaotic Strategic Environments

Must enable the distillation of simple strategic actions from the analysis of the simple, complicated, complex and chaotic world.

2.9   Positivity and Negativity

Must capture both positive and negative effects of actions.

Theme 3: Validation

3.1   Confidence in 'Doing the Right Things' as well as 'Doing Things Right'

Must focus on effectiveness (doing the right thing) first before efficiency (doing things right).

3.2   Confidence that the Strategy can Genuinely be Implemented

Must contain information and evidence that the strategy can be implemented.

3.3   Risk and Uncertainty Management

Must identify exactly where risk and uncertainty lie within a strategy and hence provide guidance on where more information and evidence may be required to fully validate the rationale of the strategy.

3.4   Effective Ways for Stakeholders to Contribute

Must enable key (or all) stakeholders to view, comment on and edit the strategy so it benefits from their collective wisdom and knowledge.

Theme 4: Prioritisation

4.1   Straightforward Prioritisation

Must display each strategic idea in the same format, including a full cause-and-effect sequence from inputs to outcomes plus compelling evidence that this sequence is viable plus compelling evidence that the idea is worth implementing.

4.2   Stakeholders Clustering into Sub-groups to Support Sub-group Ideas

Must enable strategic issue prioritisation based on both the issue's popularity (to select the issues which are the least controversial to the whole group) as well as on issues which are crucial to sub-groups.

Theme 5: Implementation

5.1   Implementation

Must create strategies that link the high-level aspirations directly to actions which can be directly implemented.

5.2   Delivery

Must create strategies which make crystal clear what can be achieved by service providers and what must also be done by end-users of a strategy if it is to be successfully implemented.

Theme 6: Performance Management

6.1   Indicators for Effective Performance Management

Must encapsulate clear information about what needs to be measured and monitored so as to confirm whether or not the strategy implementation is 'on track'.

6.2   Targets for Effective Performance Management

Must be clear about performance targets.

6.3   Actual Measurements for Effective Performance Management

Must clearly encapsulate and collate actual performance measurements and enable their comparison with targets.

6.4   Where to Take Action to Improve Performance

Must make it explicitly clear where actions need to be taken in response to any measurement which demonstrates that targets are not being met.

6.5   Reporting, Audit and Scrutiny

Must enable simple and clear reporting on performance and progress towards desired outcomes.

6.6   Defending a Strategy through Audit and Scrutiny

Must encapsulate the reasons for each strategic decision and back them up with a compelling rationale and evidence.

6.7   Linking the Performance of Individuals, Stakeholders and Organisations to the Performance Management of the Strategy

Must enable the distillation from the strategy of the roles and related performance measurements of individuals, stakeholders and organisations as they contribute to the implementation of the strategy.

Theme 7: Outcomes Focus

7.1   Outcomes which are Customer, Citizen, Community and Environment-centric

Must reflect and encapsulate an in-depth understanding of end-users' needs and wants.

7.2   Improvements in the 'Four Well-beings' (Economic, Social, Environmental and Cultural)

Must enable the encapsulation of the four well-beings as desired outcomes.

7.3   High Levels of Uptake by End-users of Services and Products

Must create strategies which lead to sufficiently high levels of end-user uptake to justify the resources which are committed to the strategy development and implementation.

7.4   Vision

Must encapsulate a 'vision' for the strategy.

Theme 8: Stakeholder Engagement (Planning Together)

8.1   When Developing Strategies, to Engage Easily and Sustainably with Provider Organisations

Must make it easy for stakeholders to plan together while at the same time enabling them to be held accountable for their silo-based actions and budgets.

8.2   When Developing Strategies, to Engage Easily and Sustainably with End-users

Must make it easy for end-users to engage with the strategy development process, ideally at all levels of engagement as defined by the IAP2 standard.

8.3   When Developing Strategies, to Engage with All Levels and Types of Stakeholder, Irrespective of Their Education and Own Agendas

Must enable stakeholders with widely varying skills, experience, interests, enthusiasms and time to engage effectively in strategy development.

8.4   When Developing Strategies, to Enable Stakeholders to Achieve Clarity about Their Roles and How Their Roles Contribute to the 'Big Picture'

Must explicitly show how each organisation's and stakeholder's actions contribute to the big picture defined by the overall strategy.

8.5   When Developing Strategies, to Enable Stakeholders to Understand and Appreciate Other Stakeholders' Roles and How They Fit into the 'Big Picture'

Must explicitly show how each organisation's and stakeholder's actions join with other stakeholders' actions to contribute to the big picture defined by the overall strategy.

8.6   When Developing Strategies, to Enable Stakeholders to Easily Scan a Strategy so They Can Quickly Decide If, Where, When and How to Contribute to the Process of Strategy Development

Must enable stakeholders to easily identify areas of direct interest to them and then to contribute in ways that suit them.

8.7   When Developing Strategies, to Share Sub-strategies' Ideas in a Controlled Manner

Must enable ideas to be kept confidential to a submitter until such time as the submitter is happy for them to be more widely shared (such confidential ideas may or may not be part of the overall strategy).

Theme 9: Stakeholder Collaboration (Working Together)

9.1 When Implementing Strategies, to Enable Stakeholders to Collaborate 'across Silos' While Retaining Organisational Accountability

Must enable stakeholders to implement and resource a strategy together while at the same time enabling them to be held accountable for their silo-based actions and budgets.

9.2 When Implementing Strategies, to Enable End-users to be Actively Involved in the Implementation of Sub-strategies

Must enable end-users to contribute to the implementation of a strategy and not just be passive end-users of assets and services created by others.

9.3 When Implementing Strategies, to Enable Stakeholders to Work Collaboratively, Irrespective of People's Different Personality Types, Skill Sets and Agendas

Must enable stakeholders to work around personal and organisational differences by, if possible, being as objective as possible and by being crystal clear on how outcomes will be achieved and who will benefit from them.

9.4 When Implementing Strategies, to Enable Stakeholders to Easily Plan Collaboratively but Nevertheless Implement Sub-strategies Individually and/or in Small Groups

Must integrate the contributions of each stakeholder group to the implementation of a strategy so that the overall strategy implementation is cohesive and achieves the desired outcomes.

9.5 When Implementing Strategies, to Enable Stakeholders to Easily Scan a Strategy so They Can Quickly Decide If, Where, When and How to Contribute to the Process of Strategy Implementation

Must be structured so as to enable stakeholders to identify areas of direct interest to them (including performance management) and then to contribute in ways that suit them.

Theme 10: Interlinking

10.1   Interlink High-level Aspirational Strategies with Grassroots Operational-level Strategies and Everything in between

Must enable the seamless integration or interlinking of strategies from high-level aspirational strategies down through mid-level guidance strategies to grassroots-level operational strategies so that it is crystal clear which high-level strategies each operational-level strategy is contributing to.

10.2   Interlink Strategies across Multiple Themes

Must enable the seamless interlinking of strategies on related themes.

10.3   Interlink Strategies across Multiple Organisations

Must enable strategies from different organisations to be seamlessly interlinked in order to optimise outcomes.

10.4   Interlink Strategies across Multiple Demographics (User Groups)

Must enable strategies which have been initially developed for specific end-user groups to be seamlessly interlinked with strategies for other end-user groups.

10.5   Interlink Strategies Sequentially

Must seamlessly interlink strategies which are implemented in sequence.

Theme 11: Governance

11.1   Clear Governance for the Development, Implementation, Performance Management and Reporting of Strategies

Must be explicitly clear about who is responsible for which actions during both the strategy development and strategy implementation phases.

11.2   Clear Organisational Sovereignty

Must explicitly enable stakeholders and organisations to manage their own sovereignty as they see fit and to enable leaders to 'earn the right to lead, not take control'.

Theme 12: Libraries of Validated Strategies

12.1   Master Library of Validated Strategies

Will ideally enable successful public strategies and their SubStrategies to be made visible to others interested in the same topics, perhaps in the form of an international library of proven successful SubStrategies.

Theme 13: Integrated Strategy Development

13.1   A Single Simple System so Stakeholders can Improve Their Organisation, Meet Stakeholders' and End-users' Expectations and Make the World a Better Place

Will ideally be a single simple and robust system which enables all strategy-related actions to be seamlessly integrated.

Index

action plan 15–16, 46–7, 58, 202, 228, 239
    see also Operational Strategies
actions, necessary and sufficient 217–18
active vs. passive Use 80–82, 197
    definition 197
aggregation/disaggregation (of strategies) 22, 48–53, 113–14, 125, 165, 170–75, 184, 191
Aspirational Strategies 15, 57–67, 122, 167–8, 201
    definition 197–8
    and Guidance Strategies 201
    Project-verbs for 59–67
    taxonomy 57–9, 72
assets 26, 27, 28, 31–3, 166–7, 190, 237
    and Benefits 128
    creation xiv, xv, 5–9, 18, 21, 23, 26–8, 31–2, 38, 77, 80, 134, 136–7, 188, 193, 209
    handover 28, 31–3, 81, 166–7, 190, 237
    and results 42, 69, 77, 87, 101–2, 134
    'right' assets 31–2
    Users 27, 31
    see also Benefits, Projects, Results, Users, Uses, PRUB
auditing OpenStrategies 109, 232–3

Benefits 7, 24, 25, 27–8, 31–8, 41–4, 53, 60, 66, 71, 77–80, 82–6, 101, 103–5, 122–3, 148, 153–5, 160–61, 188, 190, 198, 235–6

and BURP 38, 77–80, 198
compound 103–5
vs. costs 26, 36, 153–4, 160–61
creation vs. realisation 24
definition 28, 198
'delivery' 41–4, 66, 190
final 83
focus on 122–3
introduction 25
justification 82
and language 60
and Links 33–4
measurement of 83–4
multiple 101
cf. outcomes 33
ownership of 84–5
performance management 35, 36–8
and Projects 27
and PRUB 41–4
and PRUB-Validate 153–5
and Results 27–8, 31, 32
specificity level 85–6
starting with 77–80
User-created 83
and User uptake levels 235–6
and Uses 24, 85
and Value 36, 148, 153–5, 160–61
and Vision 53, 71, 82
well-beings 82–3, 235
    see also assets, costs, outcomes, PRUB, Results, Value
Benefits Realisation Management 2
boundary conditions 166–7, 190

For Product Safety Concerns and Information please contact our
EU representative GPSR@taylorandfrancis.com Taylor & Francis
Verlag GmbH, Kaufingerstraße 24, 80331 München, Germany